EAST GERMANY'S ECONOMIC DEVELOPMENT SINCE UNIFICATION

STUDIES IN ECONOMIC TRANSITION

General Editors: Jens Hölscher, DAAD Senior Research Fellow in Economics, University of Birmingham; and Horst Tomann, Professor of Economics, Free University Berlin

This new series has been established in response to a growing demand for a greater understanding of the transformation of economic systems. It brings together theoretical and empirical studies on economic transition and economic development. The postcommunist transition from planned to market economies is one of the main areas of applied theory because in this field the most dramatic examples of change and economic dynamics can be found. It is aimed to contribute to the understanding of specific major economic changes as well as to advance the theory of economic development. The implications of economic policy will be a major point of focus.

The first title is:

Jens Hölscher and Anja Hochberg (*editors*)
EAST GERMANY'S ECONOMIC DEVELOPMENT SINCE UNIFICATION: Domestic and Global Aspects

East Germany's Economic Development since Unification

Domestic and Global Aspects

Edited by

Jens Hölscher
DAAD Senior Research Fellow in Economics
Institute for German Studies
University of Birmingham

and

Anja Hochberg
Lecturer in Economics
European Business Management School
University of Wales Swansea

First published in Great Britain 1998 by
MACMILLAN PRESS LTD
Houndmills, Basingstoke, Hampshire RG21 6XS and London
Companies and representatives throughout the world

A catalogue record for this book is available from the British Library.

ISBN 0–333–72489–5

First published in the United States of America 1998 by
ST. MARTIN'S PRESS, INC.,
Scholarly and Reference Division,
175 Fifth Avenue, New York, N.Y. 10010

ISBN 0–312–21228–3

Library of Congress Cataloging-in-Publication Data
East Germany's economic development since unification : domestic and global aspects / edited by Jens Hölscher and Anja Hochberg.
p. cm.
"Based on papers given at a conference on 'East Germany in locational competition' at the Institute for German Studies, The University of Birmingham ... in June 1996."
Includes bibliographical references and index.
ISBN 0–312–21228–3 (cloth)
1. Germany (East)—Economic conditions—Congresses. 2. Germany (East)—Economic policy—Congresses. I. Hölscher, Jens. II. Hochberg, Anja.
HC290.782.E27 1998
338.943'1'009049—dc21 97–50395
CIP

This book is printed on paper suitable for recycling and made from fully managed and sustained forest sources.

10 9 8 7 6 5 4 3 2 1
07 06 05 04 03 02 01 00 99 98

Printed and bound in Great Britain by
Antony Rowe Ltd, Chippenham, Wiltshire

Contents

List of Tables

List of Figures

Acknowledgements

This volume is based on papers given at a conference on 'East Germany in Locational Competition' at the Institute for German Studies, University of Birmingham, which took place in June 1996. The workshop was initiated by lectures serving for the German Academic Exchange Service (DAAD) in the United Kingdom and organised by the editors. Included are also papers given by guest speakers to the Institute for German Studies' 'Open Seminar Series'.

The editors gratefully acknowledge the far-reaching support provided by the University of Birmingham's Institute for German Studies and the financial help given by the DAAD. An exclusive reception at the University's Barber Institute of Fine Arts greatly contributed to the spirit of the conference.

The editors are particularly happy to see this volume published, being in the eminent position of starting this new series of 'Studies in Economic Transition'.

Notes on the Contributors

Jens Bastian is a Lecturer at the European Institute/Department of Government of the London School of Economics and Political Science. His principal research areas are comparative labour–market policies, and the political economy of transition in central and eastern Europe. He previously lectured at Nuffield College, University of Oxford, and obtained his doctorate at the European University Institute Florence.

James Coop is a doctoral candidate at Imperial College, University of London.

Marc Herzog is a Lecturer in Business Administration and Marketing at University College, Dublin, and a Senior Research Fellow in Marketing at the University of Lüneburg, Germany. Prior to this he spent a number of years at the University of Bayreuth, Germany, where he obtained an MBA in 1992 and a doctorate in Business Administration in 1996. His main research interests lie in the area of international marketing with special emphasis on how small and medium-sized enterprises internationalise, international marketing communication strategies for SMEs, and international marketing research.

Anja Hochberg is a Lecturer in Economics at the European Business Management School, University of Wales, Swansea. From 1991 she studied economics at Berlin Free University where she obtained her degree in 1993. Then she continued her studies at the College of Europe, Bruges, where she obtained an MA and a DEEA in European Economic Studies. Since 1995, also being a doctoral candidate, her main research interests include regional policy and European economic integration.

Jens Hölscher is Senior Research Fellow and co-ordinator of economic research at the Institute for German Studies of the University of Birmingham. Previously, he taught at the University of Wales Swansea and the Berlin Free University. His research interests concentrate on the economic theory of money and development, with special reference to the German economy and economics of transition in Central–East Europe, a subject of particular interest during a stay as Visiting Professor with the Halle Institute of Economic Research. Besides various articles, his recent book publications are *Entwicklungsmodell Westdeutschland*, (as co-editor)

Bedingungen ökonomischer Entwicklung in Zentralosteuropa, vols I to V, (and as co-editor) *The German Currency Union of 1990*.

Michael Hüther is Secretary General of the German Council of Economic Experts for which he served as staff member previously after he was assistant lecturer at Gießen University. His main interest concentrates on fiscal policy.

Michael Kaser is Honorary Professor in the Institute for German Studies of the University of Birmingham, and General Editor of the International Economic Association, since retirement from Oxford University in 1993. He is Emeritus Fellow of St Antony's College, Oxford, and Reader Emeritus in Economics. Under various academic, official and international auspices he has since 1949 frequently visited the communist and post-communist states of eastern Europe and Asia, visits to eastern Germany covering the Soviet Occupation Zone, the GDR and the new Länder. He has published widely on their economies.

Thomas Lange, a German economist and statistician by training, is Reader in Economics at the Robert Gordon University in Aberdeen, founding Head of the International Labour Markets Research Network (ILM) and Contract Professor in Managerial Economics at the Polytechnic University of Bucharest in Romania. He also works as an advisor to the Education and Industry Department of the Scottish Office, and has published widely in the field of labour economics and industrial relations. He is co-author of *The Economics of German Unification* (1997).

Eric Owen Smith is Senior Lecturer in Economics at Loughborough University, a Visiting Professor at the University of Trier and a Visiting Fellow of the Institute for German Studies at the University of Birmingham. His research interests are in German economic performance and comparative studies of collective bargaining in Germany and Britain. As well as numerous publications in these fields, he has written the definitive English study on *The German Economy* (1994). He is also an independent chair of the Appeals Committee of the Open University, an ACAS arbitrator and a member of Industrial Tribunals.

Karl-Heinz Paqué is Professor for International Economics at the University of Magdeburg. He directed the No. 1 Research Department of the Kiel Institute for World Economy and published widely on the division of labour.

Geoff Pugh is Principal Lecturer in European Economics at Staffordshire University Business School and a visiting professor at the universities of Warsaw and Tirana. He teaches courses on the German economy and the economics of the European Union, has published on the social market and the implications for trade and employment of a single European currency, and is co-author of *The Economics of German Unification: An Introduction* (1997).

Johannes Stephan is Research Fellow at the Halle Institute for Economic Research. He became a doctoral candidate at the Institute for German Studies at the University of Birmingham after studies at Berlin Free University and University of Middlesex, London.

Rudi Vis was elected as Member of Parliament for Finchley in May 1997. He was previously a Lecturer in the Department of Economics at the University of East London.

Wolfram Waldner is Assistant Lecturer in Law at Erlangen University and Visiting Lecturer at Warwick University.

Introduction

This work provides an exercise in the theory of economic development applied to the economy of East Germany seven years after unification. Above all, it responds to a widely perceived need for an assessment of the current stage of that difficult transformation process and of the multitude of related policy implications. Representatives of very different schools of thought submit their individual perspectives and analyses to the reader of this volume: the hotly contested issue of aggregate demand management versus supply side economics is addressed at length, motivated also by the need to place certain developments within the German economy in their proper international context. On the one hand, the economic development of East Germany can of course be viewed as a frame of reference for the transitions of other Central and East European Countries (CEECs). On the other hand, the extensive discussion of lessons of German unification for European integration aims to provide a broader perspective of these socio-economic integration processes.

The book is conceived in three parts, each of them addressing specific key issues of German unification and its world-wide impact.

Part I, The German Economy and the New Länder, starts out with macroeconomics. Two of the most serious current developments within the German economy, namely a high level of unemployment and wholly unsatisfactory investment ratios, are portrayed against the German economy's historical background and its traditional features. The approach of the Council of Economic Advisors suggests a supply-side oriented solution to this dilemma.

Part II, Microeconomic Problems and Privatisation, looks at underlying reasons. Privatisation and 'marketisation' represent the two major tasks in the transformation process, with private property and a functioning price mechanism serving as cornerstones of every market economy. Basic problems of re-establishing a system based upon private property rights are thoroughly explained, as well as the specifics of the Treuhand model. The question as to what determines entrepreneurial success in East Germany leads to an analysis of the economic impact of different privatisation strategies.

Part III, New Institutions and Economic Policy, deals with German unification in terms of its policy implications. Institutional aspects such as the organisation and behaviour of special interest groups play an important role in the politically charged process of economic convergence, leading to a lively discussion of wages and labour policy, and the role of the welfare state is revisited. Ultimately, these and several other economic aspects of German unification are shaped into a concept paradigmatic for providing lessons for the design of a better framework for European integration.

Chapter 1 by Karl-Heinz Paqué traces the historical roots of the successful German economy of the past. He concludes that the German model, in its specific mix of structural economic determination and institutional mechanisms, is likely to prove its strengths even under presently adverse circumstances. However, the outcome in terms of international competitiveness will depend on how Germany will be able to face unification's daunting triple challenge: its huge fiscal burden, a less-than-comfortable current account balance, and the probable necessity of substantial changes in fiscal federalism and collective bargaining.

The analysis of the German model described in Chapter 2 by Jens Hölscher and Johannes Stephan – as an export-based economy relying upon an undervalued currency – requires a different approach. First, some alternative views of the post-unification performance are evaluated. Second, key issues of economic convergence like socialist legacies, currency conversion rate, over-valuation of East Germany's capital stock and financial transfers are analysed. Considering the severe dilemma – of mass unemployment and the role of the Deutschmark as an anchor currency – Germany is facing in the aftermath of unification, the authors argue that a move towards an overvalued, import-based economic regime seems overdue and unavoidable.

Chapter 3 by Michael Hüther raises the issue of why the basic concept of supply-side economics is gaining importance. He exemplifies the tasks of economic policy by presenting the approach of the Council of Economic Advisors. Even in terms of a supply-side oriented economic policy, the key issue of mass unemployment is not merely a function of expansive wage policy. Rather, the discussion must focus on the notable absence of job-creating investments. As a consequence, the author indicates general opportunities to increase the potential for profitable production under the specific conditions of the present German economy.

Chapter 4 by Michael Kaser examines the situation in East Germany in the context of other transition processes world-wide. Unlike any of the other economies recently in transition, East Germany was able to acquire the entire institutional framework of the FRG virtually overnight; unprecedented transfer payments support the adjustment process in the East. But despite such unquestionable advantages, East Germany has suffered from immense de-industrialisation. Hence, issues of capacity and employment policy of the Treuhand certainly deserve closer scrutiny, and the author examines changes in the supply-side, institutional aspects and in the external effects while comparing East Germany with several other transition economies.

In Chapter 5, Marc Herzog investigates the economic situation of newly established small and medium-sized enterprises in the industrial sector in East Germany in search of factors of economic success. In his view, the specific organisation of business in the FRG's New Länder affects economic performance through peculiar characteristics of corporate structure, differences in competitive conditions and differences in corporate strategy.

Wolfram Waldner addresses the 'unknown' ownership of private property in Chapter 6. He shows that in most cases, ownership is not at all unknown but merely extraordinarily complex due to a variety of reasons, e.g., the action taken by the Soviet Military Government in 1945–9, the development of the legal system and actual conditions in the former GDR, and substantive changes in the legal system brought about by the Unification Treaty and subsequent legislation. By outlining the major developments and identifying their impacts on the ownership question, the author identifies respect of private property and special guarantees extended by the Basic Law as the structural pillars of the re-introduced market economy.

The political and economic implications of the tenuous relationship between economics and social sciences on the one hand, and socio-economic problems waiting for solutions in western industrial nations on the other hand, are discussed in Chapter 7 by James Coop and Rudi Vis. Concentrating on the influence of implicit and explicit value judgements and the validity of neo-classical assumptions, they argue against proposals from economists of the New Right to dismantle the welfare state.

Jens Bastian reflects in Chapter 8 on recent changes in industrial relations in unified Germany, with the 'alliance for jobs' as paradigm. His essay traces responses to the initiative within Germany as well as in a broader European context, and concludes with a call for caution in the implementation of sweeping structural reforms.

In Chapter 9 Thomas Lange and Geoff Pugh focus on the role of wages and wage policy in the process of catching up. They propose a two-phased approach to deriving benefits from the dynamic aspects of unification. In its initial phase, large wage increases played an important supporting role and actually helped to create the potential for a high-wage/high-tech development path. But to realise this potential, a prolonged second phase would now appear necessary, a period in which real wages would be allowed to rise only fairly moderately if at all.

The economic aspects of German unification as they relate to European integration are examined in Chapter 10 by Eric Owen Smith. The principal differences between both are explained and, after a critical review of German experiences with Economic and Monetary Union, the author shows that a number of features of the German economy have indeed already been adopted at the EU level, or certainly would easily lend themselves to future adoption. He suggests that, without adoption of the German model's fiscal and social policies, politically stable and viable progress at European integration may not be feasible.

In the final chapter, Anja Hochberg reviews the rich context of conceptional lessons from German unification. First, the author calls for a holistic approach to integration processes. Second, she discusses the applicability and different results of various Optimum Currency Area theories. Her qualification of both processes as indicative of a crisis leads her to conclude that European integration has to be understood and appreciated as a historically unique opportunity decisively to eliminate deficiencies that, for their own historical reasons, have been allowed to exist and prevail for a long time.

Aside from the substantially different methodologies and research interests of the contributors to this volume, one common denominator noticeably reconciles their individual approaches: it is their judgement that the unification process in its diversity has profoundly changed economic, social and political conditions in all of Germany, not only in the East. Until now, however, it seems that economic policy has yet to respond adequately to any of these challenges. Therefore, this book should be viewed as a critical anthology of theoretical contributions to support necessary change in economic policy priorities in *fin-de-siècle* Germany, and as a wake-up call for improved receptiveness toward already amply available practical lessons for the imminent European integration at large.

JENS HÖLSCHER
ANJA HOCHBERG

I

The German Economy and the New Länder

1 From Miracle to Crisis? The German Economy at the End of the Twentieth Century[1]

Karl-Heinz Paqué

INTRODUCTION

This chapter is intended to explore whether, as a result of unification, the German economic miracle is facing a crisis. The analysis indicates that the German economy can be expected to follow its traditional path, subject to three qualifications: the united Germany will face a huge fiscal burden, a less comfortable current account balance and, as between eastern and western Germany, a gap which may lead to changes in fiscal federalism and in the practice of collective wage-bargaining.

In the first part, the reference point will be the past, and I refer here to the long-term past: I begin by identifying the fundamental forces that turned the German economy into the rich and stable entity whose working has long been admired by many observers; I then go on to consider whether these forces are still at work, or whether they have systematically changed over time and, in the latter case, in what directions they have changed, and with what consequences.

In the second part, the point of reference will be the juxtaposition of 'united Germany' and the old 'West Germany', and I outline the long-term economic consequences of the one big discontinuity in recent German economic history: German unification and the opening up of eastern Europe. This will form a basis for considering whether that unique set of historical events will cast a 'hysteretic shadow' over the German economy for the foreseeable future or even for good, changing the fundamentals that are usually associated with the peculiar institutional setting which is sometimes called the 'German model'.

I conclude with a few speculations as to Germany's future role in Europe, at least to such extent that this role may be determined by the future of the German economy.

PAST VERSUS PRESENT

Nowadays, there is a widespread feeling among Germans that, in stark contrast to earlier times, something very fundamental is happening in the world economy which, in the long run, is working against their interests. Sure enough, this is no more than a vague sentiment, but such sentiments often arise from a background that is real enough and which thus merits some consideration. I shall explore – albeit briefly – two of the major dimensions that have played an important part in the German policy debate of the last few years: the competitiveness of German industry, and the persistence of unemployment.

German Industry: Past and Present

From a bird's-eye view and with some heroic simplifications, one may describe the last 125 years – in other words, the five quarter-centuries since the first German unification in 1871 – as a remarkable economic success story, though one with a plot of three distinctive stages:

- a first stage, up to the 1914–18 war, a period representing almost 50 years of fast economic growth which, most of the time, was well above the European average;
- a second, much shorter, stage of two decades – or three, if the two World War periods are included – in which the German economy tended to perform below the European average in terms of growth and other economic indicators;
- a third stage, again roughly 50 years in length, during which the performance was for a long time above European average in terms of growth, unemployment and inflation, although it gradually converged with that average by the time Germany had become the richest country in the European community in terms of per capita income.

In leaving the second stage – the inter-war years – out of consideration in the critique which follows, I am by no means oblivious to the likely objections of historians and political scientists. It was, however, a relatively short period of major international macroeconomic disturbances which hit Germany harder than most other European countries. It was a period of dramatic political instability and equally dramatic and abrupt shifts of economic policy, and is thus notoriously difficult to interpret in terms of long-term trends of economic growth and structural change. While the inter-war years are a time of utmost interest to those focusing on events which are certainly exceptional, and possibly unique, they are of less immediate importance to economists when analysing the workings of long-term economic forces.

By dropping out this second stage, then, the picture clears to reveal the (consistent) long-term success story of a country which transformed itself from a relatively poor and backward agricultural land into a relatively rich industrial powerhouse. Sure enough, the direction of structural change was roughly the same as in most European countries during these long-term periods of political peace and generally increasing economic prosperity. What is equally certain, though, is that the growth path of the German economy was steeper than in the other major countries: it started somewhat poorer than, say, Britain, France, Holland and Belgium but, in the end, turned out slightly richer than them all.

Looking behind macroeconomic numbers, the clue to this success is not difficult to identify: the pattern of fast-growing industries that began to take shape in Germany towards the end of the nineteenth century was particularly well-suited to profit from the waves of technical progress and the tides of highly income-elastic world demand for investment goods that were to emerge in later times. All those 'modern' industrial branches that were later to become the backbone of German economic success emerged and grew disproportionally in those years: metal manufacturing, mechanical and electrical engineering, chemicals and, later, the car industry.

As is usual in economic success stories, the roots lay in a combination of good luck and good management. It has often been suggested by economic historians that the German educational system, with its strong emphasis on technical subjects, was particularly well-structured to generate a young technical elite that was able to drive the process of industrial innovation on the plant level, and that the German apprenticeship system was a highly effective way of transmitting technical knowledge from one generation of skilled workers to the next.

On the other hand, conscious educational planning for a rosy industrial future was of itself no guarantee of above-average growth: the German mining industry, for example, is still renowned today for its superb technical skills, but this did not prevent mining from turning into a sunset industry as early as the late 1950s; the same story – though with later dates – applies to iron and steel. And these developments were certainly hard to predict at the beginning of this century. Hence a genuine element of luck was involved: the industrial structure that Germany inherited from the late-nineteenth-century 'pioneer' stage of what may be called 'scientific industrialism' contained the germ necessary for fast growth once European markets began to integrate.

That it did not prove possible to achieve this market integration during the inter-war period was, of course, a tragedy: in the 1920s, the American economy was able to profit from the remarkably fast internal expansion of the (large) internal US market; Europe, by contrast, could not liberate itself from the slow-growth trap of misguided nationalist economic policies. It was not before the 1950s – in the stable political and economic environment created by an international, non-protectionist policy of co-operation and co-ordination – that Europe, and above all Germany, could reap the profits of rapid trade-integration.

Through this process of re-integration and market expansion, the West German economy finally acquired the distinctive features that remain characteristic today: an economy specialising in high value-added, high-quality manufacturing (most notably of investment goods), with a high share of sales in export markets, and an unusually high share of very innovative small- and medium-sized firms which were able to build up strong competitive positions in a large number of segments in the world market. All this added up to shares of manufacturing in terms of total output and levels of employment that, from the late 1950s onwards, were persistently higher than in any other European country. As in other countries, those shares first stagnated and then declined during the 1970s and 1980s, but the important thing is that they were consistently the highest in Europe.

We have now reached the crucial point at which observers of the German economy – particularly those coming from an Anglo-American background – have spotted a major constitutional weakness of the German economy for the future. In view of the undeniable and inevitable trend towards further shrinkage of industrial employment in all basically rich countries (so the argument goes), such an unusually high share of manufacturing branches, no matter how successful they may have been in world markets in the past, must be a major liability for an economy in the future.

The question then becomes whether German manufacturing really is oversized. I do not believe that it is. National specialisation patterns are – at least in a predominantly free-trade environment – the long-term outcome of factor endowments and a gradual accumulation of specific knowledge and skills that develop differently in different countries and regions, often for reasons that are very difficult for economists to identify *ex post*, let alone to predict *ex ante*. Germany has developed a strong tradition in high-quality engineering, as have Switzerland and Austria, the two countries with the greatest cultural similarity to Germany and which, in terms of the manufacturing share of employment, take second and third place behind Germany within (non-eastern) Europe. As an economist, I would argue that, within the changing international division of labour, these relatively high shares of manufacturing are – and will remain – sensible equilibrium outcomes, whatever the general trends may be: just as the Danes and the French will always have a relatively large sector of high-quality agriculture, just as the Dutch will always have a large sector of highly efficient trade and transport, so the Germans, the Swiss and the Austrians will always have a relatively large sector of high-quality manufacturing, notably of investment goods.

But there is another aspect of German manufacturing that may be more worrisome in the future. Some observers claim that German manufacturing suffers from a delay in structural change. The point is that, within manufacturing itself, the world-wide growth-poles have shifted away from high-quality engineering, which generally counts as medium-tech, to genuine high-tech industries, notably all those summed up under the heading 'microelectronics' (everything from semiconductors down to microprocessors and computer software). It is in precisely these industries that, unlike the United States and Japan, Germany did not have great world-market successes in the past, and she is unlikely to have them in the future.

Again, however, this gloomy prognosis deserves some qualification. While German-style high-quality engineering may be classified as medium-tech by national accounting standards that adopt the share of research staff in total employment or the share of research and development spending in value added as the relevant criteria, the degree of disaggregation of these commonly-used statistics is insufficient to explore the fact that German industry is typically specialised in those segments of medium-tech industries that are, to all intents and purposes, high-tech in terms of their research and development (R&D) spending and staff. This also explains why the German economy as a whole has one of the highest shares of R&D spending in Gross Domestic Product (GDP) of all in industrial countries – roughly on a par with the 'high-tech champions' Japan and the United States – despite its traditional strength in so-called medium-tech industries.

If one takes these qualifications into proper account, the major question regarding structural change in Germany becomes a slightly different one: will German industry be able to emulate and apply all the rapid advances of microelectronics in those branches of manufacturing where the country has its traditional comparative advantages? Nobody can answer this question with certainty but, at least so far, there is no evidence for any anxiety in that respect: German cars, for example, are by now packed with microelectronic devices, adapted to the needs of the motor industry; likewise,

German machine tools and precision instruments are as computerised as any in the world.

In the future, however, this process of technological adaptation will work efficiently only if the education and vocational training of the labour force in all industries is modern enough to enable workers to absorb, apply and adjust new ideas quickly and precisely. In the past, the German apprenticeship system was by and large able to meet these demands although, more recently, there have been occasional complaints that the system has become too rigid and a bit old-fashioned in the *Berufsbilder* – that is, in the definitions and images of the different vocations and crafts that it projects. In this respect, some reforms may be warranted, and there is certainly no need for a wholesale revolution of the otherwise viable apprenticeship system.

To be sure, the adaptation to technological change is no guarantee for future market success: it is virtually impossible to forecast whether the German specialisation pattern is likely to generate faster overall economic growth than that of the other rich countries. There is no basis on which to predict that Germany will run ahead of the rest of Europe, but neither are there grounds for expecting it to trail persistently behind.

Unemployment: Past and Present

Structural change and technological adaptation may be no obstacle to further growth of the German economy within the caravan of all advanced economies. It will not, however, lead to any substantial long-term reduction of unemployment. In order to explain my pessimism on this count, it is necessary once again to glance back into history, and to divide the 47 years of labour-market history that have passed since the post-war currency reform in 1948 into roughly equal halves, the first running up to 1973, the second from 1973 until the present, late 1990s.

The first half began with high unemployment: due to the post-war influx of roughly ten million ethnic German refugees from eastern Europe, the unemployment rate in 1949–50 was between 8 and 10 per cent. Within ten years, however, the rate came down to 1 per cent (and even below), where it stayed until 1973, with just one, very brief, interruption in the recession year 1967 when, temporarily, it peaked at an annual average of around 2 (!) per cent.

In terms of structural change, this period can be regarded simply as a continuation and conclusion of the process of industrial growth that had been the hallmark of imperial times. High income-elasticities of product demand, technical progress and, above all, a newly emerging pattern of international trade, allowed a forceful expansion of employment in virtually all branches of manufacturing, with high-productivity investment goods such as mechanical- and electrical-engineering, metal manufacturing and, most of all, the production of vehicles, standing out in terms of output and employment expansion. Agricultural workers – in 1950 still roughly one-quarter of the total labour force – stood ready to accept the relatively well-paid industrial jobs on offer, and so did the unemployed, many of them highly mobile refugees, who were crowded in the agrarian north of the country but who could, if required, quite easily move to the growing industrial heartlands of western and southern Germany.

From the early 1960s to 1973, the state of the labour market as it had stood at the end of the 1950s was by and large conserved. With industrial employment staying more or less constant, and the domestic labour force shrinking due to demographic factors, the decline of agricultural employment could be accommodated reasonably easily. Even more than that: given the persistent state of over-employment, foreign workers took over the role of a supplementary labour force, taking up industrial job slots, now mainly in the lower-qualification segments, which were being left open by upwardly mobile domestic workers. Given the large and cyclically variable wage drift, together with the elasticity of the labour force that was afforded by the cyclical 'buffer stock' of foreign workers, the German labour market of the 1960s reached what was probably the maximum flexibility that can realistically be achieved within the constraints of a collective bargaining system.

In the last two decades, the state of the western German labour market has changed decisively and lastingly for the worse: from an average share of unemployment in the total labour force of 0.9 per cent in 1960–74 to 3.8 per cent in 1975–81 and 6.4 per cent in 1983–94. Historically, the last two decades are by far the longest period of unemployment ever experienced in Germany; if the short and erratic record of the 1920s is excluded from consideration, they are in fact the only period in German history of persistent non-cyclical unemployment.

There is now general agreement that, after two major recessions that followed severe supply-side shocks, the labour markets in most western European countries are dualised: part of the previously laid-off labour force soon found its way back into employment; a smaller part remained as a kind of sediment of long-term unemployment that lacked the (potential) productivity to be re-integrated at the then-prevailing wage level.

I would suggest that the explanation for this lies in the trend-change of industrial employment: in the first of the last two decades (1973–83), industrial employment suffered a shrinkage of two million industrial jobs; in the second (1983–94), it more or less stagnated, though its share in the economy-wide total continued to decline; in turn, employment in trade and services grew at a fairly constant trend-rate throughout both decades. Hence, while the brunt of the job losses in the first half hit industrial workers disproportionately, the subsequent growth in employment took place exclusively in service sectors. As industry is, on average, the sector that pays the highest 'premium' on physical work, this structural change meant a devaluation of the market value of unskilled labour and of everything in skilled industrial labour that is sector-specific. In addition, there was a trend towards 'servicification' in industry itself, routine physical work being replaced by machine activity which is supervised and serviced by a smaller number of better-skilled workers; this made the devaluation even more dramatic.

These trends in the labour market did not lead to a corresponding wage differentiation that might have eased the re-integration of the disadvantaged outsiders: there has been no widening of the wage differential between high-skill and low-skill workers in the way that has been so clearly in evidence in the United States. The reason for this high degree of structural wage-rigidity is very likely to be found in the combination of collective bargaining and a rather generous system of unemployment benefits. Hence, at the same time as structural change is drastically devaluing the human capital of one part of the economy's outsiders, there is little incentive for the insiders to exercise their bargaining power so as to allow for a substantial wage-differentiation, since one significant effect would be the sacrifice of the interests of those insiders with similar characteristics as the relevant outsiders (unskilled and/or older workers, for example). This is all the more so because the German unemployment insurance system allows for long periods of low-intensity job search.

In seeking the deeper 'exogenous' reasons for the drastic devaluation of unskilled labour in West Germany and other industrial countries over the last two decades, two major forces come to mind: globalisation and technological progress. The former means that a growing group of newly industrialised and developing countries reached a level of industrialisation, technical standards, and labour skills that allowed them to compete successfully in the markets for labour- and capital-intensive production and, increasingly, also in the lower market segments of human-capital and knowledge-intensive goods. The latter indicates that technological progress in industry has been labour-saving in so far as it has proved consistently profitable to replace manpower by modern (physical) capital equipment.

Which of the two forces dominated is a matter of dispute, but I would argue that, while debate on this count may be highly relevant to some of the major issues of trade policy *vis-à-vis* the developing countries, it is of far less importance in a speculative assessment of future trends in the labour market. After all, the speed and the shape of technological progress is itself to a large extent the (endogenous) outcome of a competitive race on all levels, encompassing growing intra-industry trade within and between industrial countries as well as growing inter-industry trade as between industrial and developing countries.

For the future, it is hard to imagine either a change or a significant slowing down of the trend towards globalisation in the broadest sense, not least because major population giants of the Third World – notably China and India – are now embarking on the same route as that trodden by a few much smaller Asian countries over the course of the last three decades. Hence, if anything, the process is likely to speed up, and will further accentuate structural change in the rich countries: industrial employment will continue to shrink, notably in terms of low-skill jobs; service employment – in the upper 'professional' segment and in the lower 'low-productivity' segment – will tend to grow. For former industrial workers, the upper segment will for the most part be beyond reach, while the lower segment will be unattractive.

In this sense, the long historical period of 'voluntary' structural change, characterised by the growth of a sector of high-waged unskilled labour and an almost automatic trend towards more equality of incomes, may be seen as having come to a definite end some time around the beginning of the 1970s. For a country like Germany, this has quite dramatic consequences for the viability of its labour-market institutions: while there is a permanent improvement in the quality of its labour force through a 'generational exchange' – with older, on average less-skilled workers leaving the labour force and younger, on average better-skilled ones entering it – there seems to be no safeguard in the system to ensure that this 'natural' adjustment proceeds fast enough to avoid extended phases of high structural unemployment.

For external conditions of this sort, collective bargaining and the German-style welfare state do not appear to be well equipped: the economic viability of 'egalitarian' collective bargaining combined with generous welfare state provisions is (crucially) dependent on whether or not structural change itself has egalitarian implications.

There is today a widespread, if not yet fully formulated, feeling in Germany – even among union members and leaders – that something has to change in the traditional philosophy of collective bargaining. More recently, some elements of flexibility have been injected into the traditionally rigid wage structure, such as so-called 'special rulings' for lowering the entrance wage for newly hired workers. But these steps appear to be minor and too limited in scope in the face of the magnitude of the problem. In this respect, Germany is a long way behind the degree of labour market flexibility which has always existed in the United States, and which increasingly exists in Britain (and, to a lesser extent, in the Netherlands). In my view, there are essentially two reasons as to why this should be so.

The first reason is a continued belief that some vaguely defined 'social peace' would be endangered if significantly more wage differentiation and flexibility were allowed. As far as the general public is concerned, this social peace consists essentially of two building blocks: the so-called 'autonomous wage bargaining' (*Tarifautonomie*) and a generous welfare state. *Tarifautonomie* entails a quasi-constitutional guarantee of the right of unions and employers' associations to negotiate wages and working conditions on behalf of their members; the generous welfare state is regarded as the major constituent in rendering a market economy 'socially acceptable' by providing a social safety-net to those who cannot make a decent living through their own efforts. For a pragmatic observer, it is sometimes quite distressing to see that any call for adjusting or modernising these two pillars of the social consensus is immediately denounced as an attempt at what is often described as 'social destruction' (*Sozialabbau*). This typically German attitude of turning issues which are essentially pragmatic into fundamental ideological question may not be helpful under any circumstances, but it is particularly damaging when, as today, irresistible forces of long-term structural change are gradually increasing the strains on the system. With the dramatic breakdown of the Swedish model of an overburdened welfare state in mind, it should be clear that some measure of reform is necessary.

These reforms need amount neither to a dismantling of the welfare state nor to a wholesale adoption by Germany of inequality on the American scale. After all, the United States has a system of elementary education which is unarguably inferior to that in Germany; furthermore, the US faces a persistent stream of low-skill immigrants which far exceeds the dimensions ever realistically to be expected in Germany. Hence – despite all the problems of long-term unemployment – the need for greater wage differentiation would almost certainly be more moderate in Germany than in the US.

The second reason for Germany's lagging behind in labour-market flexibility is more speculative. I think it can best be described as a general distrust of the service sector. Due perhaps to the strong manufacturing performance and tradition of the country, the service sector – with the exception of highly prestigious banking – has always been looked upon as a kind of residual sphere of activity in which money is earned not as the result of hard production work, but rather by the workings of some odd properties of invisibles that are not really the core of a 'decent and proper' economy. This attitude has consequences, some of which are serious, others which might best be described as curious. Among the latter is the service quality in Germany, which is notoriously bad by any international standard. Almost no German maxim falls as far short of the mark as does '*Der Kunde ist König*' ('the customer is king'): even a minor complaint about the food in a German restaurant will more often than not generate a protracted lecture from the waiter which, right from the outset, works inexorably towards the conclusion that the real problem is not the food but the customer's lack of gastronomic sensibility.

The more serious aspect of the anti-service attitude is that Germany has an undersized, heavily-regulated service sector, which attempts as far as possible to mirror the more rigid forms of industrial work-organisation and pay. The most obvious example is the inflexible closing hours of retail stores, which are becoming ever more anachronistic in an age of increasing female labour-participation. Until very recently, over-regulation could be found in less visible forms in virtually all service branches: from telecommunications and postal services to the retail trade; from transport on road, rail or river to catering. Due to the stifling extent of regulation, a large number of service jobs – irrespective of level of pay – simply did not emerge on to the market. More than that: by comparison with the US, Britain and the Netherlands, the service sector in Germany, implicitly protected as it was by a thick layer of national regulations, was able to survive in spite of its low level of productivity.

All this had changed considerably by the mid-1990s at least in those service sectors that have now to face up to foreign competition. The completion of the European single market can be given much of the credit for this change: in branches like transport and telecommunications, many regulations have been torn down or will be torn down before the end of the century. Of course, this does not mean the instant availability of a new source of employment opportunities: in the first few years following deregulation, firms which were formerly protected will be busy raising productivity, not least by shedding workers. In the longer run, however, there is reason to hope that the German economy will gradually close part of the 'service gap' *vis-à-vis* other countries, in terms both of the quality and the size of the sector.

UNITED GERMANY VERSUS WEST GERMANY

In the first few months, and even years, after German unification in 1990, many observers were inclined to regard that event as no more than a short-term distraction of German politics, the impact of which would diminish as the post-socialist eastern German economy was transformed. Sure enough, huge public investments – mostly financed by the former West Germany – were designed to remove the most urgent bottlenecks in the physical and the administrative infrastructure so that the extreme capital shortage of the eastern German economy would, in due course, be overcome – in, say, five to ten years. But that, it was assumed, was basically 'it'. After that, economic life in Germany would go on as it had before, with the unified Germany being simply an extended version of former West Germany – politically more weighty in the concert of European nations, but otherwise with a diet of economic assets and liabilities that was more or less unchanged.

It is, of course, much too early to judge whether this view will eventually be supported or refuted by the facts, and any attempt to evaluate it is at this stage highly speculative. That said, my own prediction is that this is a view which will prove to be mistaken in a number of important respects. There are three major economic considerations which go to support a belief that the united Germany will differ from 'good old West Germany' for a very long time, and possibly even for good.

First, united Germany will have to live with a long-term fiscal burden that does not have a precedent in the post-war history of the country's western part. Or, to put it differently: the question of consolidating public finances will become a permanent theme of German politics well into the next century. The reason is simple enough: the economic costs of unification have been grossly underestimated both by politicians and by a large percentage of the public. Instead of remaining a strictly temporary phenomenon, the large-scale transfers to the east have proved to be permanent, and the very slight trend downwards has occurred only in the most recent years.

The 'magic number' which best reflects the macroeconomic dimension of the fiscal problem is the ratio of government spending to GDP: throughout the 1980s, this ratio remained roughly constant, hovering around 41 per cent when measured on a cyclically adjusted basis. From 1989 to 1992, the ratio shot up to over 50 per cent and has remained there, as yet with no observable downward correction. The tax burden was increased moderately, and the budget deficit increased sharply so that, in the recession year 1993, a record deficit emerged. The deficit has declined since then, but this is attributable mainly to cyclical causes and because income tax was supplemented by a tax surcharge.

The huge fiscal challenge for the coming years will be to curb public spending so that government absorption of Gross National Product (GNP) can be driven back to the levels reached in the 1980s. This has to be done without resort to the emergency valve of tax increases: in terms of the tax burden – notably on business – Germany has already eroded the improvements which had been made during the 1980s. Today, the country finds itself somewhere in the middle of an international ranking of industrial countries in terms of the business tax burden, way behind important competitors for foreign direct investment such as Britain and the United States. In my view, it is still totally unclear how this enormous fiscal task will be tackled.

Second, united Germany will have to live with a much less comfortable external balance than West Germany ever did. It should be borne in mind here that West Germany had current account surpluses in all but four years between 1952 and 1990, and in three of those four years the deficit was, by any standard, very small. Between 1985 and 1990, the surpluses achieved were fairly substantial. Since 1991, united Germany has consistently had sizeable current account deficits.

Again, German unification provides a plausible – though by no means exhaustive – explanation. Through privatisation, the industrial base of eastern Germany has been reduced to a (viable) core of firms that has a reasonable chance of becoming competitive not only on the domestic market but in world markets as well. Viable though this core may be, it is nonetheless very small indeed: less than 14 per cent of the eastern German labour force is currently employed by the manufacturing industry – that is, in that part of the economy which produces the bulk of German tradable, and thus exportable, goods – and no more than 12 per cent of all manufacturing employees in Germany work in the east which, in turn, has roughly 20 per cent of the total labour force. On the other hand, consumption in eastern Germany is sustained by transfers from the western part of the country, which gives rise to a persistent imbalance between aggregate internal absorption and saving. It is thus not surprising that, as an economic entity, the German economy now runs a deficit in its current account.

It makes sense to interpret the persistent current account deficit in the German economy as the outside image of a far deeper internal problem which is likely to plague the German economy for very much longer than was generally expected shortly after 1990: the persistence of the economic divide between the former West Germany and the former East Germany. It is a gap that will dwarf all the regional gaps which were familiar in West Germany prior to unification.

This economic divide is the third respect in which united Germany is decisively different from 'good old West Germany'. Moreover, it may prove to be the most important point in the long run, for it has major repercussions on traditional institutions which have been the backbone of the German-style social market-economy throughout the entire post-war period. Two celebrated institutions will be under particular strain in this respect: fiscal federalism and collective wage bargaining.

As far as fiscal federalism is concerned, the point is simple enough. Bringing eleven states (Länder) to the bargaining table to agree a system for the equilibration of fiscal capacities is politically difficult, but not quite impossible when the states in question have per capita income levels that do not deviate by more than, say, something between the five to ten percentage points from the average as was the case in the West German past. Getting 16 states round the table to do the same thing will be much more difficult, given a situation in which a large number of them has income levels which are between 30 and 40 per cent higher than those of the others. It is almost inevitable that any compromise struck will be followed by prolonged and bitter complaints from either side – probably from both – and may well poison the political atmosphere. In this sense, Germany faces the prospect of the sort of deep, bitter and long-running interregional antagonisms with which other western nations, such as Canada, Belgium and Italy, are all too familiar.

Turning now to collective wage bargaining, the issue is somewhat more complicated, and entails even more speculation on the future course of events. The fact is that unemployment is much higher in eastern Germany than in western Germany: officially, eastern unemployment rates stand below 20 per cent; unofficial calculations that include hidden forms of unemployment produce a rate of between 25 and 30 per cent. Hence, it seems safe to predict that, even if its economy grows disproportionally quickly, the eastern part of the country will have much higher unemployment than the western part for a very long time. Nor can any relief be expected from the natural exit from the labour market of older workers in the coming decade, because a vast programme of early retirement has already removed roughly one million people form the labour force.

This persistently large labour-market disequilibrium in a substantial area of the country may have serious destabilising effects on collective bargaining: for employers in eastern Germany, it may become increasingly unattractive to join employers' associations because relatively good-quality workers are available for subcontractual wages on the free labour market; in the western part of Germany, by contrast, the skilled workers who make up a large share of a modern industrial work force can easily demand the contractual minimum wage, so that the economic rationale for staying out of employers' associations is practically nil, at least for large industrial firms.

But if the wage protection afforded by collective agreements is gradually undermined in the east, it will be hard for the west to remain unaffected by that 'Americanisation' of a near-by labour market, simply because of the high degree of mobility of capital and labour between the two parts of the country. Thus, in the end, collective bargaining may turn out to be undermined in the west as well, through the 'back door' of competitive pressures from the east.

There are other pressures working in this direction, above all migration, most notably from eastern European countries. In many respects, this is a replay of the economic situation before World War I: in Berlin, for example, there is an increasing number of construction workers from eastern Europe – also, remarkably, from Britain – some of whom will work for half the gross wage that would be payable to a comparable domestic worker in accordance with collectively-bargained, minimum-wage agreements. Of course, there are now efforts to stem this flood in as much as legal instruments are some handle on the problem, but it is unlikely that they will be wholly successful in closing the border to the east.

CONCLUSION

As we approach the end of this century, the united Germany is a country with a much larger menu of major economic problems than had the old West Germany. That old West Germany of the 1980s had already become a mature industrial country – a bit richer than the rest, but with similar assets and liabilities. On balance, all this is not quite a fall – nor even a decline – from miracle to crisis, so the question mark in the title is undoubtedly appropriate. But it is likely to be the gradual fading of a golden long-term path of above-average growth that turned the country into one of the economic motors of Europe in the 120 years which span the first to the second German unification.

This does not, of course, mean that in the course of its more normal growth Germany will lose political clout in Europe. After all, a country of almost 80 million people, located in the middle of the continent, and bordering on no less than nine different countries for whom it is bound to be the main trading partner for the foreseeable future, can hardly escape having political weight. However, there are additional reasons why this political weight is, if anything, likely to increase in the future, particularly within the European Community.

I would argue that the main reason for this lies in a gradual shift of the economic centre of gravity in Europe – roughly speaking, from the south-west to the north-east. The causes of this shift are to be found first of all in the recent enlargement of the European Union (EU) and second, and perhaps more importantly, in the disproportionately fast, and relatively long-term, economic growth that is to be expected in the countries of central and eastern Europe once the transformation crises have come to an end. Sheer geographical proximity to these countries will give to Germany – and also to Denmark, Sweden, Finland and Austria – somewhat better opportunities for trade integration with these fast-growth regions than to the rest of the EU. This opportunity, in conjunction with the persistent threat of large-scale east–west migration, will make Germany, Austria, and the eastern Scandinavian countries particularly receptive to the interests of the eastern part of the European continent.

This seemingly innocent shift may have quite far-reaching implications for the political configuration of the EU. In particular, it may in the long run undermine the cosy co-operation between France and Germany that has so far been the centrepiece of European integration. The logic is simple: an implicit coalition of interests between Germany, Austria, and the Scandinavian countries will essentially be a coalition of nations with a strong free-trade tradition that will profit from further EU enlargement, and that coalition may easily be joined by Britain and the Netherlands, two other strong free-trade advocates. Thus the natural forces of economic interests might tend to drive a wedge between the Romanic–Mediterranean camp, with its strong agricultural lobbies in favour of protectionism and its tradition of state interference in the economy, and the Anglo–Nordic–Germanic camp (plus, potentially, post-communist free-market central and eastern Europe), with the opposite interests and instincts. Other international differences in Europe – as, for example, the role of ecological considerations in policy-making, or the national consensus on the stability-orientation of macroeconomics policy – seem to run along broadly the same demarcation lines.

Note

1. A previous version of this paper has been published as *From Miracle to Crisis? The German Economy at the End of the Twentieth Century.* Discussion Papers in German Studies No. IGS 97/2, The University of Birmingham.

2 The 'German Model' in Decline

Jens Hölscher and Johannes Stephan

INTRODUCTION

The phrase, a 'German model', is adopted in the title although the existence of such a model is highly doubtful. The German economic post-war success story can be understood as a result of economic policy in a peculiar internal and external market constellation, whatever model is stylised (see Hölscher 1994). This paper argues that the market constellations faded away, but economic policy remained as if nothing happened at all. The process of changing market constellations began in the early 1970s with the breakdown of the Bretton-Woods system of fixed exchange rates, continued with 'eurosclerosis' and stagnation in the 1980s, and found its preliminary last stage in the new constellation of a unified German economy. The obvious signal of the new constellation is the coincidence of a record export performance and mass unemployment, reaching figures comparable to the world economic crises of 1933.

In the following section, the overall German economic performance will be sketched and some alternative explanations will be offered to provide the basis of our analysis. Concentrating on the last stage of the decline of the 'German model', the 'New Länder' impact will subsequently be analysed in detail to elaborate the new market constellation of the German economy at the end of the twentieth century. The section is divided into subsections on the major issues of the economics of unification, such as the legacies of the past in East Germany, the conversion rate, the overvaluation of the capital stock and financial transfers. The concluding section will describe the dilemma for economic policy in Germany and suggest an explanation for the new German 'eurohysterisis'.

ALTERNATIVE VIEWS ON THE POST-UNIFICATION PERFORMANCE

The performance of the German economy in the early 1990s is marked by a dramatic fall in employment. This is not only true for East Germany, where the peculiar situation of system transformation could be responsible for mass unemployment, but also for West Germany. As a result, the unemployment rate for the whole German economy climbed at the end of 1996 to a rate of 11.4 per cent and, if one includes 'hidden unemployment', reached a rate of 15.2 per cent. Table 2.1 shows a trade-off between open and hidden unemployment, which is not surprising, given the various forms of hidden unemployment. In particular, it is noticeable that 'hidden unemployment' is not a result of a 'qualification offensive', as column 7 shows. On the contrary, the structural difference between East and West is demonstrated by the figures for beneficiaries of early retirement schemes (column 8) and state employment measures (column 5), fields where no innovative turn can be expected. The recent all-over developments show no significant differences in the crisis within the German labour market.

It seems obvious to conclude that the 'failure to attain declared objectives with regard to employment has been, and continues to be, the most serious policy failure' (German Council of Economic Experts 1995, p. 16). Such objectives can only be formulated on the basis of an analysis of the reasons for the crisis in the labour market. One very popular view makes 'globalisation' on world markets, 'where competition is keener than ever' (German Council of Economic Experts 1995, p. 1) responsible for the German economic performance in the 1990s. The argument as such contains of course some truth, but seems to be inappropriate in the German case. For half of the last century, the then-West-German economy was export-driven, a fact that clearly indicates its competitiveness on world markets. As a trading nation, Germany was always highly integrated into the world market and a weaker performance can hardly be related to an increased degree of competition. A serious analysis of the decreasing competitiveness in world markets has to offer a better explanation and usually leads to long-standing supply-side deficiencies as main causes of the misery. This view, shared by the German Council of Economic Experts (see Hüther 1997), as well as the International Monetary Fund (see IMF 1997), advocates fundamental reforms of the 'German model', including deregulations of the labour markets, tax reductions and a 'building down' of the welfare state.

Table 2.1 Open and hidden unemployment in Germany

	Open and hidden unempl. (1)	*Registered unempl.* (2)	*Hidden unempl.* (3)	*Short-time workers* (4)	*ABM*[1] (5)	*§ 105 AFG*[2] (6)	*FuU*[3] (7)	*Early retirement* (8)
All Germany								
1994	5572	3698	1873	372	338	226	568	651
1995	5249	3612	1637	199	384	244	560	373
1996	5438	3958	1481	291	355	267	547	187
West Germany								
1994	3181	2556	625	275	57	197	309	6
1995	3193	2565	628	128	72	205	304	2
1996	3465	2791	674	218	76	200	308	1
East Germany								
1994	2391	1142	1248	97	280	28	259	646
1995	2056	1047	1009	71	312	39	256	370
1996	1973	1166	807	72	279	67	239	186

[1] ABM (*Arbeitsbeschaffungsmaßnahme*): job-creation scheme.
[2] §105 AFG (*Arbeitsförderungsgesetz*): employment promotion act.
[3] FuU (*Fortbildung und Umschulung*): further vocational training and retraining.
Source: German Council of Economic Experts, 1996, p. 111.

Surprisingly, an alternative approach from an institutionalist perspective comes to more or less the same conclusions. Here, the argument is that the institutional structure of social partnership itself is disintegrating, because employers leave the employers' association and employees leave their unions. Firms also fall short of providing sufficient training places for young employees and the apprenticeship system, as the basis for a highly skilled workforce, is threatened. The picture is completed by observations of recent failures in corporate governance, and a shift towards deregulation seems to be inevitable. This view is sharply rejected within the institutionalist approach itself by Carlin and Soskice (1997), who argue for more flexibility within the existing institutional structures, rather than for a new deregulated system of industrial relations.

A third view diagnoses a failure in aggregate demand management in anticipation of the aim of fulfillment of the Maastricht criteria. In this view, the crisis is partly home-made, because an expansionary fiscal and monetary policy, which would be appropriate in the downswing of the business cycle, is not carried out. Even worse, the austerity programme of the German government and the *Bundesbank*, labelled Europe-wide as a 'stability pact', reduces the normal level of economic activity and causes unemployment. The policy conclusion is then either to postpone the European Monetary Union (EMU) or to achieve a design that will allow public deficit spending after EMU.

In this paper, we put forward an alternative view that combines elements of the arguments above with a particular consideration of the design of German unification as a peculiar way of transition from plan to market. We will argue that this 'transition recession' coincides with an overdue change in the West German economy from an export-based, undervalued regime towards an overvalued import-based economic regime in a mature industrialised country.

THE 'NEW LÄNDER' IMPACT

German unification constituted an unprecedented strain on the West German economy and resulted in a disastrous 'deindustrialisation' in the East. Rising interest rates eventually forced the DM to revalue substantially against important currencies. This might mark the end of the constituting feature of currency undervaluation of the 'German model'.

Economic transition in the case of East Germany aggravated the general phenomenon of 'transformational recession', as the shock integration into the competitive and higher developed West German economy was accompanied by a revaluation of the GDR-mark. Additionally, rises in wages and earnings in the East, which envisaged their convergence to western levels well in advance of the improvements in productivity, immediately revealed the stock of productive capital in the *Neue Bundesländer* as largely obsolete.

The political objective of raising eastern living standards as soon as possible to converge with those in the West subsequently necessitated strong state engagement in the economy of the *Neue Bundesländer*. Generous state subsidies were generated to promote economic activity and employment in the East. Furthermore, some measures of *Mittelstandsförderung* (the West German practice of promoting small- and medium-sized enterprises) were diverted from the West to the East. In addition, producers in the East were granted some tax exemptions. The subsequently emerging financial transfers rose to heights previously unknown, peaking in 1993 at over 6.5 per cent of all-German GDP, of which only 1.2 percentage points came back via taxes.

Tax-income from the *Neue Bundesländer* was not able to balance these new fiscal needs and the Government had to raise funds primarily on (international) capital markets. Subsequent rises in interest rates reinforced capital imports, which eventually effected pressure on the DM to revalue. The unification boom had the same effect on the DM exchange rate: a rise in demand on the goods markets and increasing wages in both parts of Germany led the *Bundesbank* to react strongly by raising interest rates. With financial requirements in the East rising rather than easing off (as initially expected), and with a rise in the level of interest rates, additional pressure was placed on the budget, especially as the government was just embarking on a new phase of fiscal austerity in line with the anticipation of EMU.

Rather than achieving 'self-sustaining' economic growth, the East even today relies heavily on the help of its 'big brother'. Whereas the shock-therapy raised hopes of a fast and efficient transition in the East, the 'high-wage' path that evolved as a result of wage rises prolonged the process of catching up (Figure 2.1).[1]

Socialist Legacies

The structural pattern of the GDR economy had developed as a result of the determination and control of economic activity by the plan that governed supply and demand at practically every level. The paramount aim of the plan – to promote and secure political and ideological ends – gave rise to a price regime which was completely detached from the one on the

Figure 2.1 Development of East German GDP (1991 DM prices)

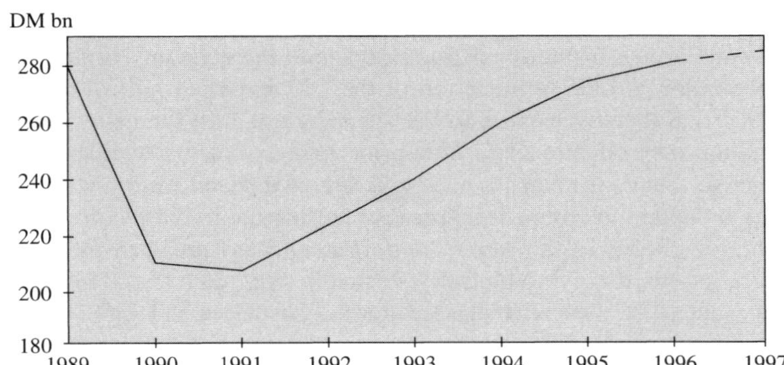

Notes: Figure for 1989 represents an estimate from the DIW, Berlin; figure for 1997 is a prognosis for a real GDP-growth of 2.0%.
Source: Deutsche Bundesbank and DIW.

world market, and furthermore led to the development of a rather peculiar pattern of production.

With the economic plan's pure supply-side orientation and due to the lack of consumer's 'feed-back' through the price mechanism, production in the GDR largely did not match demand, some products did not have any markets, whereas others suffered from poor quality. The productive sector was dominated by the production of material goods, suppressing the supply of 'invisibles': financial as well as other services were ideologically suppressed.

The GDR's aim to maintain independence from outside sources gave rise to economic structures that were characterised by a near-complete detachment from domestic and outside markets, highlighted by the (primarily vertical) integration of production that barely left any room for competition. Firms were given a wide range of social responsibilities; private engagement and risk-taking were rendered superfluous, as the means of production were state or publicly owned. The financial structure between the state bank and the producing sector emerged from a system that compares best to western practices of corporate taxation, as credits or subsidies were granted according to cost-related financial needs rather than profitability.

Whilst similar 'socialist legacies' exist to a greater or lesser degree in all other post socialist economies (PSEs), German monetary, economic and social union led the economy of the *Neue Bundesländer* down a considerably different path of systemic transformation: German unification exposed the economy in the East to a highly competitive environment without granting it any transitional period. Whilst the implantation of the West German institutional framework into the economy of the *Neue Bundesländer* and the introduction of the DM imported macroeconomic stability[2] and thereby worked to the advantage of East Germany, the reorientation of production to a new price regime and the reallocation of productive factors to match a new structure of demand were not assisted by any reduction in competitive pressure during the initial phase. Rather, productive capital in the *Neue Bundesländer* was forced to meet high western standards of productivity virtually from day one. This is the significance of the 'socialist legacies' for the East German case.

Implications of the Conversion Rate

Whilst the 'socialist legacies' outlined above indicate a productivity gap for production in the East, the initial level of competitiveness was to be determined by the conversion rate, as it set the structure of relative prices. Hence, a conversion rate that would have devalued the GDR-mark to match the productivity gap could have made production in the East competitive. Also, after fixing the exchange rate between the GDR-mark and the D-mark, higher productivity growth in the low-productivity region of East Germany would, *ceteris paribus*, have improved the competitive position.

On the contrary, however, the conversion rate between the DM and the GDR-mark effected a four-fold revaluation[3] of the GDR-mark, in contrast to the initial and then repeated devaluation of other PSEs' currencies. A 'neutral' conversion rate, that is, a rate that would have balanced the exports and imports of East Germany *vis-à-vis* the West, was impossible to calculate in light of the profound changes in prices and structures that were to emerge in the course of the subsequent systemic transformation, and integration into the world market.

The conditions of German monetary union were meant to be designed to allow producers in the *Neue Bundesländer* to enjoy a competitive advantage (Deutsche Bundesbank 1990, p. 11): converting wages at parity, it was believed, would result in eastern wages being 'competitively innocuous compared to those in West Germany' (Kloten 1996, p. 8). Productivity in East Germany in early 1990 was estimated to be at about 30 to 40 per cent of the western level (Institut für angewandte Wirtschaftsforschung 1990 and 1991; Siebert 1990), whilst gross wages per working hour were assumed to have amounted to only 25 per cent of the level in the West (Kloten 1996, p. 8). Whereas the actual conversion rate for flows in general and wages in particular would have corresponded to the overall level of productivity and would have granted competitiveness, wages in the East, at about one fifth of the western level, were clearly unsustainable. With the paramount political consideration for an early and generous unification having been the prevention of further migration, the conversion rate had to allow for converted wages to be sufficiently high to compare favourably with the West, a fact that the *Bundesbank* readily accepted (Deutsche Bundesbank 1990, p. 11).

However, the calculations pertaining to the rate of conversion were based on a static view of the economy in East Germany at the time immediately before unification and failed to acknowledge developments after unification, some of which might have been anticipated much earlier: whilst the conversion rate initially granted the firms in the East a competitive edge in as much as relative wages were lower than relative productivity levels, the rise in wages that followed German unification effected a dramatic worsening of their competitive position. Subsequently, only such firms being capable of raising their productivity levels to match the fast and substantial increase in wages were able to survive. The rest became technically bankrupt.

Although the *Bundesbank* defended the political viability of the initial wage gap on the grounds that purchasing-power in the East would remain higher than in the West even after unification – as prices of non-traded goods would not converge for some time (Deutsche Bundesbank 1990, p. 12) – early wage settlements in the East clearly set the agenda for full convergence to the western level within an extremely short period of time. In anticipation of a complete shift in the price regime and the installation of the West German system of unemployment benefits, the bargaining parties agreed an overall wage increase of 17 per cent even before German monetary union. Thereafter, increases of between 25 and 60 per cent occurred during the second half of 1990 (Sinn and Sinn 1994, p. 64). For the economy of the *Neue Bundesländer* as a whole, the metal industry wage arrangement of March 1991 served as a reference for all subsequent rounds of wage bargaining. It was agreed to adjust East German wages to western levels by 1994 and the group of additional wage-related benefits only one year thereafter (Arbeitgeberverband Gesamtmetall 1991).[4]

Secondly, the readjustment of the economy (demand and prices) was bound to result in some frictional effects, not least in widespread unemployment. With respect to the necessary structural change in the allocation of production factors amongst sectors, Sinn (1996), *ex-ante*, estimated structural unemployment by drawing the positive differences between East and West German employment shares for different sectors. Whilst this is a very vague estimate (the figure for structural unemployment rises with the number of sectoral categories, as only positive differences are being considered) and, as Sinn points out, should not be compared to measured unemployment figures, the analysis concludes that some 25 per cent structural unemployment can thereby indicate one major source of unemployment in the East. The picture provided is supported by the fact that

> the German economy relies so much on extensive vocational training and sharp distinctions between the professions ... Germany is not America where people have learned to be flexible and are used to switching from one occupation to another in the course of their lives.
> (Sinn 1996, p. 169)

Third, with the change in the conditions of trade between East Germany and the former CMEA (the shift in payments to a hard currency and GDR-mark revaluation), external demand for GDR produce plummeted and the demise in trade between all former CMEA member-states abruptly ended the GDR's low-priced supply of raw material and energy.[5] Between the end of the years 1989 and 1991, 'East Germany's real imports from other Comecon countries fell by 50 per cent or more, while its real exports remained approximately the same' (Sinn and Sinn 1994, p. 39). Such export performance can, to some degree, be attributed to generous West German export subsidies. Considering that such promotion had been discontinued in 1991, it appears that the development of imports from the CMEA area mirrored the general development of CMEA trade, whilst East German exports followed with a lag of about 6 months (ibid., p. 39).

With respect to the conversion rate for stocks, enterprise indebtedness within the banking sector, which accumulated in accordance with the socialist system of economic planning, constituted an important disadvantage for those producers in the East affected by it. Although these debts were reduced relative to savings as well as relative to flows by a split in the conversion rate, a significant burden remained in place which is not easily justifiable within the successor system. Because they accumulated during the socialist era, the underlying credits from the banking to the 'entrepreneurial' sector had been granted regardless of the criterion of profitability. The failure to dispose completely of these stocks has been widely acknowledged as a policy error that greatly reduced the asset value of capital in the East, its prospects for privatisation, and its viability in the successor system.

Very early during 1990, the first doubts about the competitiveness of GDR firms arose: in April of that year the *Anstalt zur treuhändlerischen Verwaltung des Volkseigentums* (the predecessor of the *Treuhandanstalt*) warned that only 30 per cent of firms would be able to stand up to competition after German monetary union, and that only half of the firms in the former GDR would 'be able to reach this aim after a longer phase of thorough restructuring' (Original-THA 1990, p. 5); up to 20 per cent of eastern enterprises almost inevitably faced bankruptcy (Fischer and Schröter 1993, p. 30).[6]

The Overvaluation of East Germany's Stock of Capital

In the absence of any possibility of protecting less profitable domestic enterprises against competition from more efficient producers in the West, via restrictions and other disincentives on imports,[7] the readjustment of the whole of East Germany's economy in an environment of fundamental change resulted in the demise of production and the replacement of eastern supply by products from the West. Given unity and short geographical distances, a large number of non-traded goods were just as much affected by this competition.

The 'disaster' (in the words of the then-president of the *Bundesbank*, Karl-Otto Pöhl, see Sinn and Sinn 1994, p. 51) is therefore attributable to the fact that the conversion rate was not set at a sufficiently low level to alleviate the initial competitive disadvantage of the existing productivity gap and the additional burdens of restructuring and reorientation of production, as well as the (un)expected extent of the rise of wages.

At the overall conversion rate of some 1.6:1 to 1.8:1, productive capital in the *Neue Bundesländer* had been grossly overvalued and was immediately revealed as being 'largely obsolete' (Siebert 1990, p. 12; see also Frowen 1997; and Köhler 1997). Whilst Siebert's evaluation of obsolescence is correct beyond doubt in the light of the extent of the demise of production, his reasoning[8] neglects the rate of conversion as the final determinant of competitiveness: theoretically, there always exists a sufficiently low exchange rate, which can make production competitive, even in the extreme case, where production is value-subtracting. This is the essence of the concept of 'comparative costs'.

With respect to measures of the asset value of East Germany's stock of capital, the consolidated result of the *Treuhandanstalt* may serve as indicator. Various estimates for the net value of the GDR economy had been made: Modrow, in the year 1989, estimated it at around DM 1.5 trillion. The first valuation of the predecessor of the *Treuhandanstalt*, the *Anstalt zur treuhändlerischen Verwaltung des Volkseigentums*, calculated a gross wealth of GDR-marks 924 bn (Köhler 1997, p. 153). Subtracting the value of enterprises that were earmarked to remain in state management, the figure was still GDR-marks 620 bn (ibid., p. 153). Rohwedder, the first President of the *Treuhandanstalt*, had to bring down his initial estimates to show an equal value of assets and liabilities in the balance sheet of the *Treuhandanstalt*. The opening balance sheet in October 1992 calculated a net value of firms in the East of minus DM 209 bn (Treuhandanstalt 1992) and the closing result of the *Treuhandanstalt* in the year of 1994 shows a deficit of DM 236 bn. In 1998, 'when the final balance can be drawn, a deficit of probably 270 billion DM will emerge' (Köhler 1997, p. 165).

Financial Transfers and the Strain on the German Economy

In response to this situation, the West German government set up various special funds and credit programmes to counter the immense decline in economic activity in the *Neue Bundesländer*, of which the fund *Deutsche Einheit* was only the most prominent example and proved to be completely insufficient. Having been set up in the course of German monetary, economic and social union in June 1990, it was planned to provide decreasing financial assistance between 1990 and 1994, amounting to an accumulated total of DM 115 bn, but had to be revised twice in 1992 and 1993 to a total of DM 160.7 bn (Schaden and Schreiber 1995, p. 20).

Comparing this to the actual sums of financial transfers, which reached over DM 770 bn until 1994 (iwd 14/1996, p. 3), and an accumulated gross total of DM 1146 bn until the end of 1996, of which a mere DM 246 bn flowed back in the form of taxes (iwd 24/1996, p. 4), the miscalculated extent of the burden of German unification becomes evident.

These funds had to be raised on domestic as well as foreign capital markets, as the regular year-to-year receipts of the general budget did not grant any margin: in 1989, it was slightly in surplus for the first time after a long period of fiscal austerity, and amounted to a mere DM 2.8 bn. In the following years, it turned into a substantial deficit, at around the Maastricht criterion cut-off rate and climaxed at 4.2 per cent in 1996 (see also Table 2.2).

Hence, the public borrowing requirement virtually exploded from 1990 onwards: whereas the consolidation effort since the early 1980s brought annual rises in indebtedness of the public sector down to some 2.9 per cent, indebtedness rose instantly after unification to 13.5 per cent in 1990

Table 2.2 The burden of unification: financing West-East transfers

	1989	*1990*	*1991*	*1992*	*1993*	*1994*	*1995*
General government financial balance in % of GDP	+ 0.1	–2.0	–3.3	–2.8	–3.5	–2.4	–3.5
German public debt, % change to previous year	2.9	13.5	11.5	14.6	12.2	10.1	20.1

Source: Deutsche Bundesbank.

and peaked in 1995 at 20.1 per cent (Deutsche Bundesbank 8/1993, p. 73 and 12/1996, p. 56). In anticipation of such vast borrowing requirements, the Council of Economic Experts warned: 'The funding of German unification will leave deep marks on the public budget.... We see this high public borrowing with great concern' (Sachverständigenrat 1991, p. 22, 23).

Due to the fact that about 50 per cent of transfer payments relate to the incorporation of the East into the West German welfare and financial system, whilst only 20 per cent and 10 per cent refer to investments in the physical infrastructure and fiscal policy in the East respectively (iwd 24/1996, p. 5), a renewed effort of budgetary consolidation in Germany will prove to be extremely difficult and will not only hinge on a reduction of unemployment and rising tax receipts in the *Neue Bundesländer*, but also on the development of interest rates.

In addition to the burden of financial transfers, German unification led the economy in the West into a unification boom. With output falling in the East and with regional consumption being maintained by financial transfers, the West German economy reached its potential output (though not employment): capital utilisation in the West German manufacturing sector peaked at 90 per cent in mid 1990 (Deutsche Bundesbank 1993, p. 22). With respect to the foreign sector, Germany's long-lasting current account surpluses and net capital exports turned into current account deficits and net capital imports from 1991 onwards (Deutsche Bundesbank 12/1996, p. 68).

Reinforced by wage increases in both parts of Germany, macro-economic stability was at stake: the consumer price index rose from 2.8 per cent in 1989 to its peak at 5.1 per cent in 1993. Hence, the *Bundesbank* reacted accordingly and immediately raised its rates to peak in mid 1992 (Deutsche Bundesbank 12/1996, p. 43; see also Table 2.3).

In line with the development of interest rates, the external value of the DM rose against its major trade partners in the EU, which corresponds to nominal revaluations. Whereas the reactions of the exchange rates with the US dollar and the Yen were immediate and have a strikingly similar pattern compared to interest rate parities, the European exchange rate mechanism (ERM) prevented the revaluation of the DM until the third quarter of 1992 (Deutsche Bundesbank 1993, p. 54).[9] Only with effect from February/March 1995 can this development be seen to reverse in favour of a devaluation of the DM (Deutsche Bundesbank 12/1996, pp. 74, 75; see also Chart 2).

Table 2.3 Bundesbank interest rates

	Jan. 20 1989	*Apr. 21 1989*	*Jun. 30 1989*	*Oct. 6 1989*	*Nov. 2 1990*	*Feb.1 1991*	*Aug. 16 1991*	*Dec. 20 1991*	*Jul. 17 1992*
Discount	4	4.5	5	6	6	6.5	7.5	8	8.75
Lombard	6	6.5	7	8	8.5	9	9.25	9.75	9.75

Source: Deutsche Bundesbank.

Figure 2.2 External value of the Deutsche Mark

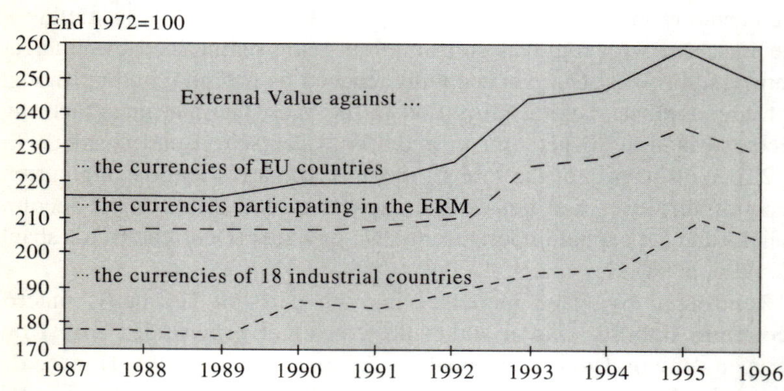

Source: Deutsche Bundesbank.

CONCLUSION

The allegation of this paper is that the 'old style' of solving the German economic problem via the export industry as locomotive of the economy does not work any more. Due to a stability orientation, which lasted too long (highlighted by the effects of German unification), the German crises consists of a dilemma marked by mass unemployment on one hand and a key currency on the other hand. The desperate attempts of the Deutsche Bundesbank to retain the old development position – of an undervalued D-Mark with consequently high export-led investment and employment growth is no longer suitable for Germany and is therefore doomed to fail: the moderate devaluation against the British pound and the US dollar at the end of 1996 and the beginning of 1997 has increased German exports, but without inducing investment for employment. A change towards an overvalued currency, which would be typical for a mature industrialised economy, would probably come too late, because the level of unemployment is already too high to cope with the negative effects on employment associated with even a small decrease in exports.

This dilemma of macroeconomic policy explains the hysterical German desire for a European currency. It is hysterical, because most of the actors do not know the economic rational reason, but have an optimistic perception of a 'European vision'. The economic rationality for a single European currency lies in the failure of a long-run monetary policy from the German central bank. If neither undervaluation nor overvaluation of the D-Mark is an appropriate policy, then, after 50 years, the good old D-Mark has served its duty. A new currency would disguise the German macroeconomic dilemma and allow for a fresh start. Of course, this teleological justification of a possible 'way out' of the German economic crisis at the end of the twentieth century does not imply any guarantees for success.

Notes

1. Depending on the estimation of a DM-value for East German GDP in 1989, this research makes a case for the late reattainment of the pre-transition level of economic activity in the *Neue Bundesländer* (in accordance with Kaser [1996], this was achieved sometime during the year 1996).
2. A discussion of possible negative effects of the implantation of the West German financial system into the economy of East Germany can be found in Robins 1995.

3. 'Enterprises were charged 4.4 mark per deutsche mark … and 4.67 mark per transfer ruble … these numbers are simply the "shadow prices" (*Richtungskoeffizienten*) used internally to price foreign goods. Since currency union, however, the cost of a deutsche mark's worth of Western products has fallen from 4.4 to unity.' (Akerlof *et al.* 1991, p. 22).
4. It was indeed thanks to the common interest of all parties involved in the bargaining process that the wage level in the East 'exploded' at this until-then unprecedented speed. While the political consideration was to prevent migration, trade unions as well as employers' associations in the West feared low-wage competition from the East.
5. The matter remains unresolved as to whether, as not least the German government stressed, the economic decline in the *Neue Bundesländer* was a result of the demise in the intra-CMEA trade or vice versa, that is, that 'the sudden and complete removal of restraints on trade between the two Germanies has made East Germany the Achilles' heel of Comecon' (Sinn and Sinn 1994, p. 28). The latter allegation of causality would mean that the collapse of CMEA trade cannot be held up as an explanation for the economic disaster in the *Neue Bundesländer* after unification.
6. Although eastern enterprises that were governed by the *Anstalt zur treuhändlerischen Verwaltung des Volkseigentums* might have had vested interests in downgrading their appearance in terms of competitiveness due to the level of subsidies received, these figures give credence to the idea that the demise in production that followed German unification could not have come as a complete surprise. 'Das Menetekel der DDR-Wirtschaft war im Frühsommer 1990 schon an die Wand gezeichnet' (Fischer and Schröter 1993, in the original German version, p. 31).
7 The argument for protection in the case of PSEs can be based on the lengthy nature of systemic transformation, the restructuring and reorientation of production to a new price-regime, and a completely new structure of demand.
8 'This is due to a number of reasons. First, the capital goods (equipment and buildings) are old … . Second, the capital stock is geared towards distorted environmental and energy costs. … Moreover, production and the capital stock were oriented to the COMECON, an external market with many distortions…' (Siebert 1990, pp. 12–13).
9 The fact that this upward trend of the DM was at least a significant contributor to the European monetary upheavals of September 1992 and August 1993, that eventually lead to the widening of the ERM bands, will not be discussed here and can best be revisited in D. Cobham (ed.) 1994, European Monetary Upheavals, MUP, Manchester.

Bibliography

AKERLOF, G. A. et al. *East Germany in from the Cold: The Economic Aftermath of Currency Union*. Brookings Papers on Economic Activity, 1/1991.

ARBEITGEBERVERBAND GESAMTMETALL *Geschäftsbericht 1989–1991*. 1991.

CARLIN, W. and SOSKICE, D. 'Shocks to the system: the German Political Economy under Stress', *National Institute Economic Review*, Cambridge, 1997. pp. 1–20.

DEUTSCHE BUNDESBANK *Die Währungsunion mit der Deutschen Demokratischen Republik*. Special print (Sonderdruck) from Monatsbericht der Deutschen Bundesbank, July 1990, Frankfurt a.M., Selbstverlag der Deutschen Bundesbank.

DEUTSCHE BUNDESBANK *Annual Report for the Year 1993*. Frankfurt a.M., Deutsche Bundesbank, 1993.

DEUTSCHE BUNDESBANK *Monthly Report August 1993*. Frankfurt a.M., Deutsche Bundesbank 8/1993.

DEUTSCHE BUNDESBANK *Monthly Report December 1996*. Frankfurt a.M., Deutsche Bundesbank 12/1996.

DIW (Deutsches Institut für Wirtschaftsforschung) *Wochenbericht 36/90*. Berlin, Deutsches Institut für Wirtschaftsforschung, 1990.

FISCHER, W. and SCHRÖTER, H. *The Origins of the Treuhandanstalt*. In Fischer, W., Hax, H. and Schneider H. K. (eds) *Treuhandanstalt – The Impossible Challenge*. Berlin, Akademie Verlag, 1993.

FROWEN, S. 'The Dimension of German Economic, Unification: Kennole Address'. In Hölscher, J. and Frowen, S. *The German Currency Union of 1990 – A Critical Assessment.* Macmillan Press, London, St. Martin's Press, New York, pp. 1–12.

GERMAN COUNCIL OF ECONOMIC EXPERTS *Facing Global Competition, Annual Report 1995/96*. Short Version. Stuttgart, Metzler-Poeschel, 1995.

GERMAN COUNCIL OF ECONOMIC EXPERTS *Pushing Forward with Reforms, Annual Report 1996/97*. Short Version. Stuttgart, Metzler-Poeschel, 1996.

HÖLSCHER, J. *Entwicklungsmodell Westdeutschland. Aspekte der Akkumulation in der Geldwirtschaft*. Berlin, Duncker & Humblot, 1994.

HÜTHER, M. *Supply side Economics: The Approach of the German Council of Economic Experts*. The University of Birmingham, Discussion Papers in German Studies, No. IGS 1997/1.

IMF 'Camdessus Cites Challenges Facing Germany and EU'. *IMF Survey*, 27 January 1997, Washington D. C., pp. 17–18.

INSTITUT FÜR ANGEWANDTE WIRTSCHAFTSFORSCHUNG *Wirtschaftsreport*. Berlin, Institut für angewandte Wirtschaftsforschung, 1990.

INSTITUT FÜR ANGEWANDTE WIRTSCHAFTSFORSCHUNG *Die ostdeutsche Wirtschaft in der Anpassungskrise*. Berlin, Institut für angewandte Wirtschaftsforschung, 1991.

IWD 'Wirtschaftsförderung Ost – Warmer Regen für die Industrie', *Informationsdienst des Instituts der Deutschen Wirtschaft*, 14/1996, p. 3.

IWD 'West-Ost-Transfers – Steiniger Weg zum Abbau', *Informationsdienst des Instituts der Deutschen Wirtschaft*, 24/1996, pp. 4–5.

IWD 'Wirtschafts – und Währungsunion – Mit Netz and Doppeltem Boden', *Informationsdienst des Instituts der Deutschen Wirtschaft*, 44/1996, pp. 4–5.

KASER, M. *Post-Communist Privatisation: Flaws in the Treuhand Model*. The University of Birmingham, Discussion Papers in German Studies, No. IGS 1996/10.

KLOTEN, N. *The German Currency Union: Challenges for Both Parts of Germany*. In Hölscher, J. and Frowen, S. *The German Currency Union of 1990*

– *A Critical Assessment*. Macmillan Press, London, St. Martin's Press, New York, 1997, pp. 177–99.

KÖHLER, C. *The Privatisation of the East German Economy and the Role of the Treuhandanstalt*. In Hölscher. J. and Frowen, S. *The German Currency Union of 1990 – A Critical Assessment*. Macmillan Press, London, St. Martin's Press, New York, 1997 pp. 151–68.

ORIGINAL-THA (Anstalt zur treuhändlerischen Verwaltung des Volkseigentums) *Report on the Work of the Institute for Trustee Administration of State Property from 15th March to 18th April 1990* (signed by Dr Moreth). Berlin, Anstalt zur treuhändlerischen Verwaltung des Volkseigentums, 1990.

ROBINS, G. S. *Banking in a Transition Economy: East Germany after Unification*. PhD thesis, Templeton College, University of Oxford, 1995, forthcoming in *Studies in Economic Transition*, London, Macmillan Press.

SACHVERSTÄNDIGENRAT ZUR BEGUTACHTUNG DER GESAMTWIRTSCHAFTLICHEN ENTWICKLUNG *Jahres-gutachten 1991/92*. Stuttgart, Metzler-Poeschel, 1991.

SCHADEN, B. AND SCHREIBER, C. 'Unerwartet hohe Transferzahlungen – Ein Ende in Sicht?', *ifo schnelldienst 17–18/95*, pp. 19–23.

SIEBERT, H. *The Economic Integration of Germany, An Update*. Institut für Welt wirtschaft, Kiel Discussion Papers No. 160a, September 1990, Kiel, Institut für Weltwirtschaft, 1990.

SINN, G. AND SINN, H.-W. *Jumpstart. The Economic Unification of Germany*. MIT Press, Massachusetts, 1994.

SINN, H.-W. *Macroeconomic Aspects of German Unification*. In Welfens, P.J.J. (ed.) *Economic Aspects of German Unification: Expectations, Transition Dynamics and International Perspectives*. 2nd edition, Berlin, Heidelberg and New York, Springer-Verlag, pp. 135–89.

TREUHANDANSTALT *DM-Eröffnungsbilanzen zum 1. Juli 1990*. Berlin, Treuhandanstalt, October 1992.

3 Economic Policy for the New German Länder: Supply-Side Economics Needed

Michael Hüther

GERMAN UNIFICATION AND THE TASKS OF ECONOMIC POLICY

Unification changed substantially the conditions for all fields of economic policy in both parts of Germany, but the basic concept of supply-side economics gained even more importance. In eastern Germany as in Western Germany investment activity has played a key role since 1991, and economic policy could and can best support growth by ensuring both that investment conditions do not worsen in the western part of Germany and that they rapidly improve in the eastern part. The core problems of the German economy are rooted in the supply side, not in the demand side.

Since 3 October 1990 the crucial point was to stimulate private investment in the new Länder. At the beginning economic policy had to focus on barriers to investment that result from both unclarified property ownership and the negative legacy of the former economic system and had to improve very quickly infrastructure by public investment. Six or seven years on, the problems are different: on the one hand infrastructure as well as public administration have improved remarkably, the bulk of unclear ownership has been clarified, a lot of private investment has taken place, the privatisation agency Treuhandanstalt has succeeded – with few exceptions – in bringing economic privatisation to a close. On the other hand the process of normalisation for eastern Germany is still a very long way from achieving the ultimate goal: especially in the labour market the situation is disastrous, even in the seventh year after unification. The East German Länder will still need substantial financial support in order to be able to continue with their reconstruction and the building up of their economic potential. The awful slowing of the process of reconstruction in

1996 and in 1997, together with the fact that many firms are in dire straits, undoubtedly provides grounds for considering the basic economic policy approach. This would create a substantial barrier to the improvement of the East German position to compete for business locations.

The German Council of Economic Experts (*Sachverständigenrat*) has argued since the beginning of the unification process in favour of this approach to supply-side economics. In January 1990, the Council published a Special Report, 'Zur Unterstützung der Wirtschaftsreform in der DDR: Voraussetzungen und Möglichkeiten', which was based on the assumption that both German states would coexist separately into the near future. This report focused only on the need for fundamental reform in East Germany. In the following 1990 Annual Report the Council started to discuss not only the transformation problem for the east but also the integration problem for the west. Economic policy as growth policy deserves high importance if one would try to solve both problems. And the Council was optimistic: 'If everything goes well the economic development in the new Länder might already have taken a turn for the better by 1991' (1990 Annual Report, item 304). But only five months later the Council was forced to publish another Special Report, 'Marktwirtschaftlichen Kurs halten. Zur Wirtschaftspolitik für die neuen Bundesländer' (13.4.1991) because of the fear that the economic crisis in East Germany would push the politicians to a strategy of high subsidisation and of preserving the old structures, especially the enterprises. In the face of the extraordinary extent of the adjustment needs the demands to limit them became louder and policy became actually more willing to succumb to them.

In the 1991 Annual Report the Council argued again that since unification the Federal Republic had changed in nature, and it required a change in thinking in the old Länder as well. Therefore in many spheres what was urgent and what had to wait needed to be reassessed. Concerning the basic concept of economic policy for the new Länder the Council discussed two different approaches:

> It is correct that the state has to take actions for renewing the economy in the new Länder. After all, the state does not just stand on the sidelines in a free market economy either. As little as it can be inactive, however, it can and must it accept a dirigistic role or dissipate its efforts in a multitude of uncoordinated individual measures dictated by the needs of the moment. It must be clear which strategy the government is pursuing and what the underlying perspectives for the economy in eastern Germany are.

Two conflicting strategies are possible:

- The first strategy is growth-oriented. Through its fiscal policy the state ensures favourable tax conditions for investment as well as for the rapid development of the infrastructure in the new Länder. Financial resources are raised in such a way that, given a strict monetary policy aimed at price stability, investment is not crowded out elsewhere. Within this strategy the primary task of labour-market policy is to foster retraining and training activities. Wage policy takes care that it does not further exacerbate the employment problems that already exist and that it does not make the social policy measures accompanying the process of adjustment even more expensive. The common objective behind this strategy is to do everything conceivable to improve the competitive position of the East German economy as rapidly as possible. The free play of market forces will determine the resulting new structure of the economy.
- The other strategy is more strongly oriented towards preserving existing economic structures. Although it also has the objective of improving the competitive position of the new Länder, it gives the state an active role in dismantling old jobs and in developing new ones. One aim is to limit the necessary adjustment burdens on the individuals. This strategy includes the idea of preserving as many old jobs as possible as long as there is a lack of new ones. In doing so, the fact is accepted that the state or the social insurance systems have to make up for what the market cannot pay in wages, and that the reorganising of old enterprises that cannot be privatised might turn the Treuhand agency into a permanent institution as a state holding company. Our political leadership cannot simultaneously pursue both strategies; there has to be a clear decision in favour of one of them.

(1991 Annual Report, item 262)

This request of the German Council was based firstly on a comprehensive and continuous analysis of the East German transformation process and secondly on the experience of the west German economy in the eighties. Since the beginning of the 1980s the federal government adopted a supply-side oriented strategy which was elaborated by the German Council after the recession of 1975. The recovery from the 1975 recession, which had looked quite promising during the later part of 1976 and early 1977, had come to a halt in the second half of 1977. Despite the fact that the government had followed a relatively strong expansionist fiscal policy, overall demand had increased only slightly. Due to the slow recovery of Germany's main trading partners export growth had been lower than the previous year. Industry had remained highly cautious and there was more restraint in its investment intentions than at similar points in previous cycles, with the consequence that the lag in investment continued. Economic growth (measured by the expansion of the production potential or potential output) was insufficient to make a dent in the unemployment figure, which had not fallen below one million people since the end of the recession in 1975. At that time in public debate the opinion had gained ground that economic policy immediately following the recession should have been directed towards a more expansionary demand policy. The Council argued that any evaluation of the fiscal policy of that period could not be restricted to the foregoing two years, because in 1975 fiscal deficit was of an unprecedented magnitude but without stimulating a self-acceleration within the cycle. So what was wrong with the German economy and German economic policy?

STRESSING THE SUPPLY SIDE: WHAT DOES IT MEAN?

The starting point for the concept of supply-side economics was the central problem of economic policy: the evil of unemployment. For the German Council the lack of jobs is related to an expansive wage policy, a policy that disregards the fact that wages are a cost factor.

Why? It is obvious that if you want to buy goods and you are willing to work for that, you must have a job – and in an economic system characterised by division of labour you will find a job only if you do not demand a higher wage than others are willing to pay for the result of your work. A permanent oversupply of manpower thus must be connected with excessive wages. There is a lack of employment, thus there is a lack of income and, consequently, of demand. Behind that is a wage policy which disregards the extent of wage increases that is justifiable in terms of the overall economy, that is, the increase of labour productivity.

Although no one (including the Council of Economic Experts) will pretend that unemployment in its entirety may be caused by wages in real terms, wage policy does play a key role with regard to the reduction of non-cyclical unemployment, because it is the wage policy that fixes the price of labour. But choosing only this approach would mean thinking in static terms (that is, based on the existing capital stock) and in a monocausal dimension.

Examining investments opens up a more comprehensive economic approach; all conditions of private-sector initiative have to be included, in particular those that are set by government action. The question is how sustained employment can be created or, to put it in other words how can unemployment be substantially reduced? The contribution of wage policy to solving that problem does not really regard the origins of unemployment in the past – because enterprises adapted to the excessive wage level a long time ago; it rather consists in safeguarding a considerable job-creating effect in future investments.

After this argumentation detour, the real focus now is on the origin of the lack of investments or, to put it more precisely, the lack of job-creating investments.

The issue of a sufficient level of investment activity leads to a particular problem of co-ordination: even a free-market system does not have any reliable mechanism that would ensure that the total of all future-oriented production plans of businesses – as expressed by their investment activities – always meets the total of the employment and production wishes of those who form the labour force potential. What is the underlying problem? The actual problem is that of sufficient profit expectations, without which investments will not be profitable. To put it in other words: the problem of the real cost level or, more precisely the problem of the remuneration claims of those involved directly or indirectly (government via taxes) in the production process in relation to the production revenue. Solving the co-ordination problem gets more difficult where uncertainties are involved. For this reason alone, any investor has to accept the possibility of losing his money. This risk may be counteracted in two ways. First, the other parties involved – in particular employees and the government – can arrange their claims in a way that permits the (external or internal) investors to maintain a satisfactory relation between opportunity and risk. Second, the investment project can be cancelled; in a market economy, no-one is obliged to make investments. The full extent of the co-ordination problem becomes obvious if one thinks of the dimension of uncertainty. What is meant here is mainly uncertainty with regard to the overall economy, expectations concerning future changes in the speed of growth, future struggles for income, and future shocks from the global economy.

What can be achieved by economy policy?

There is on the one hand demand-oriented economic policy in the Keynesian tradition. Under the term 'demand management', an attempt was made to manage the overall level of demand to achieve a smooth development, that is, to reduce cyclical fluctuations by creating additional loan-financed government demand to compensate for a temporary lack of internal or external demand. What is very important here is the aspect of temporariness. If the government follows this strategy, it gives a long-term guarantee of profitability to the businesses by stabilising demand; thus uncertainty about how the overall economy will develop is reduced or even eliminated. The idea is that the government's greater confidence in the future, which is expressed by its readiness to incur debts, should be transferred to the private sector.

Applying demand-oriented economic policy means distributing presents; however, those receiving the presents must not realise that finally it is them who will have to pay for the presents. If this illusion is destroyed as a result of the government's failing to secure financing in good times and permanently distributing presents irrespective of the general economic situation, the effect of demand-oriented policy will be reversed. Instead of reducing uncertainty, it will create new uncertainty because it will be unclear when and how the presents will have to be paid for, and how long the government will be able to act in terms of fiscal policy.

Let us examine the issue from a second aspect: according to economic theory, the underlying reason for demand-oriented economic policy is the possibility that weak private demand may lead to a recession through processes that reinforce each other – exports are collapsing, investment plans are reorganised, the work force is cut down – without any hope that a new upswing may start after quantities and prices have been adjusted. However, this is just a *sine-qua-non* condition, because not every temporary weak-demand situation entails the risk of a cumulative downswing, and every weak-demand situation has causes that can be counteracted by demand-oriented measures.

The experience of the 1970s shows that permanent use of demand-oriented tools and, in particular, the abuse of demand-oriented policy to counteract instabilities whose origins are not on the demand side – such as the oil shortage in the mid and late 1970s – lastingly impairs the efficiency of such a policy. The budgetary room for manoeuvre was reduced to such an extent that burdening the population with higher taxes or cutting expenditure in the field of immaterial or material infrastructure were unavoidable. Thus, giving priority to demand-oriented considerations and failing to take account of the costs of such policy caused long-term damage and deprived demand-oriented economic policy of any efficiency. Olaf Sievert – who was chairman of the Council of Economics Experts for many years – put it like this: 'The pleasure of giving aid to a fiery horse has turned into the agony of making Rosinante take even the smallest hurdle'.

This experience and the knowledge acquired about the practical problems of Keynesian demand management – which means overcharging the political system – induced the Council of Economic Experts to develop the concept of supply-oriented economic policy. This was first presented in the 1976 Annual Report, that is, long before the American idea of supply-side economics emerged.

Let us recall again what is the underlying problem of overall economic instabilities. The free-market system may be described as a control system, that is, a system of interdependent markets whose functioning is controlled by prices or, to put it more precisely, by price formation on the markets. If it turns out that the underlying assumption – that this control system is able to absorb and neutralise shocks – is not correct, this can only be due to inappropriate prices and wages, that is, these regulation variables obviously transmit wrong signals. If a distinction is made between current prices and prices expected for the future, an additional element of uncertainty is involved, that is, uncertainty about how to use one's property, the question of whether one should make an investment or put it away in savings. From an economic aspect, prices and wages are claims to the revenue that can be realised or are expected on the markets. To put it in other words, prices and wages determine the remuneration that can be expected for the risk run by those who are ready to provide property for future production, that is, those who invest. This is exactly where supply-oriented economic policy approaches the problem, because through reliability it tries to contribute to a situation where no one involved makes excessive claims to the output. This means two things: first, the claims of those directly involved in the production process should be based on their own efficiency, while wage demands should be based on labour productivity; and second, the claims of those indirectly involved, which are managed by government intervention (taxes and other fiscal charges), should take due account of the relation between the investors' risk and opportunities.

This is the logic of supply-oriented economic policy. Its strategy is to correct claims on the output and to improve production conditions so that more potential production will become profitable, which – from market aspects – will then justify more employment and finally more income. Supply-oriented policy is the attempt to repair damage and provision of the means not to fall behind in international competition. It is true that supply-oriented policy is less attractive than demand-oriented policy, which promises to increase claims rather than to reduce them. Moreover, making people understand and accept supply-oriented policy is more difficult than for demand-oriented policy since the lines of action of the latter appear to be shorter and more direct – but this applies only if one disregards the costs of such strategy in the form of long-term damage.

What are the opportunities of supply-oriented economic policy for increasing profitable production possibilities?

(1) Preventing price formation on the product markets that is not in line with market conditions, that is, that is not in line with scarcity:
   (a) by competition policy which prevents positions of power that are not justified by market conditions,
   (b) by policy committed to price stability which prevents the emergence of fear of inflation.
(2) Preventing excessive claims to the output by wage policy which focuses on safeguarding employment rather than safeguarding income, that is, on a permanent basis.
(3) Taking due account of entrepreneurial risk, that is, the risk of making investments
   (a) by reducing the taxation of investments and the revenues flowing direct from them,
   (b) by making employees share the investment risk (models of profit sharing with limited liability).
(4) Facilitating the search for and application of new production methods and products by avoiding unreasonable restrictions (licensing procedures and so on) and a general climate that is hostile to technology.
(5) Restructuring government activity by a strategy of qualitative consolidation:
   (a) Increasing the support of education and science, as well as research and development in the businesses,
   (b) providing sufficient material infrastructure,
   (c) decreasing consumption expenditure, that is, reducing those claims to the output that are managed by the government by means of public benefits and social transfer payments.

Since supply-oriented economic policy is based on market efficiency, it generally accepts the market principles of income distribution. This means two things: first, income is not distributed according to needs, but according to efficiency in the production process; and second, under these conditions, income from profits is justified by the efficiency of those who advance capital and take risks.

This would certainly not be satisfactory, because it would mean that anyone who is not able to be efficient will not get anything. What are the conclusions of the German Council? We need a social policy that follows the idea of subsidiarity while never disregarding the fact that individual freedom and responsibility or liability for one's own actions are an integrated whole, that social policy must not destroy this connection. Moreover, it is also from aspects of distribution policy that we need an efficient competition policy which allows monopoly profits on a temporary basis only.

Once again, supply-side economics is not as simple as demand management and less attractive. The politicians need more staying power because the advantages of such a policy are lying in the medium term future and sometimes not within the legislative period, whereas the burden of repairing damage will occur immediately. This characterises the chances to implement supply-side economics. For competing parties it is easier to impress the public with rapid, vigorous action that has a direct impact than with long-term concepts whose effects are difficult to assess and will only be felt some time in the distant future.

A SHORT REVIEW OF THE PRESENT-DAY SITUATION OF THE GERMAN ECONOMY

Given these political restraints against following a strategy of supply-side economics, it is surprising that in 1983 the new government of Chancellor Kohl was able to translate the main idea of this approach into public policy and put it into action. It is interesting to look at New Zealand, Sweden and the Netherlands where comprehensive economic reforms took place that can be characterised as supply-side economics. The necessary condition to start such a programme is obviously a situation in which the foundations of wealth are put at risk as a result of a lasting policy of distributing presents. Anyone with eyes to see will realise that economic policy in Germany came to a dead end. Present-day Germany got into such difficulties because the majority of the West German population did not realise, or did not accept, that German unification changed fundamentally the conditions for economic life in the western part of Germany as well as the eastern. Politicians and the public had the illusion that the economic impulse of unification would create a self-sustaining path of economic growth which would allow a decoupling from the world-wide economic cycle.

This was the background for some important mistakes:

(1) the federal government realised too late the financial burden caused by the programme of economic revitalisation in the east;
(2) the implementation of the West German system of regulations in the East;

(3) the introduction of the already ill-considered system of social security in the new Länder;
(4) the system of collective wage bargaining led to a wage level in East Germany which caused unit labour costs of 130 per cent of the West German.

These decisions prevented fundamental reform and caused the illusion that the traditional West German systems were functioning well. The outcome has been tremendous, well-documented problems on the supply side of the economy: high taxes, a high level of public debt, high labour costs per unit, and a social security system of disincentives.

These are the main causes that reduce the willingness to invest in a situation of intensified global competition, and economic policy up to now has not started a substantial programme of budget consolidation to gain room for a substantial reduction of taxes and levies. But, more importantly, it is vital to establish a lasting and reliable framework for market processes and to redress undesirable developments, not by ad hoc treatment of symptoms but by means of fundamental corrections.

Due to these facts the present-day situation of the pan-German economy is characterised by a remarkable weakness of investment and a very poor situation on the labour market (Figures 3.1 and 3.2). Business expenditure on new machinery and equipment, which slumped in 1993 by more than in any other recession (18.2%), is still well below the level that had been reached before the collapse. The prime motives for investment have been cost reduction and replacement, with the creation of new productive capacity a relatively unimportant factor. This weakness in investment is above all a reflection of the negative impact of state intervention and wage bargaining on the medium-term prospects for earnings. The negligible growth in the potential output during the mid 1990s reflects this lack of investment.

The other side of the sluggish growth is the fact that the labour market has not experienced the improvement that might have been expected in view of the time that has now elapsed since the recession. Unlike the other two previous cycles in West Germany, in which employment figures rose after the bottom of the trough had been reached, this time the number of employed people has continued to fall. All in all, the situation on the pan-German labour market, with more than 4.3 million in registered or hidden unemployment, is grave.

Recent economic development in East Germany can hardly be regarded as satisfactory; GDP has grown by only 2 per cent in 1996 and for the first time since 1992 the growth of aggregate output will not exceed that in the

Figure 3.1 Cyclical comparison of private investment in machinery and equipment[1] (seasonally adjusted)

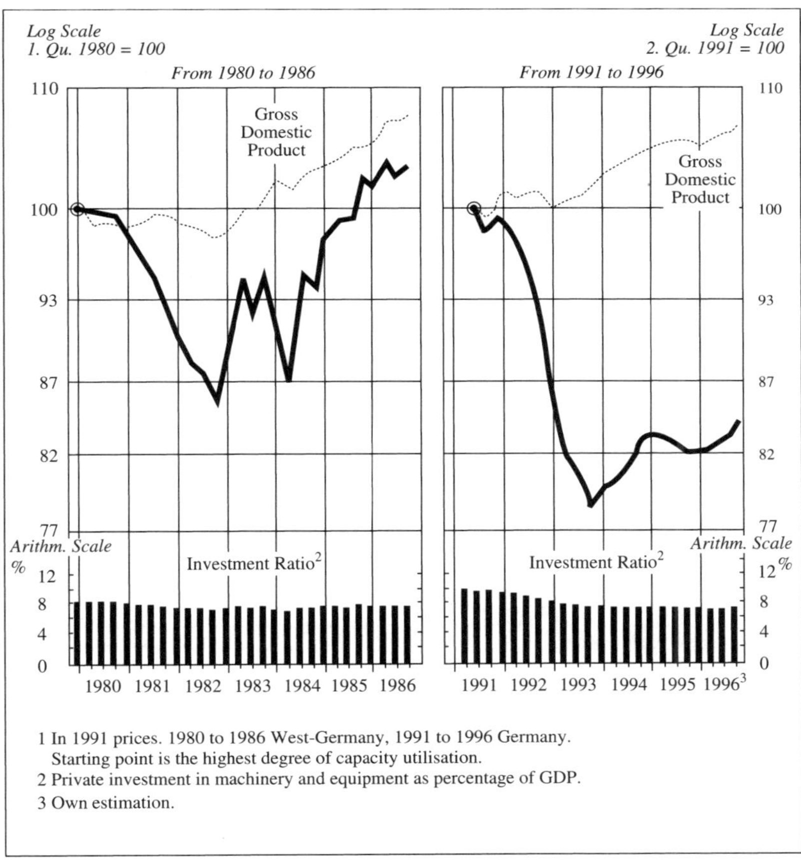

1 In 1991 prices. 1980 to 1986 West-Germany, 1991 to 1996 Germany.
Starting point is the highest degree of capacity utilisation.
2 Private investment in machinery and equipment as percentage of GDP.
3 Own estimation.

west in 1997. On the one hand, the construction industry has lost momentum and no other sector has been able to take over as a driving force whilst, on the other hand, the process of reconstruction in the east has increasingly been influenced by developments in the West German economy. It has become all too clear in the course of 1996 and 1997 that it can no longer be assumed that it will be possible in the future to maintain the high growth rates for GDP initially registered in the new Länder. In the long run, transfer payments will not provide sufficient compensation for the negative impact of unfavourable conditions on the supply side, such as

Figure 3.2 Cyclical comparison of employment[1] (seasonally adjusted)

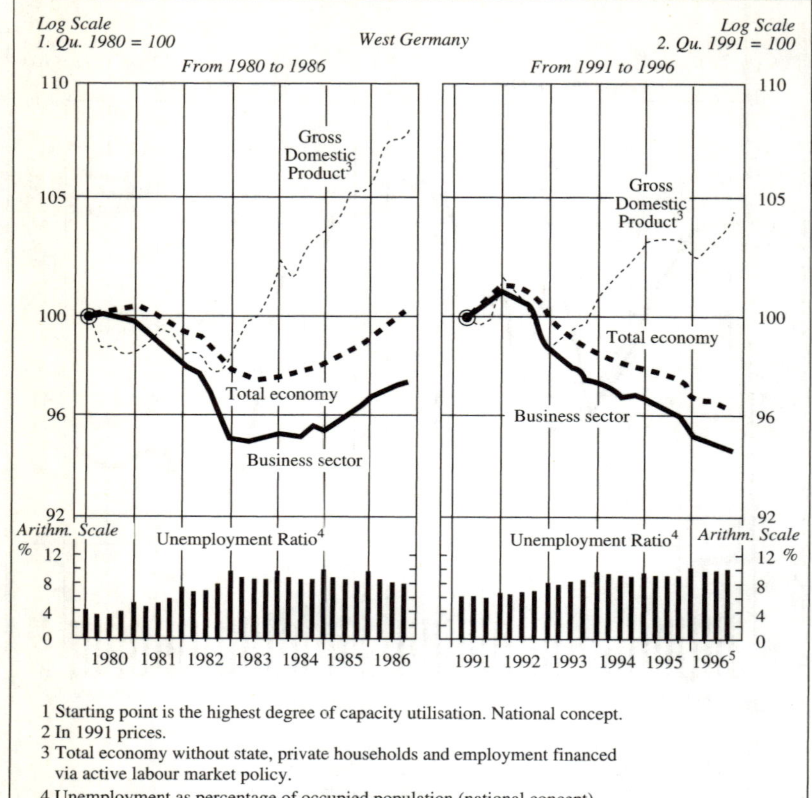

1 Starting point is the highest degree of capacity utilisation. National concept.
2 In 1991 prices.
3 Total economy without state, private households and employment financed via active labour market policy.
4 Unemployment as percentage of occupied population (national concept).
5 Own estimation.

current wage policy, and deficiencies in East German enterprises, such as management problems and the lack of innovation. All too often firms become accustomed to subsidies and this prevents them from undertaking the measures that are necessary in order for them to be able to adapt to their new situation.

The fact that the process of reconstruction is steadily slowing down does give some cause for concern. But the creation of strong and self-supporting economic regions in the east requires economic and wage policies to create a framework of supply-side conditions that will bring the East

German economy back on to an appropriate growth path and create more employment. This will be the best strategy for finding a route to normality. Normality means that companies can survive, without subsidies, on the market and thereby commercially earn the means to pay the salaries of their employees; that those who want to work are in the vast majority able to find employment; that the state concentrates its attention on the tasks most appropriate to it – education and training, and expansion and maintenance of the infrastructure – and that it finances its activities out of its income and, to a reasonable extent, through borrowings at market conditions.

II

Microeconomic Problems and Privatisation

4 The Eastern Länder as a Transition Economy

Michael Kaser

INTRODUCTION

This chapter places the German eastern Länder in the context of the almost thirty countries of Europe and Asia which have accompanied the collapse of exclusive communist rule with systemic change towards the market. It compares the Länder as a group within unified Germany against the broadly-accepted benchmarks of the process in other transition economies. Eight years after the political transformation began in the Warsaw, Budapest, Berlin and Prague of late 1989, the economies – Poland alone excepted – have not regained the level they had then. All had become market economies, the German eastern Länder more thoroughly a market economy than any, notably because the federal set of laws and institutions were applied immediately on unification and because the privatisation was more thoroughgoing. Nevertheless, the eastern Länder 'deindustrialisation' that resulted from the operation of the Treuhand could have been less severe under alternative possible policies, and the output recovery after the nadir of recession has been heavily dependent on resource inflows from the western Länder. At no time in the transition, past or future, could equivalent external support be expected for other countries.

The eastern Länder patently differ from post-communist situations elsewhere. Not only are they sub-national entities, whereas all other transition economies operate under a national government,[1] but they are just six among 17 Federal Länder and as a group have no constitutional structure. Land governments differ in political composition (CDU/CSU or SDP majorities) among themselves and from the Federal government; they are only informally in unison as a sub-national group. Thus in the summer of 1997 CDU deputies from the eastern Länder in the Bundestag jointly protested against cuts in federal funding for the east. The dispute was settled on a compromise negotiated with the Federal Economics Minister by the economics ministers of the eastern Länder as a group.

Sub-national status brings statistical problems. Sole among the international economic agencies, the UN Economic Commission for Europe

(ECE) tabulates the German eastern Länder among the transition economies. Aware that no government wishes one of its regions to be treated as a nation, it separates the data as a 'memorandum item'. For the same reason the European Bank for Reconstruction and Development (EBRD) has 26 members classified as 'countries of operation', Germany being a providing member, and by that remit cannot assess the eastern Länder, although its staff pioneered the technique of evaluation in progress towards a normal market economy.[2] Of the transition economies, the EBRD excludes, as non-members, the present Yugoslavia (Montenegro and Serbia) and neither it nor the ECE has as a member-state Mongolia, on some counts the freest economy in the world, levying neither import nor export taxes. Of the world-wide agencies, annual publications of the World Bank, the International Labour Office and UN Headquarters make member-states the basis of their analyses, while of course referring to sub-national issues where justified by the context.[3]

Academic accounts of transition have mostly focused upon national economies or smaller groups of them – the Visegrad entente, the Baltic States, Slavic members of the CIS and Central Asia, to name the favourites – or, where the eastern Länder are embraced, upon transnational features – comparisons of privatisation, labour and social policies or foreign investment. Few cross-country evaluations of the pace of systemic change have included the eastern Länder,[4] and it is to this aspect that the present chapter seeks to contribute.

Three caveats must be noted. The first concerns the calibration procedure itself. Peter Rutland cogently expressed such criticism to a NATO Economics Colloquium at which nearly all transition economies (except the eastern Länder)[5] were analysed:

> It is particularly pernicious to draw up a scorecard ranking the various countries in terms of the speed of transition they have attained. Observers zero in on a handful of easily-monitored indicators, and keenly report who is ahead in currency convertibility or reducing budget deficits, while eastern governments anxiously await their latest bond rating from Standard & Poor's.[6]

As a reviewer of that book observed, the critique should rather be directed at those governments furnishing advice or assistance – who seem to base policy on such 'checklists' and to ignore the specific national starting-points and evolving conditions.[7]

A second limitation is the nature of the various indicators: the EBRD staff emphasise that progress in characteristics of institutional change cannot be encapsulated in a single figure and that their own assessments are approximate.

A final consideration is the statistical foundation of indicators which are quantifiable (or are at least within acceptable margins of error) in established market economies. This is of particular moment with respect to two of the standard transition criteria, the end of recession and the share of the private sector. Each depends on estimates of national income and product and – in addition to familiar objections to their use as indicators – may fail within a transition process to measure a greater proportion of some 'comprehensive' aggregate than was the case in a planned economy. For example, newly-created businesses are difficult for transition governments, themselves under change,[8] to monitor, especially those that seek to escape taxation or the arm of the law. Explicitly on an output index for regaining of the level of the last planned-economy year (1989), the mix of goods and services provided under repressed inflation, arbitrary pricing and enterprise production-constraints must have differed greatly from that which would have operated under present parameters. The mix and relative valuation of demand and supply was profoundly affected by the greater share of government in procurement (of defence goods and services, farm produce and producer goods); its control over foreign trade and payments; and the absence (or provision in quite other forms) of many goods and services, such as finance and advertising.

OUTPUT AND INCOME EFFECTS OF UNIFICATION

All transition economies suffered recesssion in aggregate production after the collapse of exclusive communist rule and the adoption of marketisation. Table 4.1 reproduces estimates of GDP in 1996 for Central and eastern European states, and shows that Poland alone exceeded the 1989 level – by 4 per cent – and that only the Czech Republic and Slovakia were within 10 to 11 per cent of that benchmark. Unfortunately the German Statistische Bundesamt does not supply national accounts for the two groups of old and new Länder back to 1989, its series starting in July 1990 and ending in 1994.[9] All estimates show a nadir in 1991 of a GDP at least one-third lower than in 1989 and subsequently growing, but one of the most influential commentators on the two economic groups, Hans-Werner Sinn, estimates real GDP barely to have exceeded 70 per cent of 1989 in 1994.[10]

Recession was deliberate in the programme of the Treuhandanstalt, colloquially summarised as 'sell or slaughter'. Its first director, Detlev

Table 4.1 Indicators of aggregate economic activity in 1996
Index numbers, United States dollars and percentages

Country	*GDP (1989 = 100) in 1996 (1)*	*GNP per capita ($) (PPP) in 1995 (2)*	*Percent unemployed in 1996 (3)*
Germany: West	120	21 960	9.4
Germany: East	93	11 940	15.5
Hungary	86	6 410	13.6
Poland	104	5 400	15.1
Czech Republic	89	9 770	3.5
Slovakia	90	3 610	12.8
Russia	51	4 480	9.3
Romania	88	4 360	6.3
Bulgaria	68	4 480	12.5

Source: Statistische Bundesamt, *Daten Report* and *Wirtschaft und Statistik* extended back to 1989 on DIW estimates in Lutz Hoffmann, in Joint Economic Committee of Congress, *East-Central European Economies in Transition*, US Government Printing Office, Washington DC, 1994, pp. 65–6. Estimates at purchasing power parity from World Bank, *World Development Report 1997*, distributed between East and West Germany from *Informationsdienst des Instituts der deutschen Wirtschaft (IWD)*, no. 39, 1997. Other transition countries also from EBRD *Transition Report Update 1997*, and *ECE Economic Survey of Europe in 1996–1997*.

Rohwedder (sadly, assasinated in his first year of office), wrote: ‘Privatization is the most effective rescue operation … the closure of enterprises should form the core of new activity’.[11] But it was carried to the stage of ‘deindustrialisation’: the workforce in industry dropping from 3.2mn in the GDR to 0.6mn in the eastern Länder in 1994. It correspondingly brought mass unemployment – higher than in the other East European transitional economies (Table 4.1). Temporary respite was accorded by the offer of a special ‘short-time allowance’, which at a peak in April 1991 was being received by two million workers; it was withdrawn at the end of that year.[12] For the country as a whole, unemployment peaked in the winter of 1996/7: although it subsequently fell in the West (to 10.5 per cent by September 1997), it continued to climb in the East (to 18.3 per cent), despite aggregate growth in both regions. It is a contrast with other transition economies that the eastern Länder have the highest registered unemployment but a better record of growth out of post-communist recession. The nadir for GDP was reached earlier – in

1991[13] – than by any other transition state, for although Poland turned upward in 1992, only three did likewise in 1993 and seven in 1994. GDP growth per capita since 1991 has been higher in the eastern than in the western Länder, but thereby only modestly closed the gap between them. In 1996 western GDP per capita was DM 47 317 against an eastern DM 25 739 (54 per cent of that in the western Länder). Dispersion among constituent Länder was, however, much narrower in the East than in the West.[14] The more rapid real growth, the nominal wage increments described below and the large social security transfers combined to ease the incidence of 'income poverty', but it remained worse than in the west: 27 per cent were below a poverty line in 1990, but 15 per cent in 1994 – the western Länder equivalent was 11 per cent in both years.[15]

It was only in 1995 that the eastern Länder regained the 11 per cent of all-German GDP that it had in the heyday of the GDR, but far below the 28 per cent it had generated before the Second World War; the East GDP had been a mere 7 per cent of the west in the second half of 1990.[16] But whereas the GDR had been highly self-sufficient, the regained level was heavily dependent on imports. Imports used to be less than one-fifth of GDP in the late communist period and, apart from inner-German trade, were approximately balanced by exports. After the collapse of 1990–1, however, the eastern Länder had net imports from the western Länder and from abroad of 74 per cent of GDP (1991) and were still importing a net 65 per cent in 1994. The 1995 net West-East German transfer of resources was 39.4 per cent of the East's GDP, down from 59.1 per cent in 1991; throughout 1991–5 these transfers constituted between 4.8 and 6.1 per cent annually of western Länder GDP.[17] The net inflow of resources is so large partly because of the East's poor export performance. Merchandise exports were only 2 per cent of the German total in 1995.[18] Quite apart from the cost of restructuring the economy for privatisation and the budget deficit caused by government social and other spending in the East, the eastern Länder are still far from paying their way.

Such massive outside support is of course well above the external flow gained by other transition states. The ECE tabulates net capital flow into 13 such economies: in 1995 the most was proportionately received by the Czech Republic – 19.3 per cent of GDP; three others received more than 10 per cent of their 1995 GDP – Hungary (16.0), Lithuania (14.2) and Croatia (12.7).[19]

Alfons Weichenrieder, using ECE estimates of foreign direct investment (FDI) into 14 transition states and the Treuhand's final report,[20] shows that up to the end of 1994 direct investment in eastern Germany from outside the territory was one hundred times the average of per capita

FDI into those 14 states. FDI per capita from 1989 to end-1994 relative to direct investment into eastern Germany ranged from 0.1 per cent into Ukraine to 12.2 per cent into Hungary.[21]

There are both moral and 'kinship' reasons for such substantial support. The latter term is due, in the economic literature at least, to Jürgen von Hagen, who likens the western Länder to a rich uncle desirous of dissuading his poor nephew from settling in with him. Von Hagen points out that when Chancellor Kohl made the first announcement of monetary union early in 1990, about one-half million immigrants had already moved. Thus, the uncle's part in the deal that followed was to halt immigration and rebuild the East rather than to pay for the settlement of large numbers of immigrants in the West.[22]

The reconstitution of jobs in the eastern Länder was, as already indicated, not achieved, and by 1996 some 2 million migrants had moved from East to West. But the majority had migrated by the end of 1991, and subsequently the westward flow was substantially offset by an eastward flow.[23] The 'moral' dimension may be a compensation for the 'deindustrialisation' effected by the Treuhand, the policies of which are considered in the following section.

PRIVATISATION PROCEDURE

Treuhand policy differed from that in most transition states. First no gratis (or nominally-priced) vouchers were distributed to citizens to buy equity in state enterprises being privatised. Of the 28 other transition economies only four issued none.[24] Secondly, the Treuhand restructured state enterprises before privatisation; elsewhere, save in Estonia and Poland, private-sector participation came first and the new owners were intended to execute the restructuring they wanted and could afford. Thirdly, the Treuhand made no distinction between domestic and foreign buyers (though in the event few of the latter took on ownership), but all transition governments, save Estonia, Hungary and Poland, applied some differentiation.

The Treuhand's objectives were formulated in the Treuhandgesetz, the Trusteeship Act, passed by the first freely-elected Parliament of the GDR on 17 June 1990:

> The Treuhand is an independent government agency established for the privatisation and use of state-owned assets based on the principles of the social market economy. The Treuhand promotes the structural

adjustment of the economy to meet market requirements by developing potentially viable firms into competitive enterprises and then transferring them into private ownership.[25]

The 'structural adjustment' amounted to deindustrialisation[26] and it reduced capital assets and employment below the levels needed to facilitate greater competitiveness in labour costs. Many factors had brought high costs in the GDR period – on the capital productivity side, the technology adopted and slow capital replacement, and on the labour productivity side, pre-unification wage rises, currency unification at par with the D-Mark and by the extension of federal collective-bargaining to the eastern Länder. Both the currency appreciation and western-led wage increases took place on political considerations – eastern voters made a short-term gain on their cash and savings and western voters could expect a sharp slackening in the immigration to their region of new fellow-citizens. Unionisation and the federal form of corporate governance fostered a management–labour relationship which prioritised wage remuneration over corporate saving and hence enhanced neither international competitiveness nor the rate of investment needed to draw the East from a 'Mezzogiorno' lag behind the western Länder. The form of East European (and the Russian) privatisation which gave equity to staff ('insiders') could have countered the incentive to migrate and would certainly have maintained more capacity in operation. Finance for management or labour buy-outs was limited by the weight accorded to commercial banks (despite some encouragement of development banking)[27] in Treuhand decision-making (and similarly may have constrained access to international financial markets). Profit forecasts, furthermore, were clouded, first, by worldwide recession; secondly, by the breakdown of the East's former markets in the former Council for Mutual Economic Assistance (CMEA) and the USSR; and thirdly, by the high unit wage-costs induced by the exchange rate. Enterprise sales prices may have been pitched too low, and the consequential federal indebtedness left too high. Dieter Bös elaborates the problem as an 'incomplete contract' between government as owner which may either undertake the heavy cost of restructuring before sale or exact a contractual investment by the private buyer: before privatisation an enterprise's profitability is uncertain, but restructuring outlay is already sunk when the disposal is effected.[28]

The Treuhandanstalt was initially created in the GDR to unbundle and corporatise the Kombinate into which the communist-monopolised government had grouped large industry in the late1960s and early 1970s. When given the wider brief, its first survey of the portfolio was relatively optimistic: 30 per cent of enterprises were capable of standing up to competition after monetary union, 50 per cent would be 'able to reach this aim after a longer phase of restructuring' and 20 per cent were effectively bankrupt.[29]

When converted into a Federal institution, the Treuhand's responsibility towards its enterprises was more extensive than that of any single state agency in the other transition economies. It had first to guarantee bank credit for working capital to maintain an enterprise in operation or until definitive closure: the new Länder did not therefore experience, as elsewhere, the accumulation of inter-enterprise debt and of tax arrears ensuing from the initial post-communist recession in economic activity. Secondly, it was required to assure new owners with unencumbered title, thus protecting them from former owners or from claims for environmental damage. Finally, it had to assume that part of the cost of shedding labour which Federal German law enjoined.[30]

The Treuhand was given four types of state property. First, as a task accomplished by 30 June 1991, it took on 23 422 small retail and catering outlets, hotels and warehouses, of which 15 520 were privatised and the remaining 34.9 per cent liquidated or not privatised. The former restablished a private small and medium enterprise sector (*Mittelstand*),[31] which the GDR government had nationalised in 1972 (at that time 11 000 businesses occupying 440 000 people). Treuhand enterprises in this category which were not privatised[32] went mainly into Land or municipal ownership and are only now – as throughout Germany – being considered for privatisation. They are smaller in the eastern Länder than in the western: in per capita terms such enterprise assets ranged from DM 117 in Land Brandenburg down to DM 45 in Land Sachsen, but nearly all these ratios were lower than in the western Länder, the range of which was from DM 1 387 in Hamburg down to DM 61 in Land Schleswig-Holstein.[33] Secondly, the Treuhand had 13 815 large enterprises, of which 6 321 had by 31 December 1994 been fully privatised (45.8 per cent) and 265 given to municipalities (1.9 per cent); 1 813 had been partly privatised or taken back into public hands (usually for failure to adhere to post-privatisation contracts), and 3 718 (26.9 per cent) had been, or were then being, liquidated.[34] Thirdly, it had overview of the disposal of one-third of the region's agricultural land and two-thirds of its forests. Fourthly, it received the property of Party and Party-sponsored mass organisations, public utilities and surplus military and security service assets. To eliminate a possible contention that it was selling the 'property of the people' (*Volksvermögen*), all enterprises and properties were converted into joint-stock companies in which the Treuhand held all the equity.[35]

The Treuhand created specialised branches for the retail group, for real estate and for agricultural land and forests: most such assets were quickly disposed of, but agricultural land will need another decade for resolution, partly because of the complexity of restitution claims and the confinement of transfer of tenure to a maximum of 12-year leases.[36] An important clarification was made by a judgement of the Federal Administrative Court in February 1995, stating that industrial and landed property which had passed into state hands very shortly after the establishment of the GDR on 7 October 1949 (valued at some DM 40 bn in the cases reviewed) had nevertheless effectively been ordered by the Soviet occupation authorities.[37] To indicate the federal government's recognition of the legitimacy of the Soviet occupation, restitution under the 1990 German Unification Treaty was confined to owners expropriated by the Nazi government, 1933–45, and by the GDR, 1949–90. Due partly to unresolved restitution cases, many of the former LPG (*Landwirtschaftliche Produktionsgenossenschaften*) were transformed into co-operatives (of tenants, where land title was *sub judice*). Average farm size (co-operatives, businesses and individual holdings) is just over 100 ha in the east, against 35 ha in the west; these larger farms, however, earn about the same as the much smaller western farms. Mean annual income per farm ranges from DM 62 000 in Mecklenberg-Vorpommern to DM 90 000 in Sachsen-Anhalt, against an average of DM 80 000 in the western Länder.[38]

The recession in capacity and employment was concentrated on the second group, which employed almost 4 million at takeover. When examined by the Treuhand, nearly 90 per cent were insolvent (*akute Zahlungsunfähigkeit*). They were, moreover, mostly within huge Kombinaten – (nine out of ten employees worked in just 270 of them), which had been created deliberately to stifle managerial initiative at the enterprise level, when the modest liberalisation of the early 1960s was reversed. It had surprisingly been the GDR which spearheaded CMEA-wide economic reform, beginning in 1963 and terminated by the crushing of the 'Prague Spring' in 1968.

The first task was to unbundle some into saleable units and to merge others, as a result of which the Treuhand initial manifest of 13 815 became 12 354 enterprises. By the end of its mandate in December 1994 liquidation, or the restructuring of those to be privatised, brought three million redundancies in an initial workforce (including small business) of four and a half million – and that in a total eastern Länder employment of eight million.

The Treuhand had a remit broader than the corresponding agencies of other transition economies, which were principally sellers of physical assets. The Treuhand called itself an intermediate owner (*Zwischeneigentümer*) which itself bought management expertise, technology, access to markets and above all purchaser obligations. Contracts were concluded with about 70 000 investors, who promised 1.5 million jobs and DM 211 billion in investments. Of the 85 per cent of firms which went to western Länder owners, nine out of ten were mergers with enterprises in the same industry – bought, that is, mainly as a defence against potential competition. Nearly 10 per cent went to foreigners and fewer than 6 per cent were bought by eastern Länder residents.[39] Foreign purchasers undertook labour and capital obligations (respectively 10.3 and 12.2 per cent of all pre-commitments) in a greater proportion than their number and their sales (respectively 5.7 and 8.0 per cent) and more than did German buyers.[40] The eastern residents among the latter were 'insiders' through management or labour buyouts and constituted a rather narrow base for a new *Mittelstand*.[41] Of the employment promises, 974 389 jobs were covered by contract and 760 862 were safguarded by penalties, but some contracts were renegotiated and in others the contractor paid the penalty. A third purchaser obligation was environmental restoration and the Treuhand paid DM 100 billion to cover such liabilities and indebtedness. When the Treuhand ended in December 1994, its remaining enterprises (63 firms employing some 200 000 staff) were allocated among four management corporations (*Kommanditgesellschaften*), to be dealt with at a slower pace (1995 to 2000), but at at a much higher unit cost. The DM 45 billion earmarked represents DM 225 000 per job (a minimum, because but not all jobs would be saved), against some DM 180 000 per job maintained hitherto.[42]

It happens that federal expenditure through the Treuhand and other subsidies, and the funding of social security to the eastern Länder as a 'safety net' already equals the forecast value of the GDR assets through privatisation. These flows could hence be considered fulfilment of a promise in the Unification Treaty that proceeds from the sale would be 'exclusively and only' used for the benefit of the new Länder (stronger words than had figured in the earlier State Treaty, 'with priority'), although it was then envisaged that citizens would receive personal dividends in proportion to their then savings balance in GDR Marks.[43] Theodor Waigel (a signatory of the State Treaty, Finance Minister then and at the time this chapter was written) spoke of proceeds of 'several hundred billion DM', and the first Treuhand chief, Detlev Rohwedder, spoke of DM 600 billion receipts. This order of magnitude was a gross value of GDR state enterprises of 924bn GDR Marks, or 620bn GDR Marks after deducting the value of those to be retained by a government (mostly local) authority.

In the event, as already indicated above, the capitalisation of expected profit-flow was much lower – due to restructuring, closures, and the uncompetitive exchange rate – and revenue from privatisation was DM 28.3 billion within a total revenue of DM 41.7 billion.[44] The Federal Unwelcome Legacy Repayment Fund is shouldering a debt of DM 270 billion; by the end of 1995 DM 644 billion was the aggregate of all West–East transfers, thus nominally exceeding (at the 1 : 1 exchange) the 620 billion GDR Marks promised.

In socio-economic terms, the Treuhand made scant contribution to creating a *Mittelstand*, but many small *ab initio* businesses have been created. Between 1990 and mid-1995 1.24 million new or privatised business were registered: 0.53 million were not set up or cancelled their registration.[45] About 0.4 million were operating in 1996.

CAUSES OF CAPACITY UNDER-UTILISATION

The recession cannot of course be wholly attributed to the closure of productive capacity. Other causes are to be found in changing demand, but more are attributable to changes in supply. On the demand side, the planned economy, which was rightly termed a 'shortage economy', absorbed whatever was produced: as in all Soviet-type economies, production, not consumption, was the goal. Production cuts and factory closures where goods produced simply were not wanted, or were of poor quality or performance, were rational once that plan obligation ceased. East Germany lost most of its export markets in CMEA, first as East Europe dispensed with communism and CMEA alike, and then as the Soviet Union broke up. All those former markets went into recession, but aggregate production in East Europe and the Baltic States had shown positive growth since 1993, although in the CIS it was still declining (in 1996 by 5 per cent according to EBRD, but only by 2 per cent according to the ECE). Military demand collapsed – not so much from the departure from Germany of Soviet occupation forces, who had been highly self-sufficient, but as Warsaw Pact orders disappeared. Russia has regained many of its clients for defence goods ($3.5 billion exports in 1996) and imports none from Warsaw Pact allies. NATO's decision to offer membership to some Central European 'Partners for Peace' requires them to re-equip their armed forces from the big western suppliers – not from the German East Länder. On the demand side also, East Länder households simply stopped buying their region's consumer manufactures: with DM in their hands, they spent in the first couple of years almost nothing on East

Länder manufactures where a western Länder or foreign product was available.

The crucial problem was, and remains, on the supply side. Whereas every other transition economy allowed its currency to devalue as it marketised, the eastern Länder currency, the GDR Mark, was revalued. Thus the Russian rouble fell to one quarter of its real value against the US dollar in the first four months after price liberalisation, but the unit of East Germany went in precisely the opposite direction: it was at a stroke quadrupled in value against the DM. As if this were not enough, the exchange rate of the DM itself appreciated by 5.2 per cent in nominal terms (and by 8.6 per cent in relative unit labour costs in manufacturing)[46] between the end of 1990 and the end of 1992 – the crucial dates for potential German and foreign buyers to consider purchases from the Treuhand.

The one-for-one currency exchange was disastrous in the longer term, although it was welcomed by GDR citizens, for it protected their savings (above a certain limit deposits were exchanged at a 2 : 1 rate); it gave political support in the subsequent elections to the government party; and – as already stressed – it inhibited East–West migration. A possible alternative would have been converting wages paid at a different rate of exchange from wages received – for example the employer would convert wages at DM 0.50 per GDR Mark (not far off the productivity differential) but a 100 per cent wage subsidy would yield the employee a rate of 1 : 1; the subsidy could have been annually diminished (intendedly in line with productivity gains). Such a wage subsidy might have been in aggregate smaller than that of unemployment benefit eventually paid, and would have afforded weak enterprises a substantial breathing space for restructuring with better sales prospects.[47] Other options included retaining a renamed GDR Mark with a flexible exchange rate to the DM; issue by a currency board backed by DM reserves; and parallel circulation with the DM.[48] The immediate embedding of eastern German economic inferiority by the 1 : 1 rate of exchange was not for lack of warning – eastern productivity was something like one-third of western and the purchasing power parity of a GDR Mark was a quarter of a DM (4.5 GDR Marks to the DM). Two factors, already briefly recounted, would simultaneously offset part of the productivity gains being made by the Treuhand through shaking out overemployment and closing uncompetitive plants. The first factor was the wage and salary increments which 'insiders' awarded themselves as soon as the merger of the GDR into the wealthy and supportive FRG became evident. Despite a production and a productivity decline, the wage and salary bill in the first half of 1990 in eastern Länder manufacturing was 13 per cent higher than in 1989.[49] To pay themselves such increments, they stopped transferring profit to the state and drew down working capital. As a second, and far more substantial, factor, the trade unions of the western Länder in autumn 1990 extended their wage negotiations to the eastern Länder under the standard collective-bargaining procedures. The aim of the western unions, organised in the DGB, was to obtain wage parity in the East as part of 'social unification'. Thus in the metal-working and electronics industries a 'stepwise plan' (Stufenplan) was agreed in March 1991 between IG Metall and five Land employers' associations to the effect that wages in the East would be brought up in steps to the western level by 1994: money wages would rise irrespective of comparative productivity. One argument then deployed was that raising the eastern wage would inhibit a feared major influx of easterners into the western labour market which would in turn trigger a western wage decline.[50] Wage adjustment towards the western level was indeed correlated with the precipitate decline in east-to-west migration.[51] In the East GDP per gainfully-occupied person (as a surrogate for labour productivity) was in 1991 a mere 31.0 per cent of that in the western Länder, while labour costs per employee (reflecting the average wage) were 46.7 per cent of that in the West. Arithmetically, dividing the latter by the former showed wage costs per unit of product as 1.5 times those of the western Länder. But once the threat of mass migration seemed lifted, western employers had second thoughts. Thus those in metal-working and electronics reneged on their Stufenplan in January 1993, and were thereupon confronted with the first major eastern Länder strike (IG Metall of May 1993); a compromise was reached to defer the equalisation date to April 1996 and to insert a 'hardship clause' for low-profit firms. Pressure for equalisation was also moderated by the withdrawal of some privatised firms from their association – the Treuhand had enrolled all its enterprises as association members and some *ab initio* businesses never joined. In 1997 fewer than two out of five firms in metal-working and electronics were in their association.[52] The speed of wage equalisation varied (fully achieved in in metal-working and electronics and in banking by 1997, but postponed to 1999 in construction) and decelerated – wages were 67.5 per cent of the West in 1993, 70.4 per cent in 1994 and 72.5 per cent in 1995. In the same three years productivity in the East improved at – coincidentally – the same rate: following greater investment per employee in the East than in the West, it was 50.7 per cent of the West in 1993, 53.0 per cent in 1994, and in 1995 was 54.4 per cent. The two trends brought labour costs per unit of product in the East down to 1.3 that of the West.[53] The average of gross salaries and wages per employee in 1995 in the East was already 75.3 per cent of the West German, against 72.9 per cent in 1994.[54] Against the narrowing wage gap must be set the longer work-hours, shorter holidays and fewer fringe benefits of the eastern enterprise.

Even so, there are two other factors which affect the competitiveness of eastern Länder production: it is less competitive within Germany by being less capital intensive and in international competition by the strength of the D-Mark. At unification in 1990 the value of capital assets per worker in the East was only 29 per cent of that in the West.[55] In the two subsequent years total new investment per capita was lower than that in the western Länder and in the following two years was sufficiently above the western rate to bring the increments to eastern assets per capita back to the level of 1990 – that is notionally to around 30 per cent of the western Länder. But these four years were those of the Treuhand closures, which liquidated 33.4 per cent of its initial assets.[56] Furthermore, investment data are gross, and depreciation would certainly have offset some of the new capital formation – asset withdrawal through obsolescence would have been large, especially as GRD depreciation allowances assumed much longer asset lives than under western practice. It is unlikely that the efficiency of eastern assets installed since 1990 is greater than those concurrently being installed in the western Länder, although it is higher than average capital productivity in the west. It can safely be concluded that the eastern Länder will for long have fewer assets per capita than the western Länder. The second issue concerns the blunting of competitiveness due to the strength of the D-mark.

Table 4.2 allows for the longer hours worked in the East by being per hour, at which the eastern Länder's wage costs are much higher than those of other transition economies – in 1994 at prevailing exchange rates. Restructuring and exchange-rate depreciation enabled the other European transition economies to achieve highly competitive unit labour costs with respect to western Europe. The margin with other transition economies seems wider on purchasing power parities (PPP), using an Austrian comparator. The Wiener Institut für Internationale Wirtschaftsvergleiche demonstrates unit labour costs (Austria = 100) in 1995 as 12 in Ukraine, 15 in Bulgaria, 23 in Slovakia, 26 in Romania, 29 in the Czech Republic, 33 in Russia, 34 in Hungary, 36 in Poland and 59 in Slovenia.[57] Austria may be taken as surrogate for the German western Länder: the World Bank's PPP estimate for 1995 GDP per capita ($21 250) is very close to the West German $21 960 and the Austrian schilling shadows the D-mark. Hence East German unit wage costs (including social costs, from Table 4.2) are 78 to the 100 of either West Germany or Austria (ignoring

Table 4.2 Average wage and social charges per hour worked in 1994
DM at prevailing exchange rates

Country	*Wage per hour* (1)	*Social charge per hour* (2)	*Column (2)/(1)* (3)
Germany: West	24.21	19.76	81
Germany: East	15.48	11.05	71
Hungary	2.35	2.28	97
Poland	2.06	1.71	83
Czech Republic	2.02	1.35	67
Slovakia	1.70	1.20	71
Russia	0.85	0.59	69
Romania	0.88	0.53	60
Bulgaria	0.76	0.57	75

Source: OECD, Deutsche Bundesbank and *Informationsdienst der deutschen Wirtschaft (IWD)*, no. 6, 1996.

the 3 per cent differential as being within the margin of error for all these estimates). Table 4.2 also shows that, in proportionate terms at least, social charges in the eastern Länder are not only lower than in western Germany but lower than in some of its East European competitors (Hungary, Poland and Bulgaria) and equal to that in Slovakia.

A further disadvantage to eastern Länder firms of the tie to western Länder wage rates was the rescaling of skill differentials. The structure of wages had been ideologically skewed in favour of physical work, and the first stage of collective wage bargaining with western union participation demoted that work in favour of the white-collar and intellectual groups which rank high in the West.[58] But because the Treuhand aimed at a 'high-wage-high tech' model,[59] and eastern unions feared a 'long work-bench' (that is low skilled jobs within west Länder firms), knowledge-based industrial processes and services in the East would have benefited from the pre-unification remuneration ratio. Such industries have tended to be discounted in finding expansion finance at the same time as their potential competitive edge in 'high-tech' salaries has been constrained. Maintenance of the skill differential would have kept some commuters living in an eastern, but working in a western, Land.

Although there is some cross-border commuting and quasi-permanent migration between transition states and EU states (Poles into Germany, Croats into Austria, Albanians into Italy and Greece), a more fundamental difference between the labour markets of East Germany and transition states is the absence of multiple job-holding. At least in 1993, when a survey was conducted on this topic, respondents were asked whether their earnings sufficed ('enough to live on') from their main job. In the western Länder the answer was positive for 91 per cent and was only a little fewer – 86 per cent – in the eastern Länder. But among those in other transition economies, the nearest were Czechs at 58 per cent, Slovaks at 46 per cent and Poles at 43 per cent. The most disgruntled and dependent on second or even third jobs were Hungarians at 34 per cent and Russians at 15 per cent.[60]

It is worth reiterating that although some transition economies experienced a real appreciation of their currencies during transition, all began with a significant devaluation, and their central banks retain the power of depreciation. It is the preclusion of such devaluation in the interest of competitiveness that has helped to keep a 'Mezzogiorno problem' within Germany. The reference is to the 50 years since the end of the Second World War during which southern Italy has lagged behind the North, despite heavy subsidies from the North to the South. Estimates of when the East could converge with the western Länder range from 40 down to ten years.[61] Continuing fiscal transfers and a higher rate of investment in the eastern than in the western Länder are clearly required. Carlin and Richtofen have taken the financial system of Italy as applied in the Mezzogiorno as comparator for the Federal and eastern Land banking system, and conclude that both in Italy and in the eastern Länder the financial system has indequately funded high-risk projects where investment in intangibles is central.[62] Boltho, Carlin and Scaramozzino accept that North–South Italian divergence has been virtually permanent – there was a brief GDP per capita convergence in the 1960s – despite heavy investment and supportive policies, but contend that recent trends in investment, productivity and wage-setting suggest more promising prospects in the East–West bifurcation of Germany.[63] Because, as noted above, the rate of investment in East Germany is above that of West Germany, they pointed to evidence of significant positive correlation in industrial branches between cumulated investment and productivity catch-up.[64]

IMPACTS OF THE WEST TO EAST RESOURCE FLOW

Between 1990 and 1996 each West German has 'paid' DM 3000 annually to the eastern Länder and each East German has 'received' DM 12 600 annually. A particular personal impact has been felt from the 'Solidarity' supplement on income tax which had to be reimposed in January 1995 (at 7.5 per cent, but scaled down to 5.5 per cent in January 1998). In 1995 50.6 per cent of GDP was absorbed as general government expenditure, a ratio that year exceeded in the European transition states only in Hungary (56.1); the percentage in the Czech Republic was 50.4, in Croatia 47.5, Slovakia 46.7, Slovenia 46.2, Bulgaria 41.7 and Estonia 41.5.[65]

The familiar consequence has been slow emergence from recession throughout the European Union, as public sector borrowing and taxation have crowded out potential private investment. The German fiscal deficit will persist under continuing West-to-East transfers, debt service and the loss of revenue from the extension to 1998 of the 50 per cent tax write-off for investment in the East. In the much shorter term there was a beneficial, if transient, consequence to the fiscal transfers in the West German partial recovery in 1994: neither personal consumption nor net exports contributed to it, but construction in, and Western exports to, the East were (with stockpiling) the significant factors. The maintenance of higher capital formation in the new Länder – to which execution of the Treuhand investment guarantees has contributed – is needed, as already noted, to close the Mezzogiorno-type gap. GDP growth is also likely to remain higher as its composition in the east shifts towards services, neglected in the GDR period and with lower capital-to-output ratios than in the expansion of physical production. The reequipment by Deutsche Telekom (now itself privatised) of the Eastern telecommunications network is one of many investments that supports the forecast that significant components of infrastructure in the East could reach per capita equality with that in the West by about the year 2000.

Capital and current inflows from outside have been massive since unification: no other transition economy could have had the resources that the West furnished the East in Germany. At the other extreme, the Soviet-type Asian economies of Mongolia and the Central Asian successor states had large inflows abruptly cut off when they began their revolutionary change.[66] Nor could any transition state other than East Germany have had access to a pool of entrepreneurship and corporate capital which could be drawn on without a barrier of language and cultural comprehension: only China, attracting overseas Chinese, was able to marketise with such an influx. In Germany some of this cultural benefit has been offset by mutual psychological disapprobation: 'Wessies' see themselves as paying heavily for eastern economic adjustment and 'Ossies' deprecate the strata of managers and officials who have taken the place of locals. Clashes –

arising *inter alia* from a 'know-all' attitude on the part of those disparaged by 'Ossies' as 'Besserwessi' – led the Treuhand to appoint mediators (*Vertrauensbevollmächtigte*) to iron out trouble.[67] More generally, such a takeover by 'outsiders' may have precluded some 'insiders' becoming entrepreneurs for the enterprise with which they were familiar; in other transition economies, managements taken over from a state enterprise operation could be either a plus (by reason of training and talent) or a minus (where they kept up their bureaucratic methods and association with the local bureaucracy). Restitution to former owners, practised in Czechoslovakia, Hungary and the Baltic States as well as in Germany, may on balance have been entrepreneurially positive.

The institutional impact of private-economy institutions was of course quicker and more thoroughgoing in the eastern Länder than in any other transition economy: GDR legislation and state institutions were immediately subordinated to Federal law upon unification. Although there was a 'learning curve' in practice, in form there were no delays or reversals in the legislative process of marketisation as occurred in other transition states. One practical consequence was that the German Government was under little pressure to implement a targeted anti-monopoly policy when its eastern part abandoned the administrative economy. One reason was unwillingness to inhibit the purchase by West German (or EU) firms of a Treuhand plant – often the regaining of a possession from pre-1945 Germany. Only subsequently have the effects of such purchases been monitored, but the federal government does not seek to inhibit by break-up the general drive to greater international competitiveness. A second reason was that any enterprise which was in such a monopoly position in the GDR was immediately exposed on unification to competition from business in the western Länder and the EU as a whole. The admission of selected transition economies to the EU will exacerbate such competition.

For the western Länder, both demand and supply conditions evoked transfer of some of their exports from the rest of EU and the world to the eastern Länder. Its share of total world export markets has dropped two percentage points since the late 1980s and external surpluses then of some 4 per cent of GDP have reversed into current account deficits of around 1 per cent of GDP.[68]

The application of federal German law to the new Länder was a short cut to the protection of property and contracts and to the prudential and regulatory provisions which cost other states much time and effort, and through the interstices or inadequacies of which crime and fraud penetrated. Corporations from established market economies could enter into ownership or commercial relationships within those Länder with foreknowledge of the protection available. Such predictability – so important for investment – was also assured, for example, of tax regimes and profit convertibility. Against such gains must be set the over-meticulous nature of federal legislation, created over the years in response to specific problems in business and general activity in the West, and the cost to the eastern enterprises of consultancy, legal and other services involved in adaptation to the new practices. The almost overnight availability of western financial services had its advantages – as contrastingly shown by the unruly banking situation in Russia and the weakness of financial institutions in the Czech Republic, Latvia and Kazakstan – but has been criticized for a bankers' dominance and 'house banking' (*Hausbankbeziehung*), which may have reduced the flexibility that profound economic restructuring requires.

CONCLUSIONS

Among the issues discussed in this chapter, three may be singled out for evaluation against other transition experiences: the effects on employment, the beneficiaries of property transfer, and corporate governance.

First, unemployment in the eastern Länder remained in 1996 not only much higher than in the western Länder, but high in relation to other Central and eastern European states. Indeed in all the transition economies the high unemployment of the eastern Länder in 1996 was exceeded only in the former Yugoslav states and with 'hidden unemployment' in Central Asia and Mongolia. The trade-off was of course that labour 'shake-out' has, together with the heavy resource flow from West Germany, enabled the workplaces that remain to assure the upturn of the East Land economy, but by 1997 not to the level of the last year of the GDR. However, among transition states no other save Poland (which began serious transition a year earlier than other east European states) had exceeded the 1989 level by 1996. If the expected growth of 2.0 per cent is maintained annually (1.9 per cent in 1997, 2.4 per cent forecast for 1998), East Germany would reach its 1989 level in the year 2000 – although the product-mix would differ greatly from that under the GDR. Even so, the assurance of positive increments and the preclusion of any retrogression continue to depend upon the external resource addition. Moreover, such productivity and wage gains as ensue are likely to accrue only to those in gainful employment, widening the differential between those who are in work and those who are on unemployment benefit or who have abandoned gainful employment. It is only a consolation that (due to federal support) the social safety net extended to the eastern Land worker is higher in real terms than in other transition states. Such better standards are no more than would be expected from the differentials in aggregate per-capita product as measured by purchasing power parity exchange rates. Moreover, the incidence of income poverty (principally wages and social security benefits) is heavier in the east than in the west, except for the elderly.

A linked issue is that high unemployment ratios for long periods inevitably bring a greater proportion of long-term unemployment (which the ILO defines as for one year or more). In the eastern Länder that share has been rising from a quarter in 1992 to one-third recently. A UK study of 5200 unemployed has recently concluded that it is likely that 'employers look on potential employees who have had 12 months' unemployment as significantly less 'employable' than their counterparts who present themselves for interview at a much earlier stage in their employment history'.[69] Long-term unemployment impacts most heavily on the less skilled, and lack of work itself precludes those involved from on-the-job skill enhancement. In the particular circumstances of the eastern Länder unemployment could be holding down wage pressures and hence capping the present high unit labour costs. But, as a study of labour markets in general suggests, beyond a certain point long-term unemployment has little such effect.[70] An upper limit, which the eastern Länder unemployment rate including 'hidden unemployment' has surpassed, is suggested by another study on transition economies, which concludes that 'unemployment rates well in excess of 20 per cent … go far beyond levels which, on the experience of OECD countries, could be regarded as necessary for the efficient working of a market economy'.[71]

A second central issue concerns the beneficiaries of systemic transition. The early promise to GDR citizens of a share in the proceeds of privatisation could not be kept, although western Länder transfers to the east have already exceeded the value initially placed upon theTreuhand assets to be privatised. But nearly all other transition countries (with four exceptions) offered citizens a stakeholding, by the provision of vouchers gratis, or at a very low price, whereby citizens appropriated some of the equity created by denationalisation. In a sense, unlike transition-state citizens, East Germans may have needed no vested interest in the new system to render the political and economic changes irreversible; they did not want to revert to the German States before 1870. They were given a different 'stake', that proffered by *Mitbestimmung* to West German workers. Job security depends on the new owners and the consultation procedure. As sole and exclusive owner of the assets to be disposed of, the Treuhand was under no constraint of appeal (save on points of law or maladministration) or of workplace bargains on productivity and labour practices. Had such negotiation been imposed, as in Poland, commitments to forgo current earnings in favour of corporate investment could have formed a first phase – the 'breathing space for restructuring'. The Czech Republic experienced a mere 8 per cent decline in employment between 1989 and 1995,[72] and has the lowest unemployment rate of any transition state. Yet its capital stock was vintagewise older than, and its technical level about the same as, that of the GDR.

The third, and for this chapter final, issue can only now begin to be explored. In the terms introduced by Michel Albert,[73] Germany is generally in the 'solidaristic' mode of corporate governance, just as the Czech Republic has taken primacy among transition states in following the 'individualistic' path. Russia has created its own style of 'collectivistic' operation.[74] Research is needed to determine the relative influences of 'stakeholders' or 'social partners' in the typical eastern Land firm, but a preliminary consideration suggests that neither banks nor employees are undertaking the function they have come to perform in the western Länder. Despite the fostering of 'development banking', there is evidence that medium-sized privatized and newly-established firms are not securing adequate finance. Commercial banks, acting as agents for the development banks, are seen as balking at risky ventures, even if the risk premium is high; especially among knowledge-based firms, a lack of physical assets to serve as collateral deters bank support. More generally, the influence of banks over management, minimizing the role of shareholders, appears to inhibit a firm's access to international equity-finance markets. The displacement of those who managed enterprises under GDR state operation in favour of imported western managements precluded the 'insider' or 'solidaristic' model. The evolution of corporate governance in the coming years must be one of the most important constituents of the political economy of unified Germany.

Notes

1. This statement must be modified for political separatism – the Croat–Moslem and Serb Entities in Bosnia–Herzegovina, Abkhazia in Georgia, Transnistria in Moldova, Chechenya in Russia and Badakshan in Tajikistan.
2. The ECE and the EBRD are the principal agencies regularly and systematically reporting on transition, the former in its *Economic Bulletin for Europe* and *Economic Survey for Europe*, and the latter in its *Transition Report* and *Transition Report Update*.

3. A notable World Bank analysis was *From Plan to Market. World Development Report 1996*. The International Monetary Fund (IMF) generates *Staff Country Reports*, which are of great value for the study of transition macroeconomies and external economic relations, as well as of established market economies. Its Report, *Germany – Recent Economic Developments and Selected Issues* (No. 96/111, October 1996) provides some separate assessments and statistics for the eastern and western Länder; its *International Financial Statistics* do not of course separate the Länder, but cover many transition states.
4. Some multi-national comparisons cover more than twenty countries, but not the eastern Länder, e.g. Stanley Fischer, Ratna Sahay and Carlos Végh, 'Stabilization and Growth in Transition Economies: The Early Experience', *Journal of Economic Perspectives*, vol. 10 (1996), pp. 45–66; Darius Rosati, 'Output Decline during Transition from Plan to Market: A Reconsideration', *Economics of Transition*, vol. 2 (1994), pp. 419–42 takes the former CMEA members in Europe, but not the ex-GDR. A notable comparison between East Germany and a set of transition states is in Hans-Werner Sinn, *Factor Price Distortions and Public Subsidies in East Germany*, Centre for Economic Policy Research (CEPR) Discussion Paper Series no. 1155 (May 1995). See also Hans Werner Sinn and Alfons Weichenrieder, *Foreign Direct Investment, Political Resentment and the Privatization Process in Eastern Europe*, mimeo for an EBRD Conference, 26–27 April 1996 (the writer is grateful to John Bennett, University of Wales Swansea, for a copy of this paper).
5. It is fair to point out that the NATO Colloquium of the year before had specifically covered the Länder (Wolfgang Vehse, 'Privatization German Style', in Reiner Weichhardt (ed.), *Privatization in NACC Countries: Defence Industry Experiences and Policies and Experiences in Related Spheres*, NATO, Brussels, 1994).
6. Peter Rutland, 'Successes and Failures: Privatization in the Transition Economies', in Reiner Weichhardt (ed.), *Status of Economic Reforms in Cooperation Partner Countries in the Mid-1990s: Opportunities, Constraints, Security Implications*,' NATO, Brussels, 1996, pp. 157–8.
7. Martin Myant's review in *Europe–Asia Studies*, vol. 49, no. 1, 1997, pp. 152–4.
8. The present writer drew attention to this in 'Integration and Homogeneity in the Transition Economies', in Jens Hölscher, Anke Jacobsen, Horst Tomann and Hans Weisfeld (eds), *Bedingungen ökonomischer Entwicklung in Zentralosteuropa*, vol. 5, *Economic Policy and Development Strategies in Central and Eastern Europe*, Metropolis-Verlag, Marburg, pp. 207–28.
9. The IMF, *Germany – Recent Economic Developments and Selected Issues*, p. 65, n. 3, crisply observes: 'Publication of disaggregated data on a national accounts basis for East Germany came to an end in 1994, hampering analysis of developments in the Eastern Länder and comparison with the Western Länder'. This is just one of the statistical discontinuities which trouble the economic analyst. The Bundesbank *Monatsbericht* stopped publishing employment in eastern 'industry' in November 1990 and resumed with a narrower 'manufacturing' in January 1991 without any overlap to

allow 'splicing'. Dr Johannes Stephan (Institut für Wirtschaftsforschung, Halle) helped the present writer in finding which official time series were published.

10. Sinn, *Factor Price Distortions*, Fig. 2.
11. *Treuhandanstalt, Entschlossen sanieren*, April 1992, cited by Claus Köhler, 'The Privatisation of the East German Economy and the Role of the Treuhandanstalt', in Stephen Frowen and Jens Hölscher (eds), *The German Currency Union of 1990: A Critical Assessment*, Macmillan, London, 1997, pp. 154–5.
12. Lutz Bellmann, 'Labour Market Policies in Germany', *MOCT–MOST: Economic Policy in Transitional Economies* [hereafter *MOCT–MOST*], vol. 5, no. 4, 1995, pp. 153–9, describes the many allowances of the time and tabulates numbers of recipients.
13. Horst Brezinski and Michael Fritsch, 'Transformation: The Shocking German Way', *MOCT–MOST*, vol. 5, no. 4, pp. 1–25 (Figure 2); Lutz Hoffmann, East Germany in Transition', Joint Economic Committee, US Congress, *East-Central European Economies in Transition*, US Government Printing Office, Washington DC, 1994, p. 664.
14. *Informationsdienst des Instituts der deutschen Wirtschaft (IWD)*, no. 39, 1997. Its data at the nominal exchange rate exceed the values in Table 4.1, which are at purchasing power parity (PPP); the range of individual eastern Länder is from DM 24 244 to 26 658 plus Berlin-Ost at DM 32 200, but the western Länder ranged from DM 37 744 to 79 989.
15. Joachim Frick, Richard Hauser, Klaus Müller and Gert Wagner, 'Income Distribution in East Germany after the Fall of the Wall,' *MOCT–MOST*, vol. 5, no. 4, 1995, pp. 79–108.
16. Data for 1995 from Statistisches Bundesamt, *Volkswirtschaftliche Gesamtrechnungen* (earlier tracking from Deutsche Bundesbank, *Monatsbericht*). Estimates for 1936 and 1980 were compiled by Michael Kaser, 'The Economic Dimension', in Edwina Moreton (ed.), *Germany between East and West*, Cambridge University Press, Cambridge, 1987, pp. 123–4 and 138–9, from sources there stated.
17. Federal Ministry of Economics, *Wirtschaftsdaten Neue Länder*, April 1996.
18. ECE, *Economic Survey of Europe in 1996–1997*, p. 32.
19. ECE, *Economic Bulletin for Europe*, vol. 48 (1996), Table 5.2.1.
20. The Final Report was published in June 1995.
21. Sinn and Weichenrieder, *Foreign Direct Investment*, Table 1.
22. Jurgen von Hagen, *East Germany: The Economics of Kinship*, CEPR Discussion Paper Series no. 1296 (November 1995).
23. Friedrich Sell, 'The Currency Conversion Controversy', *MOCT–MOST*, vol. 5, no. 4, 1995, Figure 8.
24. Macedonia, Turkmenistan, Uzbekistan and Yugoslavia (Montenegro and Serbia); there was only a partial distribution of vouchers in Croatia, while Hungary issued vouchers as property restitution but offered concessional loans to citizens to buy into privatisations.
25. *Daten und Fakten zur Aufgabenerfüllung der Treuhandanstalt*, Treuhandanstalt, Berlin, December 1994. For a list of Treuhand reports and a tabulation of the progress of its privatisations, see Herbert Brücker, 'Selling Eastern Germany. On the Economic Rationale of the

Treuhandanstalt's Privatisation and Restructuring Strategy,' *MOCT–MOST*, vol. 5, no. 4, 1995, pp. 27–53.

26. Early perceived by Wendy Carlin, 'Privatization and Deindustrialization in East Germany' in Saul Estrin (ed.), *Privatization in Central and Eastern Europe*, Longman, London, 1994, pp. 127–53.
27. The Federal Government complemented bank credit for small and medium enterprises through the 'development banking' programme of the Kreditanstalt für Wiederaufbau (KfW).
28. Dieter Bös, *Privatization and Restructuring: An Incomplete-Contract Approach*, Rheinische Friedrich-Wilhelms-Universität Bonn, Discussion Paper no. A-523 (the writer is grateful to the author for supply of this paper).
29. Wolfram Fischer, Herbert Hax and Hans Karl Schneider, *Treuhandanstalt: The Impossible Challenge*, Akademie Verlag, Berlin, 1996, p. 30; they term the first incarnation the 'Original-Treuhand', to distinguish it from the federal agency it became.
30. Lesley Lipschitz and Donough McDonald (eds), *German Unification: Economic Issues*, IMF, Washington DC, 1990, pp. 7–9; Vito Tanzi (ed.), *Fiscal Policies in Economies in Transition*, IMF, Washington, 1992, pp. 69, 73–4.
31. Small and medium enterprise (SME) is usually defined as employing 1 to 499 staff, whereas the *Mittelstand* is conventionally of firms employing 100 to 499 staff.
32. Brezinski and Fritsch, 'Transformation', p. 13, imply that all were privatised.
33. Roland Tichy, 'Privatisierung und soziale Marktwirtschaft', *Basis-Info:Wirtschaft*, no. 28, 1996, p. 9.
34. Klaus-Dieter Schmidt, *German Unification: A Progress Report*, Kieler Arbeitspapiere, no. 722 (February 1996), Table 2.
35. Wolfgang Vehse in Weichhardt, *Status of Economic Reforms*, p. 64.
36. A close analysis of the forest and farm disposal and of the successor agencies to the Treuhand is in Dieter Bös, *The Treuhand: A Never-Ending Story*, Rheinische Friedrich-Wilhelms-Universität Bonn, Discussion Paper no. A-531 (September 1996).
37. Report by Judy Dempsey, *Financial Times*, 14 February 1995.
38. Report by Frederick Studemann, *Financial Times*, 20 August 1997.
39. Brezinski and Fritsch, 'Transformation', p. 13.
40. Birgit Sander, 'Foreign Investors' Activities in the Context of German Privatization', *MOCT–MOST*, vol. 5, no. 4, 1995, pp. 109–32.
41. See in particular, Dieter Bös and Gunter Keyser, *Treuhandanstalt: Heads or Tails*, Institut für Mittelstandsforschung Bonn, Materialen no. 119 (June 1996).
42. Jobs saved in the giant GDR heavy industrial investments cost most – the cost of saving the Baltic shipyards was DM 800 000 per job and in the deal for the EkoStahl metallugical works in the former Stalinstadt it was DM 680 000.
43. Wolfram Schrettl, 'Transition with Insurance: German Unification Reconsidered', *Oxford Review of Economic Policy*, vol. 8, no. 1, 1992, p. 147.

44. Schmidt, *German Unification*, Table 5.
45. Brezinski and Fritsch, 'Transformation', p. 13.
46. IMF, *Germany – Recent Economic Developments*, p. 46.
47. Maria Haendcke-Hoppe-Arndt, Michal Keren and Günter Nötzold, 'The Currency Union and the Economic Road to German Unity,' in Michael Keren and Gur Ofer (eds), *Trials of Transition. Economic Reform in the Former Communist Bloc*, Westview Press, Boulder, 1992, p. 182.
48. Sell, 'The Currency Conversion Controversy', sets out these options and notes their presentation at the time by Horst Siebert. They may not have been widely appreciated, because Siebert seems to have confined this particular presentation to his Institute's working paper series (*Kieler Diskussionsbeitrag*, no. 160a, 1990), rather than to the broadly-read professional journals to which he frequently contributes (such as 'Labor Market Rigidities', *Journal of Economic Perspectives*, Summer 1997, pp. 37–54).
49. George von Furstenberg, 'Overstaffing as an Endgame and Prelude to the Employment Collapse in Eastern Germany?', *Communist Economies and Economic Transformation*, vol. 7, no. 3, 1995, pp. 229–318 (p. 312).
50. Dieter Bös, 'Privatization in East Germany', in Vito Tanzi (ed.), *Transition to Market. Studies in Fiscal Reform*, IMF, Washington DC, 1993, p. 204.
51. Sell, 'The Currency Conversion Controversy,' points out that trade unions competed with each other in the race to gain equality with western wage-rates (p. 41).
52. The writer is grateful to Stephen French, doctoral student at the Institute for German Studies, University of Birmingham, for the detailed account of the IG Metall negotiations.
53. *Informationsdienst des Instituts der deutschen Wirtschaft (IWD)*, no. 6, 1996.
54. IMF, *Germany – Recent Economic Developments*, Table I–3 (Federal Ministry of Labour data).
55. Von Furstenberg, 'Overstaffing', p. 302.
56. Brücker, 'Selling Eastern Germany', Table A2.
57. Leon Podkaminer *et al.*, *Transition Countries: Economic Developments in 1995 and Outlook for 1996 and 1997*, Research Reports no. 225, February 1996, WIIW, Vienna, pp. 35–9.
58. Köhler, 'The Privatisation of the East German Economy'.
59. Gerlinde Sinn and Hans-Werner Sinn, *Kaltstart: Volkswirtschaftliche Aspekte der deutschen Vereinigung*, Mohr, Tübingen, 1991.
60. Richard Rose and Christian Haerpfer, 'The Impact of a Ready-made State: Advantages to East Germans', *Studies in Public Policy*, no. 238, University of Strathclyde, 1996; and in Helmut Wiesenthal (ed.), *Einheit als Privileg? Vergleichende Perspektiven auf die Transformation Ostdeutschlands*, Campus Verlag, Frankfurt am Main, 1996.
61. 'Thirty to 40 years' is estimated by A. J. Hughes Hallett and Yue Ma, 'Real Adjustment in a Union of Incompletely Converged Economies: An Example from East and West Germany', *European Economic Review*, vol. 38 (December 1994), pp. 1731–61; '20 years' is from Sinn and Sinn, *Kaltstart*; '10 years' is from T. Mayer, *Borrowed Prosperity: Medium Term Outlook for the East German Economy*, Goldman-Sachs International, London, May 1992.

62. Wendy Carlin and Peter Richthofen, 'Finance, Economic Development and the Transition: the East German Case', *Economics of Transition*, vol. 3, 1995, p. 192.
63. Andrea Boltho, Wendy Carlin and Pasquale Scaramozzino, 'Will East Germany Become a New Mezzogiorno?', *Journal of Comparative Economics*, vol. 24, no. 3, 1997, pp. 241–64.
64. Wendy Carlin and David Soskice, 'Shocks to the System: the German Political Economy under Stress', *National Institute Economic Review*, February 1997.
65. EBRD, *Transition Report Update 1997*, Appendix tables; Poland is not shown for 1995, but was 47.5 per cent in 1994.
66. See Richard Pomfret, *Asian Economies in Transition*, Edward Elgar, Cheltenham, 1996; and Michael Kaser, 'Economic Transition in Six Central Asian Economies', *Central Asian Survey*, vol. 16, no. 1, 1997, pp. 5–26.
67. Köhler, 'The Privatisation of the East German Economy'.
68. Report by David Marsh, *Financial Times*, 6 March 1995. The current account deficit in 1996 was 0.8 per cent of GDP, compared to a 1.2 per cent surplus for western Europe as a whole (OECD, *Main Economic Indicators*).
69. Peter Dolton and Donal O'Neill, 'Unemployment Duration and the Restart Effect: Some Experimental Evidence', *Economic Journal*, vol. 106 (March 1996), p. 397
70. Richard Layard, Stephen Nickell and Richard Jackman, *Unemployment: Macroeconomic Performance and the Labour Market*, Oxford University Press, Oxford, 1991, ch. 9.
71. Richard Jackman, and Michal Rutkowski (eds), 'Labor Markets: Wages and Employment' in Nicholas Barr (ed.), *Labor Markets and Social Policy in Central and Eastern Europe: The Transition and Beyond*, Oxford University Press for the World Bank and the LSE, Oxford, 1994, p. 147.
72. Podkaminer *et al.*, 'Transition Countries', p. 38.
73. Michel Albert, *Capitalisme contre capitalisme*, Seuil, Paris, 1991 (English trans. *Capitalism against Capitalism*, Whurr, London, 1993); and Colin Crouch and David Marquand (eds), *Ethics and Markets: Cooperation and Competition within Capitalist Economies*, Blackwell, Oxford, 1993.
74. See, for example, Michael Kaser, 'Privatization in the CIS', in David Dyker (ed.), *Challenges for Russian Economic Reform*, Brookings Institution, Washington DC, 1995, pp. 184–93.

5 Determinants of Entrepreneurial Success in East Germany

Marc Herzog[1]

INTRODUCTION

The central issue underlying this investigation was the assumption that the distinctive type of business formation in East Germany, or factors relating to this, have a decisive influence on the problems and the economic performance of newly established small and medium-sized enterprises (SMEs) in the industrial sector in East Germany. With data collected from an empirical study conducted in East Germany in early summer 1993 as its base, the investigation involved analysing the problems experienced by East German business, investigating their economic situation and identifying the factors which influence the performance of SMEs in the industrial sector of East Germany.

German reunification triggered a far-reaching economic turn-around in East Germany. In particular, the manufacturing sector in East Germany underwent a huge set-back – after the collapse of the socialist command economy and the abrupt transition to a social-market economy, the lack of competitiveness became apparent within a very short period of time due to the drastic job-cuts which ensued.

In an effort to overcome the consequences of the economic restructuring process, economic policy concentrated in particular on promoting the formation of SMEs because of their potential for creating new jobs. Furthermore, experience in West Germany had shown that SMEs are especially effective at adapting quickly and flexibly to changing market conditions. In addition, they often assume an innovating function in the development and manufacture of new products, that is, quite a significant number of innovations can be traced back to SMEs (Hunsdieck 1985, p. 1).

An economic structure characterised by SMEs was therefore seen as the best way in which the East German economy could cope with the inevitable adaptation needed to the changed supply and demand conditions and to the new political-economic and socio-political general economic setting.

In the former GDR, however, SMEs had been gradually eliminated through nationalisation schemes as they did not conform to the system (Haendcke-Hoppe 1982; Åslund 1985; Pickel 1992) – the centralised command economy favoured the creation of large economic units in the form of 'Kombinate'. After 1989, therefore, SMEs in East Germany had, to a large extent, to start from scratch.

In forming viable small and medium-sized enterprises in the industrial sector (BMWi 1993; Hauer et al. 1993; and Belitz et al. 1994) in East Germany – until early summer 1993 approximately 9800 small and medium-sized enterprises in the industrial sector had emerged (Kayser et al. 1993, p. 1) – three central elements were important:[2]

(1) New business formation.[3] Economically active SMEs in the industrial sector resulted, in particular, from the drive to set up new business (Hüfner et al. 1992; May-Strobl and Paulini 1990; Paulini and May-Strobl 1994). According to the findings of the Research Institute for Small and Medium-Sized Enterprises in Bonn, approximately 2400 newly formed SMEs in the industrial sector were recorded in East Germany in May 1993 (Kayser et al. 1993, p. 2).

(2) Creation of SMEs managed by private enterprise through the privatisation activities of the Treuhandanstalt (THA). At the time of investigation, approximately 12 360 businesses had been privatised by the THA Treuhandanstalt 1993, p. 5) The German Institute for Economic Research (Deutsches Institut für Wirtschaftsforschung – DIW) estimates that this resulted in the emergence of approximately 4300 SMEs in the manufacturing sector (DIW 1994, p. 322).

    Apart from privatisation through the sale of companies to mainly West German investors, the sale of a company, or section of a company, to the former management, was seen to be of particular importance – since 1991, this strategy had received special emphasis within the framework of the small and medium-sized enterprises initiative set up by the THA. Up to May 1993, a total of approximately 1200 SMEs emerged in the industrial sector of East Germany by means of the so-called Management-Buy-Out (MBO).[4]

(3) Reprivatisation of expropriated companies, in particular repossession of companies nationalised in 1972, by their former owners or their descendants (Schmidt 1992; Schmidt and Kaufmann 1991; 1992). At

> the time of investigation, 4150 companies active on the market had arisen in East Germany as a result of repossession of companies or sections of companies. Taking approximately 75 per cent as the small and medium-sized enterprise rate, there were therefore approximately 3100 reprivatised SMEs in the industrial sector in East Germany in May 1993 (DIW 1994, p. 322).

The question as to the emergence of SMEs in the industrial sector seems therefore to be still relatively easy to answer; it is, however, incomparably more difficult to determine which form of company formation is most promising for East Germany.

The existence of past company data can, for example, be regarded as an advantage of derivative formations – this can clearly facilitate potential investors in assessing the plan of formation as regards financial difficulties characteristic of newly created businesses. A further positive factor is the acquisition of what is usually a solid customer base, with whom the founder of the company – often an employee of the particular company of many years, standing – is usually acquainted. The entrepreneurial risk of a derivative company formation therefore appears to be calculable (Graf 1983, p. 255; Hunsdieck and May-Strobl 1986, p. 41).

New formations are, on the other hand, confronted with the fundamental problem of first building up effective demand for themselves. The degree of freedom and autonomy in decision-making may be larger in the development of a viable formation concept, but the probability of losses in the initial stage is incomparably higher (Hunsdieck and May-Strobl 1986, pp. 41–76).

The situation in East Germany is characterised, among other things, by the opening of the markets to the outside world and the collapse of the former Comecon markets – in the case of a derivative formation, it will therefore only seldom be possible to acquire a solid customer base. Furthermore, the information value of past experience figures will be rather limited. Given the new demands of the free-market system, it is also doubtful whether it will be advantageous to be able to fall back on a previous organisational structure.

All in all, this raises the question as to whether the advantages spoken of in relation to a derivative formation are valid in the context of the very specific situation in East Germany, or whether they may even turn out to be disadvantageous.

So, which type of company formation is the most promising? Is it derivative formations, that is, companies which were taken over by their former management, former owners or West German companies, or, is it new East German set-ups which profit from not having to carry the burden of the past?

RESEARCH OBJECTIVES AND METHODOLOGY

Underlying this research was the assumption that the distinctive type of business formation in East Germany, or factors relating to it, have a decisive influence on the problems and the economic performance of newly established SMEs in East Germany.

The objective of the research was therefore first of all to analyse the problems of companies in East Germany, and then to investigate their economic performance and identify the factors which determine the success of SMEs in the industrial sector in East Germany. It was assumed that entrepreneurial success is determined, in particular, by the personality of the entrepreneur, the structural characteristics of the company at formation or take-over, and the extent to which companies are affected by specific problems and exogenous factors. In this point, this paper complies with the complex concepts from previous research in entrepreneurship. the findings are based on data collected from an empirical study conducted in East Germany in early summer 1993.

THE MOST IMPORTANT FINDINGS

The most important result to stress is that, under the conditions of radical economic change in East Germany, important company-specific structural characteristics, different starting conditions, different company strategies and finally divergent economic performances are, in fact, all reflected in the type of company formation.

Problems of Companies Investigated

The hypothesis that difficulties are related to the particular way in which enterprises emerge was confirmed unequivocally, that is, the individual groups of enterprises can be classified according to typical problems which can be traced back to the way in which the companies emerged (Herzog 1996, pp. 79–142).

In the formation stage East German start-ups complain about financing difficulties in particular. Delays in clarifying questions of ownership and in providing suitable industrial sites are also somewhat of a hindrance. On the sales side, however, there was comparably little cause for concern. Even after the first few years of business activity this assertion still holds in principle: the main problems are still financial. Furthermore, public administration is seen as an impediment to corporate expansion. There are comparatively few problems regarding sales and other market-oriented activities, and the cost position of the company can be judged to be quite good. Finally, R&D activities are seen as a company strength.

Aspects of market development are, on the other hand, the main concern of companies taken over by or founded by West German companies at the time of emergence, while financial questions are, at most, of marginal importance – an assessment which has not necessarily changed at the time of inquiry, early summer 1993. Marketing and sales problems still dominate. In addition, pressure to rationalise, that is, to cut overly high personnel and production costs, has intensified. On the other hand, those debts which were enforced on companies by the socialist government over the previous 40 years ('old financial debts') and unclarified questions of ownership – the latter, however, only at the time of retransfer – constitute a serious burden for reprivatised companies. There appear to have been too many cuts in R&D capacity in an effort to cut costs. In addition to the usual difficulties in the area of sales, R&D capacities are often seen as a company weakness.

The formation stage was particularly difficult for companies which were privatised by Management-Buy-Out. Approximately every second company complained of difficulties both in the areas of financing and also of sales and other market-related activities. Over 60 per cent criticised the general legal and administrative setting. This assessment is still partially valid, even after the first few years of business activity. Financial difficulties and problems in marketing and sales are still being reported. Furthermore, unclarified questions of ownership and deficits in public administration (knowledge, expertise, manpower, and so on) are viewed as limiting factors. The general legal and administrative setting has however clearly declined in importance. Finally, the main problems are those of cost cutting and increasing productivity, but overly high personnel and energy costs – the latter due to lack of investment capital to modernise the plants – are particular causes for concern.

Finally, when contrasted with the initial phase, the situation of companies under the administration of the Treuhandanstalt looks totally different. Although there were very few problems apparent at the time when the legal form was changed, and no acute need for action was seen, the enterprises found themselves in an extremely difficult situation at the time of investigation, early summer 1993. Of foremost importance was the effort to attain a competitive cost position: the overly high personnel and production costs had to be drastically reduced. Added to this came the collapse of the Comecon markets and the penetration of West German competitors in the East German domestic market. This accentuated the problems of THA enterprises, in particular, because of characteristic weaknesses in marketing and sales. Furthermore, the companies were faced with the problem of having to attend to 'old financial debts' and of having to modernise the factories. The necessary investment capital was, however, only available to a very limited extent.

Economic Performance of Enterprises Investigated[5]

In this investigation, only economic indicators were used to measure performance – in other words, a company-related concept of performance measurement was chosen. The operationalisation of corporate success follows Willer's research on entrepreneurial success (Willer 1989, pp. 140–158). The indicators 'profit on sales', 'turnover performance', 'earnings performance' and 'employment trend' were used to allow conclusions to be made about the performance of the sample investigated. By using 'profit on sales' as an indicator, preliminary conclusions could be drawn at particular points in time with regard to economic performance. To ensure that maximum usage was made of all reliable data for the analysis, the development of turnover, total number of employees and profit were also individually described over the period investigated, that is, 1990 to 1993. These observations were then ranked.

The hypothesis that the type of company formation was related to company performance was confirmed unequivocally – the group East German formations succeeded in obtaining the best results overall in all the selected performance indicators, that is, profitability and corporate growth. Enterprises which had been privatised by Management-Buy-Out followed in second place, while the performance of retransferred companies revealed itself to be rather average. Finally, West German formations/take-overs and THA companies took last place over all performance indicators.

Determinants of Success

Entrepreneur

The systematic comparison of entrepreneurs showed considerable differences regarding the personal qualifications of entrepreneurs to switch to self-employment (Herzog 1996, pp. 35–64).

East German entrepreneurs become self-employed at a younger age. They also have less formal education and have somewhat less professional and managerial experience to look back on.

The owners of reprivatised companies have a higher level of formal education and can usually refer back to many years of experience in managerial functions. Despite being strongly influenced by their own or their parents' former experiences in self-employment, this group believes that they lack the skills needed to survive in a competitive market environment.

The MBO-entrepreneurs are relatively speaking the best qualified for entrepreneurial activity. Long years of professional experience in management positions nearly always follow an academic qualification. Judging from the self-assessment of their entrepreneurial qualifications, this group seems to have succeeded best in closing the gap between knowledge and experience.

Managers of companies with a West German controlling interest have clearly profited in many areas from the know-how of the parent company.

Finally the management of companies under the administration of the Treuhandanstalt takes last place as regards the skills needed to survive in a competitive market environment and also formal education.

East German entrepreneurs in particular appear, on the whole, to be less qualified to succeed in entrepreneurial activity. However, the analysis of the data collected showed that the lack of education demonstrated does not conclusively hinder entrepreneurial success. It was also shown that in the specific situation of East Germany, a certain lack of professional and management experience tends to be quite conducive to success – because the experience was gained in the old system (Herzog 1996, p. 167).

Furthermore, it is worth noting that many East Germans have ventured into self-employment, despite decades of formative socialist experience – although the present inquiry only provides preliminary proof of this phenomenon and should therefore not be generalised. To an extent, an autonomous, and to some degree very successful, group of East German entrepreneurs has undoubtedly arisen without the need to 'import' entrepreneurs from West Germany.

Company's structural characteristics

The account of the structural characteristics of the company had shown that, to some extent, considerable differences existed between the individual groups of companies within the sample investigated (Herzog 1996, pp. 65–78).

Based on the level of employment and the initial value of the company at formation, East German formations were found, without exception, to be smaller. A smaller sum of starting capital was raised.

Although the West German market is basically of primary importance, local or regional markets are particularly significant for East German formations and MBO enterprises.

In this context, the analysis of the companies' economic start-up situation verified the hypothesis that the economic situation of those companies which serve selected sub-markets (local and regional) in East Germany appears to be superior to that of companies active throughout Germany or internationally and therefore confronted with intense competitive pressure (Herzog 1996, p. 173).

Also of importance for corporate success is company size. It can be demonstrated that smaller companies in East Germany were, at the time of investigation, without exception more successful (Herzog 1996, p. 179). This result is not in line with previous findings in entrepreneurship research, which postulate that larger formations are more successful than smaller ones, and that smaller and younger enterprises find it more difficult to be successful and to maintain a hold on the market than longer-established enterprises. However, initial signs indicate that the deviating result could be due to a transitional phenomenon caused by the initial situation and that these major differences will decrease in importance in the course of further developments in East Germany. In the East German transformational economy, seemingly sound companies now find their success clearly impaired by organisational and psychological burdens from the past as well as by 'old financial debts', that is, in decisive areas they are possibly lacking the necessary agility and flexibility to succeed in competition.

Company problems

The following findings relate to the correlation between the problems and difficulties experienced by East German enterprises and performance.

Firstly, of major importance in the formation stage are the companies' financial difficulties. 'Old financial debts' hinder success. (Since these liabilities were the result of government dispositions and not debts acquired in the market process, basic debt relief would definitely have been a good idea here.)

It is quite typical for successful enterprises to have difficulties procuring loans or to have a rather poor equity position. It can be assumed that the companies concerned feel restricted in their urge to expand and that they are, to a certain extent, successful, despite these restrictions (Herzog 1996, p. 187).

Apart from the correlation of financial difficulties with success, it can also be shown that marketing and sales problems – and in particular the lack of a qualified sales force – exert a decisive influence on the performance of the companies surveyed. Those that are able to operate unaffected by such difficulties are significantly more successful (Herzog 1996, p. 187).

The same applies to problems in the area of cost reduction and productivity gains – it was demonstrated that companies which only experienced minor difficulties concerning the burden of overly high personnel and production costs, in particular, were significantly more successful than companies which had difficulties in this area (Herzog 1996, p. 188).

Finally, difficulties in the area of research and development should not be ignored. It can also be clearly illustrated that this problem area – and specifically the particular problem of developing marketable, innovative products – has a decisive influence on company performance. Companies which reported few, if any, such problems were significantly more successful (Herzog 1996, p. 190).

Reasons for differences in performance according to type of formation

The reasons for the divergent performance of the individual groups of companies can be summarised as follows.

East German start-ups enjoyed an important initial starting advantage – they were able to enter the competitive market place on their own terms, that is, they were able to choose their company size and number of employees. This, to a large extent, explains the comparatively good cost position of these companies. On top of this came the decision to concentrate marketing and sales and marketing activities more intensively on sub-markets (local and regional) in East Germany and also not to disregard R&D activities. The fact that they did not have a past – that they were able to function more or less unaffected by difficulties resulting from the legacy of the socialist command economy – proved to be just as advantageous. Finally, it was quite significant that East German entrepreneurs had apparently been influenced to a smaller extent by the socialist economic system.

The comparatively good performance of companies which emerged by means of a derivative formation by Management-Buy-Out can also be partly traced back to their market orientation. Furthermore, the efforts taken to cast off the burden of the past and to become competitive seem eventually to be paying off.

However, financial difficulties prove to be a hindrance to the further development of MBO enterprises – the lack of availability of investment capital make necessary modernisations more difficult and/or hinder any plans for expansion.

As to the case of enterprises which have been retransferred to previous owners, somewhat average performance can be traced back, in particular, to the burden of 'old financial debt'. Furthermore, in an attempt to reduce costs, R&D capacities were cut too much – the resulting lack of innovative products does not contribute to acceptance of the particular company in the market and certainly does not help to reduce the problems they encounter in the market-place.

Serious difficulties in market development account mostly for the general bad performance of enterprises taken over by West German companies. As a result of political and economic changes in the former Eastern Block, these relatively large enterprises had, to a large extent, lost their traditional market. They then had to subject themselves to predatory competition in West Germany and on the western European markets, where their weaknesses in marketing and sales became apparent. However, on the whole, due to support from the West German parent company, the enterprises have made good progress in attaining full competitiveness – corporate success appears to be only a question of time.

Finally, the failure of companies under the administration of the Treuhandanstalt can be traced back to a number of difficulties. No one problem can be isolated as being particularly life-threatening to these companies – rather, their survival is threatened by the fact that these difficulties blend and intensify each other.

CONCLUSIONS

The collapse of the socialist economic system in the former GDR created a completely new situation for the industrial enterprises there: the old 'Kombinate' were dissolved, some parts were liquidated, others became new – mostly small and medium-sized – enterprises in the industrial sector. In addition, a significant number of new companies were formed in the industrial sector. These changes of legal form and business start-ups with all their related side effects were a typical feature of the restructuring of the industrial sector in the East German transformational economy.

As the process of reorganisation and new formation occurred in different ways – each in their own way characteristic – and with different configurations of owners, it was possible to analyse, almost as a natural experiment, the success of various entrepreneurial approaches – a controversial question in the context of research in entrepreneurship and Third World development policy (creation of a self-supporting industrial sector). This situation in the former GDR – short-term as it is – was used as the basis for an empirical investigation into the formation process and its approaches, problems and successes or failures.

The central hypothesis – that the distinctive form of business set-ups in East Germany or factors relating to this have a decisive influence on the problems and economic performance of newly established SMEs in the industrial sector – was verified unequivocally. Under the circumstances of radical economic change in East Germany, important corporate structural characteristics, different starting conditions, different corporate strategies and finally divergent performances are, in fact, all reflected in the type of company formation.

Notes

1. University College Dublin/Universität Bayreuth. This article is based entirely on research conducted by the author for a PhD thesis, which was awarded by the faculty of law and economics of the University of Bayreuth in February 1996.
2. This figure has, however, to be adjusted for market exits. Assuming an exit rate of 12.5 per cent, the IfM in Bonn estimates the number of SMEs in the industrial sector in the East German market, at the time of this investigation, at 8600.
3. Here it is necessary to differentiate between new and derivative formations. The former refer to newly formed businesses; the later to businesses which had already existed, but were either taken over or underwent a change of legal form.
4. For more details, see Luippold (1991), Hoffmann and Ramke (1992), Friedrich (1993) or Kokalj and Hüfner (1994) on the importance of this form of privatisation in East Germany.
5. All findings are based, if not indicated differently, on Herzog 1996, pp. 143–66.

Bibliography

ÅSLUND, A. *Private Enterprise in Eastern Europe. The Non-Agricultural Private Sector in Poland and the GDR 1945–83*. New York, 1985.

BELITZ, H. et al. *Aufbau des industriellen Mittelstands in den neuen Bundesländern*. Unveröffentlichtes Gutachten des Deutschen Instituts für Wirtschaftsforschung im Auftrag des Bundesministers für Wirtschaft. Berlin, February 1994.

BUNDESMINISTERIUM FÜR WIRTSCHAFT (BMWi) *Unternehmensgrößenstatistik 1992/1993 – Daten und Fakten*. Studienreihe Nr. 80, Bonn, 1993.

DIW 'Aufbau des industriellen Mittelstands in den neuen Bundesländern' *DIW-Wochenbericht*, vol. 61, no. 20, Berlin, 1994, pp. 321–8.

FRIEDRICH, W. *Management-Buy-Out und Management-Buy-In in den neuen Bundesländern*. Untersuchung im Auftrag des Bundesministers für Wirtschaft. ISG Institut für Sozialforschung und Gesellschaftspolitik GmbH, Köln, April 1993.

GRAF, H. *Beteiligungs – und Unternehmenserwerb*. In Nathusius, K. (ed.) *Praxis der Unternehmensgründung*. Köln, 1983, pp. 255–76.

HAENDCKE-HOPPE, M. *Privatwirtschaft in der DDR. Geschichte – Struktur – Bedeutung*. In Forschungsstelle für gesamtdeutsche wirtschaftliche und soziale Fragen (ed.) *FS-Analysen 1/1982*. Berlin, 1982.

HAUER, A. et al. *Der Mittelstand im Transformationsprozeß Ostdeutschlands und Osteuropas*. Heidelberg, 1993.

HERZOG, M. *Determinanten des unternehmerischen Erfolgs in den neuen Bundesländern – eine empirische Untersuchung mittelständischer Industrieunternehmen in Sachsen, Sachsen-Anhalt und Thüringen*. Frankfurt am Main, 1996.

HOFFMANN, P. and RAMKE, R. *Management Buy-Out in der Bundesrepublik Deutschland. Anspruch, Realität und Perspektiven*. 2nd ed. Berlin, 1992.

HUNSDIECK, D. *Beschäftigungspolitische Wirkungen von Untergründungen und – aufgaben*. In Institut für Mittelstandsforschung Bonn (ed.) *IfM-Materialien Nr. 28* Bonn, 1985.

HUNSDIECK, D. and MAY-STROBL, E. *Entwicklungslinien und Entwicklungsrisiken neugegründeter Unternehmen*. In Institut für Mittelstandsforschung Bonn (ed.) *Schriften zur Mittelstandsforschung Nr. 9 NF*. Stuttgart, 1986.

HÜFNER, P. et al. *Mittelstand und Mittelstandspolitik in den neuen Bundesländern: Unternehmensgründungen*. In Institut für Mittelstandsforschung Bonn (ed.) *Schriften zur Mittelstandsforschung Nr. 45 NF*. Stuttgart, 1992.

KAYSER, G. et al. *Industrieller Mittelstand in den neuen Bundesländern*. In Institut für Mittelstandsforschung Bonn (ed.) *IfM-Materialien Nr. 98*. Bonn, 1993.

KOKALJ, L. and HÜFNER, P. *Management-Buy-Out/Buy-In als Übernahmestrategie ostdeutscher Unternehmen*. In Institut für Mittelstandsforschung Bonn (ed.) *Schriften zur Mittelstandsforschung Nr. 54 NF*. Stuttgart, 1994.

LUIPPOLD, T. *Management Buy-Outs – Evaluation ihrer Einsatzmöglichkeiten in Deutschland*. Bern, 1991.

MAY-STROBL, E. and PAULINI, M. *Unternehmensgründungen in den neuen Bundesländern*. In: Institut für Mittelstandsforschung Bonn (ed.) *IfM-Materialien Nr. 77*. Bonn, 1990.

PAULINI, M. and MAY-STROBL, E. *Die Entwicklung junger Unternehmen in den neuen Bundesländern*. In Institut für Mittelstandsforschung Bonn (ed.) *Schriften zur Mittelstandsforschung Nr. 62 NF*. Bonn, 1994.

PICKEL, A. *Radical transitions. The survival and revival of entrepreneurship in the GDR*. Boulder, 1992.

SCHMIDT, A. *Reprivatisierungsreport – Laufende Berichterstattung über die Reprivati-sierung von Unternehmen in den neuen Bundesländern – Januar bis August 1992*. In Institut für Mittelstandsforschung Bonn (ed.) *IfM-Materialien Nr. 94*. Bonn, 1992.

SCHMIDT, A. and KAUFMANN, F. *Reprivatisierungsreport. Laufende Berichterstattung über die Reprivatisierung von Unternehmen in den neuen Bundesländern*. In Institut für Mittelstandsforschung Bonn (ed.) *IfM-Materialien Nr. 84*. Bonn, 1991.

SCHMIDT, A. and KAUFMANN, F. *Mittelstand und Mittelstandspolitik in den neuen Bundesländern: Rückgabe enteigneter Unternehmen*. In Institut für Mittelstandsforschung Bonn (ed.) *Schriften zur Mittelstandsforschung Nr. 47 NF*. Stuttgart, 1992.

SIEGEL, S. *Nichtparametrische statistische Methoden*. 3rd ed. Eschborn, 1987.

TREUHANDANSTALT (ed.) *Zentrales Controlling – Monatsinformation der THA*. Berlin. May 1993.

WILLER, H. *Das neue Unternehmertum in Afrika*. Spardorf, 1989.

6 Private Property and the Transformation Process

Wolfram Waldner

INTRODUCTION

When you talk to someone about the difficulties regarding reconstruction in the new Länder (the so-called *Aufschwung Ost*), he or she will certainly mention the key phrase, 'unknown ownership of private property' (*ungeklärte Eigentumsverhältnisse*). This is said to be the obstacle for the investment of capital or – more often – is the pretext for idleness while other difficulties prevail.

Why is the ownership of private property unknown in so many cases? While the former German Democratic Republic (GDR) could not be labelled a state under the rule of law in our sense of the phrase, it was a state with statutes, acts and rules. There was – just as in Germany under the rule of the nazis – not pure arbitrariness, but instead the so-called socialist lawfulness (*sozialistische Gesetzlichkeit*) governed the legal relationships of her citizens. The concept of private property was well known and settled by law.

I would like to go somewhat further: the citizen of the GDR who bought a copy of the Code of Civil Law 1975 (*Zivilgesetzbuch*, ZGB) of the GDR was much more likely to understand the legal system of contracts, torts, and private property in the GDR than a citizen of the Federal Republic of Germany buying a copy of the Civil Code 1896 (*Bürgerliches Gesetzbuch*, BGB) in order to understand his legal system. Unlike the highly abstract BGB the ZGB was a clear, easy-to-understand code, even though it was quite slipshod in systems and terms, and its German left room for improvement. The Unification Contract (*Einigungsvertrag*) which came into force on 3 October 1990 did not alter the ownership of private property directly. How can the right of ownership be unknown in so many cases?

THE COMPLEXITY OF THE QUESTION

I would like to start with the following hypothesis: the common accord that unknown ownership is so frequent gives a simple answer. However, it is a complex question. Generally speaking, in such a case, simple answers are not entirely wrong, but they do not suffice. That is just the case with unknown ownership. Of course they exist, and of course statistics may prove that they exist more frequently in the new Länder, but as a rule the ownership is not unknown; instead it is complicated, difficult to find out and easily disputed.

There are a number of reasons for this complexity:

(i) the measures of the Soviet military government in their occupation zone between 1945 and 1949;
(ii) the development of the legal system in the former GDR in the 41 years from 1949 to 1990;
(iii) the development of actual conditions over the same period;
(iv) the changes in the legal system caused by the Unification Treaty and the legislation of the five years following.

Each of these reasons produced a great many of the problems we face today with ownership of private property in the new Länder.

Property under Socialist Law

After the end of World War II the two states emerging from the ruins of the German Empire (*Deutsches Reich*) disposed of a uniform civil law, the BGB, as it had been in force before the nation collapsed. It was not before 1 January 1976 that a new civil code, the ZGB, came into force in the GDR. The laws of each state had been growing apart from each other before, mostly as a result of the remodelling of the social system in the GDR. The law of property and, particularly, the law of real property, was concerned, as it reflects specifically the economic system of a society. Essays published after the unification normally describe the West German law of property rather emotionally as suitable for the requirements of a liberal state under the rule of law and a market economy.[1] That is utter nonsense, of course. The law of property of the BGB survived, substantially unchanged, the fall of the monarchy in 1918 as well as the Nazi period. It was suitable for the free market economy before 1914 as well as for the war economy of World War I and World War II and for Ludwig Erhard's social market economy of the 1950s.

Law of property is characterised by a high degree of abstraction. It says what ownership is, which limited real rights do exist, how they are acquired and lost. It does not say, however, which contracts can be formed under the legal and actual conditions of a society in order to acquire or loose these rights. In other words, the law of property of the BGB is suitable for any legal system that acknowledges that ownership is an absolute right, that is for every capitalist economic system. It is certainly not suitable for a social and economic system on the basis of Marxist–Leninist ideology.

These facts, however, emerged only gradually in the GDR as did the way this state saw itself. Thus another property law was developed and, especially, other concepts and other forms of ownership. The distinctions can only be made vivid when confronted with the law of property of the FRG.

In the FRG the Basic Law (*Grundgesetz*, GG) guarantees the right of private property (art. 14 GG) as one of the basic liberties of man. Private property is regarded as the material equivalent of the general basic right of personal liberty (art. 2 < 1 > GG). The law may restrict its use on the grounds of public or community needs and even provide for expropriation (which entitles the owner to a fair compensation). These restrictions, however, leave untouched the principle that the owner has the total factual and legal control of his object and the freedom to do as he wishes with it (par. 903 BGB). Thus ownership is effective against the whole world and is legally protected from anyone interfering with it. On the other hand, that requires that acquisition and loss of ownership are open to public disclosure: for movables, the delivery of possession (*Übergabe*) fulfils this requirement; for real estate, it can be observed in the Land Register (*Grundbuch*). Transfer of ownership of real estate requires a record in the Land Register; without such an entry the transfer is void. The registration covers not only the land itself, but the buildings as well: they are deemed essential parts of the land and paragraphs 93, 94 state that essential parts cannot be the subject of separate rights. The owner of a piece of land is owner of all the buildings attached to it, by law and automatically.

There is only one statutory exception, building lease (*Erbbaurecht*) under the Building Lease Act. A building established thereunder is not deemed by law to be an essential part of the land, but it is treated like land (*grundstücksgleiches Recht*). The building lease is recorded in the Land Register, making sure that everybody acquiring a property right (for example, a mortgage) knows that the owner of the land is not the owner of the building.

Furthermore, the rule that there can be no separate ownership of buildings attached to land does not exclude joint ownership of land, and under the Apartment Ownership Act (*Wohnungseigentumsgesetz*) joint ownership may consist of co-ownership of the common property and facilities, and individual ownership of flats and apartments. A special entry in the Land Register shows the fraction of ownership of the land and describes the parts of the building in individual ownership, thus upholding the principle of public disclosure even in this case.

The 1968 constitution of the GDR shows quite clearly the distinctions between the concept of ownership in the FRG and the GDR. This constitution gives two types of ownership: the socialist ownership of the means of production intended to strengthen the economic and political power of the working classes on the one hand, and the private property of the citizens, intended only to meet personal needs, such as real estate for housing and leisure, on the other hand. The latter was regarded as less important of course.

There were several types of socialist ownership: the national property (*Volkseigentum*) of the state, the co-operative property of the agricultural co-operatives (*Landwirtschaftliche Produktionsgenossenschaften*, LPGs) and the property of the trades and crafts (*Produktionsgenossenschaften des Handwerks*, PGHs). These types of ownership, however, were not invented by the 1968 constitution, but only renamed.

The remodelling of ownership had started as early as autumn 1945, when the Soviet military administration ordered the implementation of agrarian reform (*Bodenreform*). It was aimed at 'the elimination of feudal Junkerish big landowners' as the regulations of the provincial governments called it.

Everybody who owned more than 250 acres of land was regarded as a big landowner, and not only that land exceeding 250 acres was expropriated, but all his land, with livestock, fixtures, and fittings. Most of that land was not nationalised, but transferred to private owners or, in the words of the regulations of 3 September 1945, real estate 'shall be based on firm, sound and productive farmsteads, which are the private property of their owners'. About 13 600 farmsteads and forests with a total of about 13 million acres of productive land were transferred to about 550 000 farmers, workers, and refugees from former Eastern Germany, who had no or very little land.

The said regulations prohibited the division, demise, pawning or, of course, sale of real estate acquired in the *Bodenreform*. There is no doubt that the regulations promised private ownership to the new possessors, but this was not the ownership meant by the BGB, not an absolute right, but a title difficult to categorise in the previous system. It has been called a servitude (*Nutzungsrecht*) or worker's ownership (*Arbeitseigentum*).

The restrictions imposed made such real estate a *res extra commercium*. It was transferable by succession only, and even this was only possible when the heir cultivated the land himself and lived in the buildings attached. If he did not, it reverted to the so-called land fund (*Bodenfonds*) and could be transferred to others under the same conditions. Transfer by loan was the only way to hand it over to a third person legally, and this occurred quite frequently.

It was still in the time of Soviet military administration that the property of war and nazi criminals (*Kriegs-und Naziverbrecher*) was expropriated and substantial parts of the economy as a whole were nationalised. This was especially true for all the heavy industry, the banks and the insurance companies, but also in part for medium-sized enterprises. The payment of the reparations to the Soviets was only one of the reasons for this policy, and it continued after the foundation of the GDR. Even those plants which were expropriated for reparation were not wound up and taken to the Soviet Union, but remained in the GDR, and later were resold to her. Following the Soviet example the property was transferred to People's Own Enterprises (*Volkseigene Betriebe*, VEBs). LPGs and other co-operatives as trustees (*Rechtsträger*). When such a Rechtsträger put up buildings on land transferred to it, these buildings became national property. They could be neither pawned nor seized, and there was no way of transferring the land into private property.

Not all real estate was nationalised, however. One or two family houses and smaller farms were not infringed. In principle, the private owner was even allowed to dispose of it, but in fact there were rigid restrictions. A permission by the County or City Council (*Rat des Kreises oder Rat der Stadt*) had to be obtained, and this permission could be refused whenever the interests of the state or the society were against it or the desirable economic use was at risk. The Real Estate Transactions Regulation (*Grundstücksverkehrsverordnung*) used vague terms (*unbestimmte Rechtsbegriffe*) in order to leave it to the discretion of the state whether the owner could dispose of his estate or not. Sales contracts were obstructed by rigid price regulations. The price could not be agreed upon by the parties of contract, but was limited to the so-called standard value (*Einheitswert*), set up for revenue purposes in 1935 and thus being only a fraction of the market price.

Consequently, sales contracts were usually dealt with at a black-market price, while the regulated price was given in the document of the notary, thus leading to all the problems of a false document. Sales contracts, however, were rather rare, for rents also were kept on the level of 1935 while maintenance costs were relatively high. Thus a landlord could never make a living, and real estate was sold to the state quite often, making national property even more predominant.

Blocks of rented flats owned by people living outside the GDR were not expropriated automatically but rather put in compulsory administration. As rental income was far less than maintenance costs the state administrator took out a mortgage on the building. From 1976 onwards this system was also used for the so-called cold expropriations (*kalte Enteignungen*): As soon as mortgaging led to negative equity, calculated by the unrealistic prices of 1935 of course, the house was taken over as national property.

It is quite clear that under the circumstances described above, building did not make sense save for the client's own needs, and that as a rule it was only possible when the client was owner of the building land. The state, however, faced a dilemma: it was not able to provide sufficient homes for the population, but on the other hand national property could neither be transferred nor charged, for example by means of building leases.

The solution found was to hand over national property to socialist organisations and co-operatives and even citizens by specially designed contracts (*Überlassungsverträge*), while building land was handed over by conferring a special kind of servitude (*Nutzungsrecht*). The Nutzungsrecht was conferred under the condition that the applicant did not own another home and the Parish Council gave its consent. If so, the County or City Council issued a document for the Nutzungsrecht. Other than the building lease of the BGB the Nutzungsrecht was given for an indefinite period and generally speaking without paying rent or interest for it. The holder of the Nutzungsrecht became owner of the house he built, while the land remained national property. Thus ownership of land and ownership of building were separated.

The Land Register Regulations of the GDR provided for recording the conferment of a Nutzungsrecht in the Land Register. The entry, however, did not constitute the conferment – it was valid even if never recorded. The building was to be recorded in the Land Register as well, and a sales contract regarding the building had to be signed in the presence of a notary. A permission to sell had to be obtained, and it could be refused on the same grounds as with real estate.

Thus far, apart from the fact that it was given for an indefinite period, no significant difference seems to exist between building lease and the Nutzungsrecht, and one might think that it is just playing with names. However, when the holder of the Nutzungsrecht died, the difference was quite clear: in principle, the building could be inherited but an heir was not allowed to own more than one home. If this was the case, the Nutzungsrecht could be withdrawn and he would be forced to sell the building. The same rules applied when the owner made use of the property in a different way from what was agreed to in the conferring document.

While it would have been possible to categorise the said Nutzungsrechte in the system of the BGB property law as a somewhat strange building lease, this cannot be said for the Nutzungsrechte awarded by the LPGs. As a result of agrarian collectivisation the LPGs were granted a Nutzungsrecht regarding all the land in their possession. That could be their own co-operative property as well as transferred national property, or private property of the members of the co-operative. The LPG was authorised to allocate separate Nutzungsrechte to its members as well as to other citizens for the purpose of building a home. The allocation was put into effect by the chair of the co-operative, who signed a document that was certified by the local Council. As the LPG did not care which of its land was concerned, ownership of buildings on national real estate, co-operative real estate, and private real estate came into existence.

That was not all. Special regulations applied to leisure property (*Erholungsgrundstücke*). This was transferred to citizens by means of an Überlassungsvertrag, but without the creation of a Nutzungsrecht. When constructing a building on such a piece of land the citizen was owner of the building – meant to be a summer house or cottage, a so-called Datsche. As for selling a Datsche, the strict rules for real estate did not apply. There was no entry in the Land Register, and no specific form was required. At least after 1976, the rules for movable property were applicable.

At the end of the day, a specific form of acquisition of ownership was created by the new ZGB in 1976. It was meant to safeguard socialist enterprises when building on private land. Automatically, that is, without the need of expropriation of the previous owner, joint ownership emerged, the nationally owned share being determined by the value of the building compared with the value of the land. The joint ownership was to be recorded in the Land Register.

Day-to-Day Practice in the GDR

This juxtaposition of real estate – expropriated by the Soviet military administration or by the authorities of the GDR or by law, the different reasons for expropriation (Nazis, big land owners, nationalisation of industry, negative equity), and the different ways of transferring rights (Nutzungsrechte, Überlassungsverträge) – may look complicated enough. Nevertheless, you might hope to get the upper hand on it, provided the authorities in the GDR had stuck to their own principles. Unfortunately, that was quite rare.

The low value of land and the unimportance of the fact of being the owner of real estate led to a neglect of land survey and land registry that is hard to believe in a civilised nation. The neglect was so extreme that housing schemes of a hundred or more flats were built without taking land ownership into account and disregarding boundaries. Buildings on someone else's land were not demanded or expressly permitted by the authorities, but widely approved.

Law and reality were far apart, especially for the Nutzungsrechte. In a large number of cases houses were built on someone else's land without conferring a Nutzungsrecht, and therefore no ownership of the building emerged. Members of co-operatives built houses on land of the LPGs without prior allocation. The LPGs, on the other hand, transferred buildings owned by them to citizens, or land to the Parish Councils, and these subsequently transferred it to citizens to build on.

All this was quite frequently not recorded in the Land Register, local practices in different places being quite different. As a rule, in Saxonia, Thuringia, and in the urban districts some diligence was observed, while in the north of the GDR and especially in rural areas procedure was rather lax. In other cases, the so-called *hängende Bebauungen* (pending buildings), nationally owned or co-operatively used land was allocated for building on; the award of Nutzungsrechte was promised, but never did happen for various reasons.

As there were no administrative courts, the citizens had no opportunity to enforce the issue of documents for their Nutzungsrechte, and even if there had been such opportunity, most of them would have refrained from doing so, as there were no practical consequences of having or not having that document. The different kinds of Nutzungsrechte were not as stringently kept apart as the legal rules required. That is specially true for the Erholungsgrundstücke, where solid homes were built with the tacit permission of the authorities, the so-called *unechte Datschen* (improper cottages). Even buildings in the nationalised economic sector did not comply with the regulations. Disregarding boundaries was not an exceptional case, but something of the rule in many places.

These strange phenomena can easily be explained by the fact that in the GDR the question of ownership of land came long after the much more vital questions of how to get workers and material for building, and – for state building – to meet the output target set up by the planning department. Many people were aware that ownership problems had to be settled and sorted out – but this was delayed and then forgotten as a quite meaningless issue, and a settlement was never achieved.

All this serves to prove the hypothesis we started with: in most cases ownership in the new Länder is not unknown in the precise sense of the word, but very often complicated and difficult to find out. This is true both for the factual side, from the point of land survey, and the legal side, because of the large number of cases which are characterised by the fact that sometimes the statutes were kept to, sometimes not, and it was definitely pure chance for the citizen involved as to which category applied to his or her land or building.

DEALING WITH THE PROPERTY QUESTION AFTER UNIFICATION

It was not an easy job for the legislature to clear up this situation. The formulation of coherent and practical rules was itself a sisyphean task, let alone the delicate implications of social politics and, at first, foreign policy. Every possible solution would surely lead to conflict situations. There had never been any realistic hope before for those whose land had been expropriated to get back what they had lost, but now they scented their chance. Those to whom the socialist state had allocated land or buildings wanted to keep the property for which and on which they had worked hard. It was not only the text of new statutes that was required, but also discovering a socio-politically acceptable solution. We must not forget this difficult situation when we assess the legislation for evening out today, when the enacting of new legislation – not the evening out itself, of course – has come to an end. Statutes were enacted without a proper system, sometimes changed after a few months. Nobody could assume that any concept could reconcile the contrasting interests. Workable compromises could not be found without substantial cuts for many people involved. It is no wonder that there are some controversies as to whether the final balancing out met the expressed needs, and it may be necessary to change certain regulations in the future. We should have a look at the expropriations under Soviet military administration, especially the Bodenreform, the expropriations in the GDR and, finally, the problems caused by the Nutzungsrechte, resulting in a separation of land ownership and ownership of the buildings.

Expropriations under Soviet Military Administration

In the opinion of the last governments of the GDR, international law made it impossible for the two German states to deal with the expropriations carried out in the years 1945 to 1949, by reason of the fact that they had occurred under Soviet administration. This argument does not hold water, as it was not the Soviets, but the German authorities, who put the expropriations into effect. It should be remembered, however, that the Modrow government was successful in making the Soviet Union declare the continued existence of the Bodenreform a precondition of her consent to German unification.

Obviously, the Soviet Union not only wanted to support the standpoint of the GDR, but also rule out any idea that the measures applied under the law of occupation could be questioned under today's standards, disregarding whether the military authority itself or German authorities were to be held responsible. There is no question that even though the aims of the expropriations were legitimate, the implementation had led to many irregularities and injustices, especially when declaring people 'war criminals' or 'Nazi activists'. The principle of definitiveness of those expropriations was incorporated in the Unification Treaty, and the Basic Law was amended to ensure that its provisions would not stand in the way.

It was inevitable that the principle was taken to the Constitutional Court (*Bundesverfassungsgericht*) with the reasoning that it represented unconstitutional Constitutional Law, a term quite familiar to German lawyers. The Court however ruled against the petition in 1991 and declared the exception of return in these cases lawful on the grounds that the attitude of the Soviet Union had made it inevitable for the government to act in that way and that the delicate question of unification had not to be endangered.

In the extraordinary situation of that time this had to be accepted, even if it led to a breach of the rule of equal treatment regarding the expropriations before and after 1949. A long time after the judgement, statements from the Soviet leader Gorbachev suggested that the Soviet Union had been neither willing nor able to make unification fail, and that she wanted to do the last governments of the GDR a favour. It is a pointless issue as to whether this is true or not, as the Constitutional Court held to its opinion in a new judgement.[2]

It should be noted that the West German negotiators where quite happy with the firm attitude of the Soviets. As we mentioned, most of the expropriated land was transferred to private owners, and they or their successors mostly still owned it in 1990. It would have been unacceptable to examine every single case after more than forty years in order to find out whether the expropriation was justified.

The restrictions imposed on the owners of Bodenreform land were repealed by the new democratic government of the GDR with effect from 15 March 1990, without any interim regulation. In the heat of the moment the GDR parliament did not take into account that, due to the virtual unimportance of ownership, the transfer of possession documents provided for by law in the case of the death of a farmer had very often not been set up, and no entries in the Land Register had been made. So it proved difficult in many cases to establish who was entitled to dispose of Bodenreform land when the registered owner had died long ago.

In 1992 a very complicated regulation came into force deciding who should be the beneficiary and under what circumstances he or his successors should have to transfer ownership to beneficiaries with a better title (the so-called *besser Berechtigte*). Legally, everything is clear now; but the law assumes facts that are hard to find out, let alone prove, after up to forty years. Parliament, however, was wise enough to fix a deadline which will be of importance for another reason too: it is only until 31 December 1999 that the besser Berechtigte is given special protection. The Parish Council will be informed if someone wants to dispose of Bodenreform land; if it knows about somebody who might be the besser Berechtigte, it may suspend the disposal temporarily, giving the besser Berechtigte four months in which to pursue his claim. From 1 January 2000, he who fails to have an entry recorded in the Land Register cannot pursue his claim against those who rely on the correctness of the Land Register. From that date Bodenreform land will be fully negotiable.

Expropriations in the GDR

The legal position of those with land expropriated by the GDR authorities is more complicated. The Act Regulating Open Questions of Property (*Gesetz zur Regelung offener Vermögensfragen, Vermögensgesetz*), enacted before unification and amended several times since, says that previous owners can demand the return of their property or the removal of state administration of their property if they lost it through unlawful acts specifically related to the division of the country (*spezifisches Teilungsunrecht*).

It is clear that in the 40-year period of the GDR there have been a large number of expropriations and similar acts affecting the property of GDR citizens as well as that of West Germans and other nationals. Some of these appropriations could have occurred in West Germany, for example when land was appropriated to build roads, and some are not acceptable from the West's legal point of view. It would obviously have been impossible to revise all these measures. That is why the Vermögensgesetz decided to make restitution only in cases where property had been expropriated on the grounds that the owner's domicile was outside the GDR, or that he had left it without permission from the state authorities (so-called *Republikflucht*).

The Vermögensgesetz therefore provided for the restitution, *interalia*, of

(i) property acquired by unfair wheelings and dealings (corruption, coercion, deception by the acquirer or the state authorities);
(ii) property confiscated after Republikflucht from the previous owner;
(iii) nationalised industries;
(iv) blocks of rented flats taken over as national property after driving them into negative equity by absurdly low rents.

It goes without saying that these criteria were disputed from the beginning and one question was solved only in 1996.

Naturally, the GDR had to expropriate the land needed to build the Berlin Wall. There was no provision for restitution under the Vermögensgesetz, as these expropriations affected land of GDR citizens as well as that of aliens, and the expropriations took place in the same way as if they had been in the way of a military training area or a new motorway. On the other hand, it is obvious that these expropriations meant injustice related to the division of the country *par excellence*. And it is quite clear that at the very least the land needed for building the wall in Berlin city centre could have been sold lucratively: by square feet it might be the most expensive land in Germany, and that is exactly why the treasury was keen to keep it for itself. The Administrative Courts had always dismissed the actions of previous owners on the grounds that there was no provision in the Vermögensgesetz. Now, a political solution has been found: the previous owners are entitled to buy their land back from the Treasury at one fourth of the market value.[3]

The Vermögensgesetz set up the rule that land should be given back to the previous owners rather than paying them compensation. Any other solution was likely to be challenged successfully at the Constitutional Court. Restitution, however, could not be provided for, if in the meantime land had been acquired by third persons honestly (*redlicher Erwerb*). If third persons had acquired one of the Nutzungsrechte in respect of a piece of land honestly, restitution meant that the Nutzungsrecht had to be taken with the land.

This issue remains in dispute. What is meant by 'acquired honestly'? It is definitely a new term in German law, and the well-established criteria of interpretation fail. The Vermögensgesetz deliberately does not say 'in good faith' (*in gutem Glauben*), but 'honestly' (*redlich*). It is quite clear that those who acquired ownership or a Nutzungsrecht from the GDR authorities in most cases knew that it was property nationalised in a rather questionable way. They were not 'in good faith', but they nevertheless acted honestly. He who lived in the GDR had to live with its conditions. When he acted correctly, given these conditions, he cannot be denied to have acted honestly. But the acquisition may date back years, or even decades, and it is difficult, if not impossible, to shed light upon the situation then.

There was no doubt from the beginning that restitution claims should not be allowed to slow down the urgently needed economic development of the new Länder. A conflict arising between possible restitution claims and investors had to be solved by giving priority to investment. But the question remained unsolved as to which kind of investment was urgent enough and best-suited to achieving these development aims, and which was the best way to decide whether a specific piece of land was essential for the investment. The legal provisions were changed several times, but inevitably they still use vague terms, and many cases find their way to the courts.

It is not only these circumstances, but also the difficulties in finding out the true owners when the expropriated person has died, that must be held responsible for the fact that many proceedings have not come to an end today, seven years after the Vermögensgesetz came into force. The pending cases are often labelled with the 'unknown ownership' formula. It should be mentioned, however, that not all the problems unsolved are a result of difficult factual conditions or points of law. At least as important is that the new Länder dealt with the problems in quite different ways – though the law is the same everywhere. In the south of the GDR – apart from the big cities of Leipzig and Dresden – all proceedings that did not result in an application to the courts are carried out substantially, while in Greater Berlin and elsewhere in the north an alarming number of cases remains unsettled, though undisputed.

Problems Caused by the Nutzungsrecht

While the act regarding the GDR expropriations came into force in 1990, and the act regarding the Bodenreform land in 1992, it was not before autumn 1994 that a legal solution was found for the problems caused by buildings on someone else's land. These buildings had made mortgaging difficult: the buildings did not constitute real property and could not be mortgaged. The land, however, was not accepted as a security by banks as nobody could predict what the holders of a Nutzungsrechte would be allowed to claim.

The reason why it took so long to hammer out a regulation was not only the rather complex factual side – as we have seen – but mostly the extraordinarily fierce lobbying by the owners of the land and the holders of the Nutzungsrechte, which in turn was due to the fact that the situation on the housing market was turned upside down after the market economy was introduced. While in the times of the GDR land ownership was virtually unimportant because of price regulations and sale restrictions, and the Nutzungsrechte and the buildings were the things that really counted, things thoroughly changed after the breakdown of socialism: land prices soared while the buildings attached did not comply with western standards of quality and proved quite often a burden on the land.

That is why the ideas of the owners and the holders of a Nutzungsrecht seemed to be irreconcilable. The holders of a Nutzungsrecht demanded to keep to these rights even under today's circumstances, that is, to some extent to preserve socialism. The owners, on the other hand, demanded the return of their property without any burden, to be allowed to do with it as they wished, that is, to force the holders of a Nutzungsrechte either to buy the land at the full market price or to pay a rent for the land as high as the interest usually earned on the said amount.

The German parliament found a solution worthy of a Solomon, not based on principles of law, but on policy: both, owner and holder of the Nutzungsrecht, shall share the gains of reunification. The holder of the Nutzungsrecht is entitled to buy the land at half the market price or to be given building lease for the expected lifetime of his building at half the usual rent.

The so-called Property Law Settlement Act (*Sachenrechtsbereinigungs-gesetz*) provides for a mediation by a notary, and, in the worst case, for an application to the court. In order to accelerate these settlements the holders of a Nutzungsrechte are encouraged to act soon and not to let things drag on: those who do not file an application for mediation with a notary by 1 January 2000 see their building at risk. Up to that day all buyers of real estate in the new Länder have to take a Nutzungsrecht into account – they cannot rely on the Land Register. From that day the Land Register will be reliable even in the new Länder, and failure to have the beginning of mediation recorded in the Land Register will mean that a buyer in good faith will not have to respect the Nutzungsrecht.

These regulations apply to holders of a Nutzungsrecht in possession of a document, or recorded owners of the building, and – as there was so much wishful thinking in GDR Law – to those who had had such a document or had been recorded owners of the building, if everything had gone the right way, and, finally, for those who built an improper cottage (unechte Datsche), that is, a real home on a piece of land designed for a garden house. These regulations do not apply, however, to those who built a real garden house or weekend cottage on such a piece of land. A separate regulation, the Obligation Law Settlement Act (*Schuldrechtsanpassungsgesetz*), was hammered out for these cases, changing them to permanent lease contracts, as a rule not terminable by the land owner before 4 October 2015. As the law of the GDR did not create ownership of the building, land ownership was given priority in these cases after unification. It was found sufficient to guarantee their right of possession – in some cases for the lifetime of the user – but they do not share what the land is worth, even when unification multiplied the price. There is no need to mention that the legitimacy of that distinction was much disputed by legal scholars as well as in parliament.

Of course, only the most important outlines of the conditions that make ownership of property in the new Länder not 'unknown', but extraordinarily complex, could be mentioned here. They have been an obstacle for the investment of capital for a long time, and in one way or another they hinder it even today. A legal system, however, respecting private property in a market economy and the special guarantees granted by the Basic Law could not find a much easier and at the same time a fair solution.

Notes

1. Pruetting in Pruetting/Zimmermann/Heller, 'Grundstrücksrecht Ost,' München 1996, Sachenrechtsbereinigungsgesetz, Einführung, Note 2.
2. Constitutional Court, Judgment 18 April 1996, Zeitschrift für Vermögens- und Investitionsrecht (VIZ) 1996, p. 325.
3. Berlin Wall Land Sales Act (*Mauergrundstücksgesetz*) of 15 July 1996 (Federal Law Gazette 1996, pt. I, p. 980).

III

New Institutions and Economic Policy

7 Problems of the Welfare State and the New German Länder

James Coop and Rudi Vis

INTRODUCTION

It is the aim of this chapter to analyse the relationship between economics as a social science – its value judgements both implicit and explicit – and many of the socio-economic problems that most industrialised western liberal democracies are experiencing, for example unemployment, uncertainty, low growth, diminishing public sector provision, and so on, applied to the European social model. Seemingly we are told that the State cannot take the burden of the Welfare State and that individuals must make provision for their own futures. According to this argument Germany should follow this prescription. It is our intention to throw doubt on this proposition.

The Anglo-Saxon stagflationary economies were running into serious problems in the late 1960s and early 1970s. The unheralded period of post-war economic growth had ended. Serious criticism began of 'Butskillism', the political consensus that had grown out of the Second World War and the social problems of the 1930s. Moreover, the Welfare State as founded by the 1945 Labour Government, it began to be argued by the increasingly vocal Right, was in their view the major contributing factor to Britain's relative and ever-increasing economic decline. This was seen as contributory to a moral decline via the something-for-nothing society, which created a 'new form of social deprivation' and a 'cycle of dependency' (Sullivan, 1996, p. 6).

The ideology behind the welfare reforms of successive Conservative governments argues that the Welfare State hinders 'wealth creation'; the dead hand of bureaucracy stifling the efforts of entrepreneurs and making the country uncompetitive. Indeed it was in the early 1970s that a still-relevant debate occurred between Rawls and Nozick concerning the role and responsibilities of the State, especially as regards its less-privileged citizens. This debate is worth revisiting, since it occurred simultaneously with a seeming crisis in Keynesian economic theory and a rising fear by the elite of the impact of the participation of previously marginalised, excluded and apathetic sections of society in the formal democratic processes, especially as regarded the Vietnam war protests and the Civil Rights movement. This ideology is relevant to that which has inspired much government welfare legislation in the mid-1990s (Rawls, 1971: Nozick, 1974).

The approach used will be historical, comparative and international, with especial reference to the UK and Germany, since this will show that what passes in the media and much of academia for a value-free scientific approach is in fact ideological in nature, in favour of what in New Right terminology are called 'special interest groups'. Why should the efficient subsidise the inefficient? By doing so nations can render themselves inefficient in competitive terms with other nations, or so it is argued. The Asian Tiger economies – Hong Kong, Singapore, South Korea, Taiwan – are presented as shining examples of what successful non-Welfare-State-based capitalist economies can achieve with all sectors of society benefiting by their spectacular rates of growth. This is contrasted with the sluggish, un-dynamic, non-entrepreneurial, stagflationary Welfare State economies like the UK. This notion and the other related lines of attack have been used by some New Right critics of the present Welfare State systems which exist in Germany and other western capitalist societies. Radical critics who attempt to construct an intellectual defence of Welfare State support systems can find themselves in immense difficulties if they do not start with the fundamental premises upon which the New Right base their attack – free trade and comparative advantage. Reasons of space dictate that we must leave out any analysis of the perfect market and of the notion of rational economic man. Critics, who construct a defence from within the present ideological system, whilst ignoring the premises upon which the New Right base their attack, can find that they are constrained into accepting their conclusions. At best any such arguments constructed will lose intellectual force. We therefore propose to examine some of these premises. We will then analyse some of the present criticisms of the Welfare State with special reference to the Rawls/Nozick debate of the early 1970s. We will synthesise this with an analysis of the holy grail of all neo-classical economists, quantitative economic growth – thus ignoring any consideration of the quality of life – before we present our conclusions (Okun, 1975).

COMPARATIVE ADVANTAGE AND FREE TRADE

The case for the notion of comparative advantage is based on the case of free trade in a national economy. As Aliber states: 'There is a basic presumption that free and voluntary exchanges increase welfare both within national borders and across national borders' (Prasch, 1996, p. 38).

The Ricardian, Ricardo–Viner and Heckscher–Ohlin models assume among other things: perfect competition; constant returns to scale; costless exchange; equivalent numbers of goods, factors and sets of taste across national borders; and capital not crossing international borders (Prasch, 1996, p. 39).

For reasons of space we will take issue with just a few of the assumptions contained in the notion of comparative advantage. The first thing to note is that not one of the countries which industrialised after Britain, particularly Germany, listened to the economic arguments of British Free Traders. All of them sacrificed short-term comparative advantage in pursuit of long-term developmental aims. For most of its history the USA has resorted to protectionist measures. Policies of strict protectionism were followed from 1816 to 1846. From 1846 to 1861 restrictions were relaxed but in 1861 a stricter policy was followed. Japan never took the economic doctrines of its rivals seriously. It would appear to be no coincidence that Japan, a non-white nation not to be conquered in the nineteenth century, was the only one successfully to industrialise. As a nation with almost no natural resources, the nationalistic Japanese elite, fearful of western domination, deliberately set out to industrialise and modernise their nation. In the three decades following the 1868 revolution this was as a matter of policy, done without foreign capital – bar a five million yen loan from Britain in 1871 to complete the Tokyo to Yokohama railway. By the end of that century Japan possessed a highly evolved efficient elite providing the necessary human capital for further development and independence (Lehmann, 1982, p. 175).

This diverges from the fate of Japan's Indian, South American, Chinese and Egyptian contemporaries. It was nationalism that provided the 'will to achieve ambitious ends irrespective of the sacrifices', and which provided the 'high degree of determination and singularity of purpose among the elite; that element was lacking in other would-be modernising nations' (Lehmann, 1982, p. 178). This contrasts sharply with the present elites who exist in many Third World countries and who may be one of the most important barriers to self-sustaining economic development linked to the needs of their people (Hunt and Sherman, 1980, p. 661).

This is especially true for those countries where the USA has sponsored coups, directly or indirectly invaded and set up puppet regimes – Indonesia, Guatemala, Haiti, Vietnam, to name just a few (Chomsky, 1992, p. 324). Ricardo assumed, when in 1817 he elucidated his theory, that men of property would be 'satisfied with a low rate of profits in their own country, rather than seek a more advantageous employment for their wealth in foreign nations' (Goldsmith, 1995, p. 18). He was wrong. Capital is being moved to the developing world in increasing amounts. In the period 1989–92 the average transferred per annum was 116 billion dollars with, in 1993, 213 billion dollars and, in 1994, about 227 billion dollars. This is occurring as international capital takes advantage of the enormously lower labour costs in developing countries, sometimes as much as forty times lower than in the home country (Goldsmith, 1995, pp. 19–21).

Neo-classical economists point to the economic success of the 'Asian Tigers' as proof and models of the virtues of comparative advantage and free international trade. They fail to point out that much of world trade is dominated by transnationals and consists of intra-firm trade. The 'Asian Tiger' countries are still dependent upon international capital and their much-vaunted exports are dominated by firms from the advanced capitalist countries who retain control over research, advertising, marketing and long-term term profits. Indeed most of their production for export is subcontracted work ranging from wholly owned subsidiaries to independent producers. This dominance helps explain why it has been possible, despite domestic political resistance, for nearly all of the US market for consumer electronic products to be taken over by imports of these products, but this is not seen as 'imports' in the eyes of corporate America. When faced with real competition which threatens their domestic interests and privilege, serious measures are taken, as illustrated by the imposition of 'voluntary' quotas when the US textile market was penetrated to less than 15 per cent of consumption, and by the 'orderly marketing arrangements', which limit exports from South Korea's steel, shipbuilding, shoe and auto industries (Landsberg, 1979, p. 61). Neo-classical theory does not match reality. As Prasch concludes: 'this lesson is supported by the conclusion that a policy of *laissez-faire* founded upon the theory of comparative advantage does not appear to be able to withstand an examination of its own foundations' (Prasch, 1996, p. 53).

The basic theoretical premise behind free international trade is transferring the concept of the division of labour from a national to an international context. Countries will specialise in those areas of the economy in which they enjoy a comparative advantage. The 'invisible hand', individual rational self-interest and a self-regulating international market would do the rest. As Ricardo stated:

> Under a system of perfectly free commerce, each country naturally devotes its capital and labour to such employments as are most beneficial to each … it distributes labour most effectively and most economically: while, by increasing the general mass of productions, it diffuses general benefit and binds together, by one common tie of interest and intercourse, the universal society of nations throughout the civilised world. It is this principle which determines that wine shall be made in France and Portugal, that corn shall be grown in America and Poland, and that hardware and other goods shall be manufactured in England.
>
> (Ricardo, 1926, p. 81)

We will illustrate with historical and contemporary examples that comparative advantage and free trade as a doctrine has never been taken seriously by the elites of western countries who actually make the decisions. Germany and the USA industrialised behind tariff and non-tariff protective barriers. In 1841 Friedrich List argued that if international free trade was established then countries who were behind in development would take a long time to catch up – if ever. He was for free trade but only after less-advanced countries had reached parity with the more advanced. He recognised the moral claims embodied in the free traders' arguments for what they were – the ideological justification of the dominant economic power of the day. As List put it: 'It is a very common clever device that when anyone has attained the summit of greatness, he kicks away the ladder by which he has climbed up, in order to deprive others of the means of climbing up after him' (List, 1904, p. 295).

History can easily show what free trade meant in practice to the elite that ruled Britain. The establishment of British control over India under the banner of free trade certainly had an impact on that sub-continent's economy. Acts passed in 1700 and 1720 forbade the importation of printed fabrics from India, Persia, and China into the 'mother country'. Simultaneously, discriminatory taxes were passed against locally produced textiles within India, which was then forced to take inferior British products. By such measures the Bengal textile industry was deliberately and systematically destroyed. In the mid-eighteenth century India was relatively well developed in textiles, shipbuilding – providing one of the flagships of an English Admiral during the Napoleonic wars – and metal and glass working. Under British rule India's development was halted and new industry stopped. In 1841 a British historian testifying before a Parliamentary Commission said: 'India is as much a manufacturing country as an agriculturist; and he who seeks to reduce her to the position of an agricultural country, seeks to lower her in the scale of civilisation' (Chomsky, 1993, p. 14).

THE WELFARE STATE

Starting with Bismarck's welfare reforms in Germany in the 1880s when, to counter the threat of socialism, the Reichstag agreed that compensation for industrial accidents was to be the employers' sole responsibility (1884); that employees be entitled to sickness benefit that covered the first 13 weeks of illness (1883); and old age and disability pensions to be funded by employers and employees with a State contribution (1889) (Gildea, 1987, p. 357).

All western governments have seen a massive expansion of their role in the economy and in society. The State has encroached into areas that had previously been left to individuals, private enterprise, and markets. The post-Second-World-War settlement saw the establishment of 'Welfare States' and a 'Keynesian consensus' when many governments saw it as their role to provide a National Health Service, State pensions, an education system, unemployment relief and to ensure that the economy guaranteed full employment. This expansion of the State's role has seen government expenditures rise from around 10 per cent at the start of this century to 30–35 per cent of GDP at the bottom end of the scale and 50–55 per cent at the high end towards the end of the century. In the 1960s and 1970s governments experienced economic and social problems simultaneously with a perceived crisis in Keynesian economic theory. It was within this context that an academic and political debate was stimulated between the critics of the 'Welfare State' and its defenders.

According to Rawls' ethical principle and theory of distributive justice the social structure should maximise the welfare of the worst-off person in society (Rawls, 1971). Governments can achieve this by direct and indirect intervention in society and the economy. This intervention can take different forms.

- **Allocation**. Governments could intervene in the allocation of capital and labour, producing directly or indirectly such goods as are needed for national defence, fire protection, pollution control, which private producers are deterred or unable to provide. Moreover, government could strictly control the quality of such goods as it provides.

- **Stabilisation**. Governments could pursue economic stabilisation policies using mainly fiscal instruments and the benefit system to create the conditions necessary for sustained economic growth.
- **Distribution**. The distribution of income, wealth and welfare provided in a competitive market situation may not be socially just. Governments could pursue a redistribution policy mainly using the taxation system.
- **Regulation**. Governments could pass legislation to protect consumers' rights, health and safety. It could control imperfections in the free market.
- **Insurance**. Governments could provide for social insurance in areas such as health, unemployment and pensions.

Nozick, on the other hand, argues that the primary role of government should be to ensure that individuals have the freedom to exercise their property rights. Governments should only provide for the administration of justice; define and protect private property rights; enforce privately negotiated contracts and safeguard the nation's defence (Nozick, 1974).

Economic libertarians like Nozick have a firm belief in the workings of the 'market' and argue that prosperity is there for those who wish to take it. If an individual acquires property and wealth by 'acquired entitlements' through voluntary exchange, then no institution or government has the right to interfere with those individual rights. No majority could legitimate such a violation of individual rights. Furthermore, libertarians argue that any government intervention beyond this is not only unjustifiable but, in the context of a free market economy, inefficient.

For libertarians the concept of social justice is illusory and even dangerous. In the long term government welfare programmes discourage individual responsibility and initiative, creating a 'culture of dependency' that will result in social problems amongst the poor such as the breakdown of the family and violence. A 'Welfare State', by shielding individuals from the consequences of their behaviour, not only exacerbates this, but would create the problems in the first place. Hayek argues that 'freedom' is threatened by policies of social redistribution and poverty amelioration, which creates dependency amongst recipients and involves coercion of taxpayers forced to meet the costs. Libertarians are critical of the economic arguments which conclude that any evidence of market failure is grounds for corrective government intervention. The 'litmus test' in any instance should be whether government bodies could deal with the problem any better than the market. Even if the answer is yes, then intervention must be kept to a minimum. The desire to privatise prisons and the suggestion that the police should be privatised indicates that no function of the State is immune from this line of argument.

TRADE REGIME AND THE WELFARE STATE

It could be argued that our method of approach – which is supposed to treat elements of welfare and value and seemingly withdraws to perspectives of the fundamental theoretical premises of international capital – has missed the point. However, we strongly believe that unless a clear analysis is undertaken, the prospects of improving individual welfare are marginalised. As implied by our method of analysis, our aim has been to undermine the theoretical framework which New Right or Public Choice theorists have used to analyse politics and society.

If the fundamental assumptions of these theorists are wrong, what validity have their versions of society or their policy prescriptions? As has been said: 'From the 1870s until today, many economists in the neo-classical tradition have abandoned any real concern with existing economic institutions and problems. Instead, many of them have retired to the rarefied stratosphere of mathematical model building, constructing endless variations on esoteric trivia' (Hunt and Sherman, 1980, p. 104).

The Germans, the Americans and the Japanese of the last and this century simply ignored the theorists. State-sponsored industrial development was the name of the game, and it has been no different this century, as any cursory glance at the role of the Japanese Ministry of Trade and Industry will attest in the re-industrialisation of that country after the Second World War (Hutton, 1996, p. 270). It is worth noting here that when every nation is seeking export-led growth then such growth attained becomes a zero-sum game. And any nation seeking to industrialise, or re-industrialise as in our case, will not be able to do so without resorting to protective tariff and/or non-tariff barriers. Free Trade is the economic doctrine of powers who expect to win the game.

It is here that the true significance of New Right political and economic ideas lies: no one in the various governing elites takes them seriously enough actually to obey their precepts if it hurts their interests. Just as neo-classical economics itself can be seen as a response to ideological attack from within on classical economics, that is, from Marx and the surplus theory of value, so New Right/Public Choice theory is a reaction to the involvement of the despised masses in democratic politics in the 1960s, especially in the USA.

The notion of free trade led to a counter-attack by the 'business community', the proportions of which are only now being understood via the institutions of ideological control, that is, the media and academia, combined with three developments within the international economy: firstly, the growth of new labour-intensive manufacturing industries, for example electronics, combined with innovations in transportation and telecommunications; secondly, the intensification of capitalist rivalry between the successful export-led advanced economies of Germany and Japan, who in the mid-1960s began to compete heavily with the USA in markets traditionally the domain of US companies – the US trans national companies (TNCs) met this threat partly by means of international sub contracting to take advantage of Third World labour costs; thirdly, US capitalists were unable to maintain high profits and cede to working-class economic and political demands. International sub-contracting was the perfect means to combat this domestic pressure and defeat the problems of full employment in the home market.

The erosion of the Welfare State and its values can be seen as a victim of this counter-attack. The massive unemployment in the western capitalist countries can be seen as a deliberate policy decision, as international Free Trade – as described in academia and the media – does not exist. The massive build-up of Third World manufacturing and consequent jobs is not the result of the neutral workings of Free Trade and Comparative Advantage, something indicated by the negative reaction in Wall Street whenever good employment figures are published. TNCs have little if any loyalty to the nations in which they are based and certainly their existence is not acknowledged in the theoretical premises of the neo-classical Flat Earthers. It is in this light that the arguments over things like the minimum wage can be interpreted. Any good neo-classical economist can tell you that a minimum wage will destroy jobs. True; but so do child labour laws.

That same neo-classical economist however has been unable to resolve the 'mysteries' of unusually high marginal tax rates for people on low incomes who receive benefits, or the massive incomes of the 'fat cats' whose pay is mainly determined by themselves. And when the State pays benefits to those on low incomes, who are the real recipients if not the employers who pay slave wages? Neither should it have escaped anyone's attention that the UK has witnessed a massive extension of fiscal privilege during the 1980s. Or, to approach it entirely differently and as John Wells put it in 1990: 'When the history of Thatcherite economic policies is written, commentators will surely rub their eyes in incredulity at how the fabulous windfall of North Sea energy resources has been squandered' (*Guardian*, 26 November 1990, p. 14).

It is on this point that the relationship between morality and the explicit and implicit value judgements of neo-classical and New Right economics are highlighted. A different conception of human nature and ethical and moral value judgements could lead to a different conception of the socio-economic order.

THE NEW GERMAN LÄNDER IN THE GLOBALISED ECONOMY

The German socio-economic model has never been one of total *laissez-faire*; social welfare has been an important factor. The rise of the New Right elsewhere in the world is no doubt mesmerising to some German industrial interests. In this brief analysis we hope to have indicated that the fundamental premise upon which the New Right case is based is questionable. Thus German policy-makers should be aware of the consequences of attempting to introduce an 'Anglo-Saxon' socio-economic model. If the new German Länder were to be left entirely to their own devices and thrown to the mercy of the 'Free Market' and international competition, the results would be predictable.

Bibliography

CHOMSKY, N. *On Power and Ideology*. Boston, South End Press, 1987.
CHOMSKY, N. *The Chomsky Reader*. London, Serpents Tail, 1992.
CHOMSKY, N. *Year 501. The Conquest Continues*. London, Verso, 1993.
CHOMSKY, N. *Human Rights and The New World*. Transcript of speech delivered at Liberty's Human Rights Convention, King's College, London, 16 June 1995.
CROUZET, F. *The Victorian Economy*. London, Methuen, 1982.
DUNLEAVY, P. and O'LEARY, B. *Theories of the State, The Politics of Liberal Democracy*. London, Macmillan, 1987.
FRIEDMAN, M. *Capitalism and Freedom*. University of Chicago Press, Chicago, 1962.
GILDEA, R. *Barricades and Borders: Europe 1800–1914*. Oxford University Press, Oxford, 1987.
GOLDSMITH, J. *The Response: GATT and Global Free Trade*. Macmillan, London, 1995.
HAYEK, F. A. *The Road To Serfdom*. Routledge, London, 1944.
HERMAN, E. S. and CHOMSKY, N. *Manufacturing Consent: The Political Economy of the Mass Media*. London, Vintage, 1994.
HUBERMAN, L. *Man's Worldy Goods*. Victor Gollancz, London, 1937.
HUNT, E. K. and SHERMAN. H. J. *Economics: an Introduction to Traditional and Radical Views*. New York, Harper International, 1981.
HUTTON, W. *The State We're In*. Vintage, London, 1996.

LANDSBERG, M. 'Export Led Industrialisation in the Third World', *The Review of Radical Political Economics*, Winter, 1979.

LASLETT, P. and RUNCIMAN, W. G. (eds) *Philosophy, Politics and Society.* Basil Blackwell, Oxford, 1978.

LEHMANN, J. P. *The Roots of Modern Japan.* Macmillan, London, 1982.

LIST, F. *National System of Political Economy.* Longmans, Green, London, 1904.

NOZICK, R. *Anarchy, State, and Utopia.* Basil Blackwell, Oxford, 1974.

OKUN, A. *Equality and Efficiency; the big trade-off.* Brookings, Washington DC, 1975.

PRASCH, R. E. 'Reassessing the Theory of Comparative Advantage', *Review of Political Economy*, vol. 8, no. 1, January 1996.

RAWLS, J. *Theory of Justice.* Harvard University Press, Cambridge, 1971.

RICARDO, D. *The Principles of Political Economy and Taxation.* J. M. Dent, London, 1926.

ROBINSON, J. *Economic Philosophy.* Pelican Books, London, 1970.

SPERO, J. E. *The Politics of International Economics Relations.* St. Martin's Press, New York, 1990.

SULLIVAN, A. 'Welfare State Reaches End of the Road', *The Sunday Times, News Review*, 4 August 1996.

SUMNER, C. S. *Crime, Justice and Underdevelopment.* Heinemann, London, 1982.

WELLS, J. 'Soft Landing Comes Down to Earth with a Bump', *Guardian*, 26 November 1990.

WOLF, R. P. *Understanding Rawls.* Princeton University Press, Guildford, Surrey, 1977.

8 The Institutional Architecture of an Alliance for Jobs[1]

Jens Bastian

INTRODUCTION

The aim of this chapter is to offer some reflections on the changing nature of industrial relations in Germany, with particular reference to the new Länder. At the heart of the exposition is the scope and content of the Bündnis für Arbeit ('Alliance for Jobs'), a union initiative on employment which was launched in November 1995. It was welcomed enthusiastically by the public – and attracted the support of the Chancellor[2] – as an innovative contribution to resolve the problem of record unemployment in Germany. While the jobless figures continue to show a deep divide between western Germany and the former communist eastern states, the Bündnis für Arbeit constituted a call on all groups – unions, employers, and government at local, state, and federal levels including the parliamentary opposition – to negotiate a trade-off between modest wage increases and improved employment levels, and turn it into political reality. The terminology that characterized the proposals – 'alliance', 'pact', 'conciliation', and 'contract' – was significant, and these were to remain key words at various stages of the negotiations. This avoidance of confrontational language emphasized the spirit in which the proposals were advanced, as did a pragmatic approach to details. The inclination toward compromise rather than divisiveness and conflict was specific to the union initiative and, in the early stages at least, the blunt instrument of threat-based bargaining *vis-à-vis* the other parties who came to the negotiating-table was notable by its absence.

The significance of the initiative was further highlighted by the extent to which it attracted attention outside Germany, and wider European support for it is evidenced by demonstrating its comparative dimension. The following account does not offer definitive answers to the challenges surrounding the Bündnis architecture, but seeks rather to provide information which will facilitate further empirical and analytical inquiry. The point to be argued out is this: while the Bündnis initiative served to focus actors' minds on the need for co-operation in pulling out of the crisis in the labour market, its candid proposals could not avoid becoming entangled in the diverse economic problems and organizational interests that exist in East and West Germany. Hence, its short-lived history not only says much about the dilemmas of the (social) unification process, but also directs attention to the risks inherent in testing innovative solutions in an economy which is characterized by deep-rooted traditionalism.

THE DYNAMICS OF ALLIANCES

The sparks set off by the Bündnis initiative were a clear indication of its originality and importance: similar proposals were tabled within and between different sectors of the German economy, and sub-central governments – a notable instance is Bavaria[3] – began to set up tripartite initiatives. By the same token, policy-makers in neighbouring European countries were quick to react, subsequently tabling their own versions of trilateral employment pacts. The background to the union initiative was as follows.

Bündnis für Arbeit was launched in November 1995 by Klaus Zwickel, chairman of IG Metall, at the union's annual conference in Berlin, and the proposals subsequently received the support of the German Trades Union Confederation (DGB) and its member unions. The IG Metall initiative focused on a tripartite arrangement, and sought to answer three interrelated questions:

- How can moderate wage-growth and job creation be ensured for all?
- How can job creation be encouraged in the future?
- How can the labour-market situation in the new Länder be improved?

Of these three questions, the last was the most pressing but, in attempting to reach a solution, the trade unions found themselves facing some highly revered sacred cows, such as non-wage labour costs and public-spending levels.

In practice, the IG Metall was willing to agree, first, to starting newly recruited long-term unemployed on a wage which was below the collectively agreed minimum remuneration rate 'for a limited period' and, second, that its members would take time off in lieu of overtime worked, so as to create what were described as 'time accounts' (*Arbeitszeitkonten*). In return for these concessions, individual member companies of the engineering employers' federation, Gesamtmetall, were to agree to three demands:

- not to create any redundancies in the course of the next three years;
- to increase the total number of vocational-training positions by 5 per cent per annum;[4] and (the most controversial of the Bündnis proposals)
- that employers in the metalworking industry would create 330 000 new jobs between 1996 and 1998.[5]

It is obvious from this list that the proposed architecture of the IG Metall initiative represented an unprecedented contribution to the German debate on job-creation policies. By the same token, its ingredients underlined the fact that the largest union in Germany was now prepared to address certain elements of the collective-bargaining process which had hitherto been sacrosanct (Hoffmann 1996, p. 5). Conversely, the trade-off nature of the proposed compromise package included commitments from the employers. The legal enforceability of those commitments was subject to intense debate: can an interest-federation bind its members to deliver on job creation when that federation does not hold decision-making authority over the prerogatives of employers at the plant level? This legal dimension has wide-ranging implications, not least for the interplay between the members of the federation and its leadership: the availability of control-mechanisms to verify that the contract is honoured, and how, is one potentially contentious issue; the negative sanctions to be imposed in the case of non-compliance is another. By their very nature, such delicate issues address the organizing principles of interest-representation among competing market actors and the logic of collective action between them (Streeck 1992, p. 76).

At the height of discussions in Germany, Zwickel proposed a Bündnis für Arbeit Ost – 'Alliance for Jobs (East)' – in recognition of the divergence of economic and labour-market performances as between the old and new Länder. Unlike its West German counterpart, the East German version included a call for a drastic reduction in working-time (from 38 to 35 hours a week), combined with partial wage compensation. Zwickel expressed the hope that this policy instrument would yield 33 000 new jobs. In order to attach institutional guarantees to his proposals, the IG Metall chairman argued in favour of 'burden sharing' between the three parties to such a Bündnis Ost. In practical terms, this meant that trade unions, the employers' federations, and the Federal Employment Agency (*Bundesanstalt für Arbeit*) in Nürnberg would have to muster savings of more than DM 1 bn in the administration of unemployment benefits. These savings would be diverted to fund additional job creation in the East.

But there was a significant omission from the union's catalogue: the IG Metall refused to reconsider delaying the adjustment of engineering wages in the new Länder to West German standards, which was due by 1 July 1996. In other words, the priority given to wage parity over employment levels in the East was maintained, albeit with limited modifications. The IG Metall argues that the living and working conditions of citizens in the East must be put on an equal footing with their colleagues in the West. In order to add substance to such an ambiguous objective, the union drew attention to Article 106 of the old West German Basic Law (the Basic Law has applied to the whole of the country since unification) which requires 'uniformity of living standards in the federal territory [to be] ensured'. Noble as this might sound, it should be added that another factor in the union's insistence on wage parity is the fear of a potential pool of cheap labour in the East competing for (scarcer) manufacturing jobs in the West.

In the view of the union, the call for feasible reductions in working hours would bring East German industry into line with its competitors in the West. But in doing that, firms in the nascent, and still very fragile, manufacturing sector in the new Länder would lose one of their few competitive advantages. Working hours, as stipulated in collective-bargaining agreements, continue to be longer (by more than 2.5 hours) in the East than in the West. Furthermore much of the 'burden sharing' proposal as applies to the Federal Employment Agency could easily turn into a double-edged sword: the federal government, desperately seeking to find additional savings for its 1997 budget, is currently considering reducing its contribution to the Agency's coffers by more than DM 3bn.

It should be clear by this stage that the East–West dimensions of the Bündnis proposals addressed different constituencies and a different set of structural problems in each case. The latter are paramount in the new Länder: despite all the DM transfers poured into the region's factories and services, they produce just 2 per cent of Germany's total exports – less than west Berlin alone. Equally, one worker in seven is unemployed in the former communist country, corresponding to a regional unemployment rate of over 16 per cent. This percentage would be much higher were it not for a variety of government-subsidized 'make-work' schemes (*Arbeitzbeschaffungsmassnahmen*), such as requalification programmes and short-time working schedules. Such work-creation measures have involved half of East Germany's work-force over the past six years. Adding to the plethora of structural problems is the observation that East Germans produce just 60 per cent of what they consume; the rest comes from a raft of subsidies paid by increasingly reluctant West Germans (*The Economist* 1996, p. 5). This is discussed further in the next section.

Against this dire economic background, the engineering union had to be well aware of the risks involved in its Bündnis Ost initiative: the union's wage-compensation proposals potentially widened a window of opportunity which employers in the East could not resist exploiting in the form of demands for adjustments in important areas of collective-bargaining agreements. Many companies in the manufacturing sector of the new Länder are either not bound by, or simply ignore, industry-wide pay agreements.[6] In particular, small and medium-sized firms circumvent national pay contracts by leaving the employers' federation and/or negotiating individual agreements with their workers at the plant level, and the Bündnis Ost initiative of the IG Metall had to take this margin of wage flexibility into consideration. By the same token, the concessions the union was prepared to make over wages and fringe benefits in the East had to avoid outright contradiction of its bargaining policy in western Germany (Gutmann 1995). What this delicate balancing job illustrates is that the engineering union has neither a coherent negotiation strategy nor a uniform demands structure for East and West Germany. The two bargaining arenas differ in terms of the problems they have to address, the sequencing of negotiations, and the constituencies to which they respond. In short, these differences accentuate the divisions apparent in the social unification process.

The European dimension was a further characteristic of the general dynamic generated by the Bündnis discussions. The appeal of the initiative quickly gained cross-border momentum and gave rise to a plurality of alliance and pact proposals. In Germany, Belgium and Portugal in particular, the debates reflected a trend towards 'Europeanisation' of the agenda. In March 1996, for example, the deputy SPD leader, Wieczorek-Zeul, demanded a Bündnis für Arbeit in Europa; the social-democrats argued that such an alliance should emerge as one of the results of the deliberations at the Intergovernmental Conference (IGC) of the European Union (EU), and went on to issue a veiled threat on behalf of the social democrats by suggesting that any change(s) to the Maastricht Treaty – these require a two-thirds majority in each of the Bundestag and Bundesrat (the lower and upper houses of parliament respectively) – would have a 'difficult chance' of approval if they failed to incorporate new EU commitments towards employment.[7]

Perhaps the most convincing evidence that the issue had established itself on the European agenda came when the president of the European Commission, Jacques Santer, proposed a 'European Pact for Employment and Confidence' in his address to the European Parliament in January 1996. His conception of a 'pact' included joint initiatives on youth job-creation, qualifications and training, together with the implementation of flexible work-patterns, particular attention being given to the expansion of part-time work. But Santer failed to address a key problem which must be resolved before the EU can be turned into a motor for job creation: the EU's lack of resources – political and financial – in this field. The entire EU budget amounts to just over 1.2 per cent of the bloc's economic output. Hence, Santer's modest proposal in February 1996 to spend an extra 1.7 billion European Currency Units on trans-European research projects and road and rail networks died at birth, a victim of the lack of political will on the part of the member countries to commit resources on that scale (Lemaitre 1996, p. 2). As Werner Hoyer (the deputy foreign minister who negotiates for Bonn at the IGC of the EU) emphasized: transferring responsibility for job creation from national capitals to EU headquarters in Brussels 'leads to absolutely incalculable financial risk'.

That the concept of employment pacts had Europe-wide appeal was further reinforced in February 1996 when the Belgian government under prime minister Jean-Luc Dehaene and the social partners issued a joint declaration regarding the details of an employment accord. The so-called 'Contract for the Future' included:

- the keeping of wage growth in line with development in neighbouring countries – after the three-year wage freeze which expired at the end of 1996, pay rises should not exceed the average hike in France, Germany and the Netherlands;
- moves to redistribute work and to encourage part-time work;
- a commitment (unspecified in terms of numbers) to job creation.

But the absence of a target number on employment led the FGTB union[8] to vote against the declaration being turned into a formal agreement. In spring 1996, a tripartite 'Short-Term Social Conciliation Agreement' was signed in Portugal. Based on a framework of macro-economic references, a set of guidelines on wages, jobs, labour relations, fiscal issues, and social-security measures was laid out in the pact (ETUI 1996).

This listing of various initiatives and proposals serves to illustrate the intention of this chapter: so viel Bündnis war noch nie.[9] Rarely in the past 20 years has so much 'alliance talk' featured in German and European industrial relations – or so prominently. While the practical details of the various proposals relate to employment levels and the establishment of industry-wide wage agreements, and lay particular stress on the consensual architecture of industrial relations, the Bündnis initiatives also carry wider implications regarding the nature of contemporary macroeconomic policy-making. The Belgian case further illustrates how the tripartite compromise explicitly includes provisions that limit wage increases to the average rise in the neighbouring countries of Germany, France and the Netherlands.

On the one hand, the alliance projects sought to balance liberal economics with equitable social policies at a time when global orthodoxy seems to be suggesting that this is neither possible nor even appropriate. Put otherwise, what is termed 'social-market economy' (*soziale Marktwirtschaft*) in Germany, and 'social contract' (*pacte républicain*) in France, is linked with the image of a process of consensual industrial governance (Séguin 1996). Through that lens, the Bündnis initiatives can also be regarded as an attempt to address the normative dimensions of job creation under conditions of mass unemployment. At the level of the individual firm, on the other hand, the bold IG Metall plan highlights both the need to, and the difficulties of, persuading blue-collar constituencies to share the costs of liberal economic restructuring. While the former perspective addresses labour-market prescriptions that defend both a social and societal model in Europe, the latter exposes the potential, and the risks, of 'burden sharing' when it comes to making job creation a determining factor in policy decisions. Seen in this light, the Bündnis initiatives cast a net which is, potentially, extremely wide: they seek to establish the institutional preconditions for a process of social learning in European societies whose citizens are slowly, and at times reluctantly, beginning to understand that major changes in their future expectations regarding employment are in order, if not overdue.

It is perhaps a further illustration of its initiator's understanding of the German institutional architecture, and the broad discussion the IG Metall proposals sparked off, that the intra-union Bündnis debate has not been linked with the stringent deadlines and policy objectives of the EU timetable as set out in the Maastricht Treaty. Indeed, the Bündnis debate has had curiously little effect on union attitudes towards the single currency's budgetary disciplines. By contrast, in a country like Belgium, which is itself trying to finalise a tripartite 'Employment Accord for the Future', such initiatives were linked immediately with the controversies surrounding the meeting of the Maastricht criteria. In the sections which follow, discussion will focus primarily on the German Bündnis debate. Although its reception was initially favourable, the proposal had to contend with institutional as well as legal constraints and, equally important, has become subject to a decline in political will. The dynamics of this evolution are addressed in the sections which follow.

THE CONTEXTUAL BACKGROUND

The leitmotiv of the Bündnis initiative in Germany centred around the observation that both parts of the country – East and West – are in a state of sustained economic and social crisis. To appreciate the state of the German economy, it is necessary to call attention to a few statistics. On a seasonally unadjusted basis, unemployment reached a record level of 4.3 million, or 11.1 per cent of the labour force, in March 1996. But the truth is worse even than the statistic would indicate. With a further 1.5 million people kept off the register by early retirement, short-time working, and similar expedients, Germany's overall unemployment rate during the first two quarters of 1996 is closer to 15 per cent of the labour force.[10] In the country's showcase industry, plant and machinery, employment has fallen from 1 250 000 in 1991 to 980 000 in December 1995. Since manufacturing (including construction) generates 35 per cent of employment in Germany – an exceptionally high share for an advanced industrial country in Europe – it is hardly surprising that the employment record has been poor. In other words, what is currently taking place in the German economy poses a challenge, the terms of which extend beyond the purely economic.

Viewing the situation from that perspective, the Bündnis proposals sought to uncover the implications of this profound structural crisis for the country's political and institutional definition of compromise and social peace (*sozialer Frieden*). Put another way: are we possibly witnessing the demise of what the French author, Michel Albert, labelled 'Rhein capitalism' with its unique architecture of social compromise, a welfare state, and consensual federalism (Albert 1991)? That model may itself be less suited to the challenges of the future than it was to those of the past. Judging from public debates since the beginning of 1996, this architecture is increasingly being called into question by employers, representatives of the CDU/FDP governing coalition, and even by members of the opposition SPD (such as Gerhard Schröder, the state premier of Lower Saxony).

The emergence of answers to the Bündnis inquiry is particularly pertinent because they will help to establish whether German democracy, anchored as it was in the western part of the country under conditions of economic prosperity, a distributional wage policy, and a welfare state, can be implanted in the former GDR at a time when there is little, if any, room for income increases (Bastian 1996, p. 297). The principal government response to this conundrum has been twofold: first, the 50-point 'Action Programme for Investment and Jobs' (*Aktionsprogramm für*

Investition und Beschäftigung) of January 1996, which embodies a series of supply-side reforms including deregulation, reform of corporate taxation, and incentives for company start-ups; second, a finely named 'Programme for More Growth and Employment' (*Programm für mehr Wachstum und Beschäftigung*) of April 1996 which seeks DM 70 bn (£30.43 bn) in public-spending cuts, to be spread among the federal, state and local authorities, and Germany's social-security funds.

The latter package includes a two-year pay freeze for public-sector employees, reductions in pension outlays, and a delay in increasing monthly child-benefit allowances for families. The scheme further aims to price workers into jobs by reducing high, non-wage labour costs, such as social-security contributions, sick-pay allowances, and holiday provisions.[11] Read in conjunction, both programmes are geared to a reduction in the excessively large role of the state in the German economy. In practical terms, the objectives are to bring public-spending levels down from over 50 per cent of GDP in 1996 to 46 per cent by the year 2000. The goal of pushing social-security contributions below a (still staggering) 40 per cent of gross wages by the end of the century remains unchanged. In terms of justification, it is instructive to note that Chancellor Kohl has been careful to portray the two packages as vital contributions towards rendering German firms more competitive and cutting unemployment. The programmes have not, therefore, been presented as a means of securing Germany's place in the European Monetary Union – that is, to fulfil the Maastricht convergence criteria.

The Kohl government's February 1996 commitment to reduce record unemployment by 50 per cent within the next four years,[12] while seeking at the same time to finance unification without further increasing taxes, raises the issue of social solidarity to one of the highest priorities on the political agenda. How this is to be achieved remains vague, but is nonetheless an enormous bone of contention – all the more so against the background of the employment situation in the new Länder, which exemplifies a market without a self-sustaining economy. Between 1991 and 1996, one-third of the jobs in eastern Germany have been lost, with agriculture and manufacturing hit particularly hard. 80 per cent of all working people have either changed jobs or lost their jobs, and the projections for 1997 are anything but encouraging. Eastern Germany's growth has slowed down drastically: it is not just lagging behind the vibrant economies of Poland, the Czech Republic, and Hungary, but its growth rate is even predicted to fall below that of West Germany in 1997. The six leading economic research institutes in Germany sounded the alarm bell in their traditional autumn forecast when they claimed that, for the first time since 1991, economic growth in the new Länder would be inferior to that in the West. The implications of such a scenario for the East German labour market are dire, some sources predicting a further loss of up to 600 000 jobs for 1997 (Focus 1996, p. 22).

So far, the momentous changes in the East German labour market have been sustained partly through various government 'make-work' schemes, early retirement, and retraining programmes. Growth may be bounding ahead in eastern Germany, and scattered islands of prosperity are visible, but all in all there is little evidence to suggest that the East is close to standing on its own feet. The six new German states are as dependent as ever on western support: revenue transfers are expected to exceed $698 billion by the end of 1996,[13] and the flow of subsidies is likely to equal about 6 per cent of West German GDP. Initially, the flow of subsidies was supposed to be limited, both in scope and in duration; that they now account for more than 40 per cent of eastern Germany's GDP has fuelled debate on whether the subsidies are actually hampering development of eastern Germany and creating long-term economic dependency and, in 1995, the Bundesbank itself warned of the danger of a 'subsidy mentality' taking root in the East (Ridinger 1995).

The prospect of pumping cash indefinitely into a region that shows no clear signs of becoming a net producer rather than a net consumer of tax revenue causes concern in Germany, and invites direct comparison with Italy: the German situation bears no small resemblance to the Italian north–south divide which exists between Milan and Naples, and the assertion of an Italian historian, Angelo Bolaffi, that a possible scenario for development in the newly unified country is a German mezzogiorno (with the cleavage running east–west), is becoming increasingly credible (Bolaffi 1995, p. 157). The eastern states have 20 per cent of Germany's population, but account for less than 9 per cent of the country's economic output. In light of budgetary problems, and a growing reluctance amongst the western states to contribute to the financing of subsidized jobs in the East, the Kohl government is considering a substantial reduction of resources for labour-market policies in the new Länder.

THE INSTITUTIONAL RISKS OF THE ALLIANCE PROPOSALS

To expose the complexities of the issues with which the Bündnis proponents have to contend is not necessarily to subscribe to gloom-and-doom scenarios. It does, however, underline the fact that, while German capitalism delivered the goods in the past, and helped to consolidate democratic development, energy alone can no longer mask the tensions in society that have accumulated since reunification in 1990. Even if social turmoil does not boil over into the streets as it did in France at the end of 1995, the mixture of problems and challenges has already started to fray the consensual architecture which has lain at the core of the German political machinery for the past half-century and which underpins the culture of corporate governance. Perhaps the vaunted Bündnis campaign may inadvertently have accelerated a process of change that carries longer-term implications: German business has effectively been handed the opportunity to loosen even further the network of employment rules by dealing directly with the workers' councils in individual enterprises rather than with the IG Metall union itself. Under the banner of the broad and increasingly ambiguous Bündnis für Arbeit, a plethora of company-specific accords have been agreed, each negotiated with in-house workers' councils and not with the national union leaders.

This flurry of accords may, over time, contribute to the cracking of Germany's system of universal wage contracts, a time-honoured system of collective bargaining that has dominated labour relations in what, since the end of the Second World War, has been a highly unionized nation. Such a shift from national wage contracts to agreements concluded at the corporate level constitutes a major change in the underlying negotiating situation of the Bündnis initiative. If the trend intensifies, it is likely gradually to erode the tradition of central bargaining. The classic national contract may survive in spirit, but its letter will be faced increasingly with plant-level pressures to include sufficient latitude for individual companies to modify the national contract so as to incorporate their own terms, such as opt-out clauses for weak companies.

Two recent collective-bargaining agreements illustrate the argument which is being advanced here. The March 1996 agreement in the textiles industry exemplifies precisely this dual process of decentralization and insertion of opt-out alternatives. So-called 'opening' clauses (*Öffnungsklauseln*) are permissible for companies 'in difficulties'. Based on a settlement with the respective works council, the nationally agreed wage increase, which compensates only for a rise in price inflation, can be postponed for a maximum period of one year. During that period, the companies subject to the contract are prevented from making personnel redundant. Furthermore, the agreement introduces so-called 'year-long working-time accounts' (*Jahresarbeitszeitkonten*) for employees which permit the rescheduling of weekly and monthly working time without having to resort to overtime work.

The March 1996 agreement in the chemical sector provides a good illustration of the conflicts and difficulties which arise when attempting both to create jobs (one of the IG Metall objectives) and to preserve them. As the first major wage- and employment-settlement of the 1996 bargaining-round, the agreement commits both sides of the industry to count employees on an industry-wide basis after 1 July 1996, and to hold employment at that level until the contract expires on 28 February 1997. Under this joint pledge, individual companies that are faring poorly after the July deadline can still lay off workers as long as the industry as a whole can maintain total employment at the July 1996 level. As far as wages are concerned, the contract provides for a moderate 2 per cent pay-rise for 1996–7, which in effect sets a benchmark for wage negotiations in the public sector and in the construction industry.

The contract negotiated in the chemicals industry has three main mechanisms for the staunching of job losses:

- employers promised to allow workers to retire at age 57 in order to make room for a younger generation of workers;
- both sides agreed that overtime hours would be compensated by time off rather than by additional wages, thus freeing-up hours for potential recruitments and exempting employers from paying the usual overtime bonus; and
- establishment of a 'Round Table for Labour Market Issues' (*Runder Tisch für Arbeitsmarktthemen*) which is to discuss and monitor the implementation of the contract.

These new provisions are commensurate with the flexible working practices laid down in earlier contracts negotiated by the industry; it can, for example, re-hire its long-term unemployed at 90 per cent of normal wage levels.

The decentralization impetus, while neither created nor advocated by national union leaders, is enhanced by the scope and content of the Bündnis initiative and such collective agreements as can be placed in that context (as in the two examples above). Initially, Bündnis für Arbeit was one of the most impressive public relations successes in German industrial relations in the 1990s, reversing the scathing criticism of the IG Metall's 1995–6 wage-increase agreement with Gesamtmetall.[14] But that positive reception changed in the course of discussions of the Bündnis proposals in different sectors and regions of the German economy.

A number of consequences have followed from this. Basically, the process spun out of the unions' control. Not only did employers prove unwilling to honour their commitments, the Bündnis discussions kicked the door wide open for the revival of demands such as reduction of payroll taxes for companies, and curtailment of sick-pay benefits. More generally, demands of this nature combine policies of fiscal consolidation with calls for deregulation of labour- and product-markets. The DGB chairman, Mr Dieter Schulte, characterised the window of opportunity created by the initiative as follows: 'Employers are pulling all the old demands out of the drawer ... they are belly-aching again ... we cannot deal with each other in that way'.

It should come as no surprise, therefore, that IG Metall and Gesamtmetall quickly became locked in a bitter public rift over the future and/or end of the Bündnis project. Gesamtmetall, thrilled at the pockmarks in the face of the centralized bargaining system, declared the formal Bündnis talks 'dead' in March 1996. Its president-elect, Mr Werner Stumpfe, criticized the union's bargaining position as having degenerated from a Bündnis für Arbeit to a mere 'Alliance against overtime work'. The engineering federation went on to argue that struggling companies should have the right to pull out of existing blanket contracts. Furthermore, the bargaining parameters were gradually enlarged to incorporate what, from the employers' perspective, was the most pressing issue on the agenda: the need to reduce labour costs in the industry by 20 per cent.[15] IG Metall's reaction was to threaten industrial action if an agreement did not materialize, but the union had to contend here with two unknown quantities. The first was whether its members actually would go on strike against overtime work: for many, regular overtime was a means by which to compensate for previous wage-losses, and had thus become part of the income expectations of a sizeable proportion of union members.[16] Second, agreeing overtime levels and extra shift working is an important prerogative of the consulting works councils. It is a bargaining resource which provides them with considerable leverage in plant-based negotiations with employers, and any suggestion that it be relinquished would face strong opposition against the IG Metall central office in Frankfurt.

With the search for a Bündnis compromise reaching an impasse, German companies jumped into the vacuum and exploited the initial momentum of the Bündnis movement. Significantly, the company-specific deals disregard the union-supported guidelines for a pact. In the East German engineering and construction industries in particular, sectoral agreements are regularly and systematically undercut by plant-specific accords. Most notably, instead of job-creation targets, the companies are adamant that their more modest accords will merely preserve existing jobs within a specified time period.

This approach highlights the sweeping changes that are taking place in the German labour market, but their effects are felt more quickly and more dramatically in the new Länder given the nature of the economic transition, the main characteristics of which are the shift from low to high performance yield among small enterprises, the declining demand for unskilled jobs, and the need for more highly trained and flexible workers.

A two-speed labour market is thus emerging in the new Länder. On the demand side, there is a high-speed labour market driven by technological innovation and competition between enterprises in domestic markets (and, to some extent, in global ones as well).[17] But the speed is much slower on the supply side because the systems of education and training remain limited, as too is the ability to meet the demands for new skills in the short term (Wegner 1995). Briefly stated, the segmentation of the East German labour market is reinforced.

Technically, Bündnis talks continue among the union's 17 regional bargaining districts in hopes that one of them will reach a pilot agreement that can provide the lead for adoption at national level. Conversely, with each new company agreement, a national employment pact becomes more difficult to negotiate, let alone implement, and, it would seem, increasingly redundant. It follows from such a dynamic that Germany – East and West – is facing the need for structural reform of the labour markets in order to stimulate job creation. In the parlance of the Bündnis advocates, the magnitude of the task lies in coming-to-terms with a new definition of the balance between economic requirements and social policy objectives.

In general terms, the Bündnis initiative provided a much-needed opportunity to refocus German attention on the growth of unemployment and the serious risk of social exclusion, even if it failed to produce any tangible programme for meeting either challenge. For some, however, the debate about the Bündnis initiative is a debate about Germany having for too long afforded a 'dictatorship of conciliatory understanding' (Swiss finance economist J. Wittmann). What such critics emphasize are the overriding imperatives of consensus and security that have been manifested by industrial-relations actors in Germany over the past two decades; they then go on to argue that these have come to result only in ambiguous compromises and what, in practical terms, is an imposition of limitations on the scope for innovation. In terms of policy prescription, this critical assessment implies – as the so-called 'five wise men' (the independent economic advisers to the government) advocated in

April 1996 – that the government should cease its policy of seeking trade union agreement to any proposed changes of regulation in the labour market, irrespective of cost. In short, the consensual approach which has been the hallmark of the German post-war economic system is being fundamentally questioned. If core policy issues are not to be decided by consensus when the institutional pressure to do something is as pressing as it currently is, a close examination of the alternatives becomes imperative.

THE EMPLOYERS' WINDOW OF OPPORTUNITY

For many employers involved in the German system of collective bargaining, further strivings towards compromise and consensus are being seen increasingly as far too time-consuming and even as counter-productive. Their criticism, most vocal in the engineering federation, Gesamtmetall, focuses on the degree of centralization in, and top-down approaches to, the regulation of wages and working-time. To put it metaphorically, the institutional architecture of social peace is being refurnished from round to rectangular tables – and the corners of those tables are becoming ever sharper. The reception of the engineering union's Bündnis proposals demonstrated that round tables are an expedient piece of 'political furniture' for employers' federations whose own disgruntled members are making threats to 'vote with their feet' and, in some cases, actually do leave the federation. Such (former) members then voice urgent calls for taking advantage of the window of opportunity presented by the economic quagmire.

The March 1996 agreements in the chemical and textiles sectors described above are heralded as the torch-bearers of a new age of collective bargaining in Germany. But, in each of those industries, the union opponents of the 'new trends' – if indeed that is what they turn out to be – read them as nothing short of an intention to remove the 'social' parameter from Germany's social-market economy. What Germans describe as America's 'hire-and-fire' system of capitalism is increasingly the subject of discussion within the employers' federations. Many of their members are stressing a (perceived) need to introduce the flexibility of labour markets and lower non-wage costs which pertain in the US and in Britain into the German system of collective bargaining. It is a line of argument which bodes ill for the German system of framework agreements and tends, instead, to underline the extent to which that model has turned into a 'disease', with intransigent trade unions and a hesitant regulatory government at the root of the problems.

Solutions offered subsequently have highlighted the need for wholesale change, as opposed to incremental adjustments at the fringes. The engineering employers' federation, Gesamtmetall,[18] presented a catalogue of demands in June 1996 which would subdivide the centralized system of framework collective-bargaining agreements (the so-called *Flächentarifvertrag*),[19] into two separate sections, one binding on all signatories, the other extending the window of opportunity for plant-level agreements. It is part of this concept that future collective agreements should have the authority to regulate seven different areas from percentage changes in nominal wages to the total number of working hours, annual holiday entitlements and redundancy procedures. But regulation of the duration and distribution of working time is reserved exclusively to the individual firms. In other words, collective agreements provide both a framework and an incentives structure which can be shaped according to the specific requirements of the enterprise, increasing the capacity of the latter to stipulate the precise rules of the game.

Proposals of this nature do, however, carry a number of challenges in their wake, and their implications should be clearly understood. Perhaps most critically: to impose limitations on the scope and content of framework agreements is to beg the question as to whether such agreements continue to be needed at all. Any answers to that intriguing question must take a crucial factor into consideration: the more framework agreements are subject to legitimacy problems, and thus reduced in their capacity to shape conditions of industrial governance, the more their *raison d'être* is called into question by the interest groupings who are parties to them. In other words, employers' federations and trade unions would limit, if not lose, the major regulatory element that defines their authority and shapes their resources above the plant level. Consequently, the constitutional recognition of *Tarifautonomie* would have to be reassessed (Zohlnhöfer 1996).

Brief consideration of two of the areas which would be affected by radical reassessment should serve to illustrate the magnitude of the task and the possible ambiguities that would follow from it. First, the future role of the state in German industrial relations would make its way back on to the legislative agenda, with all the complex questions that even hard-line employers have so far failed to answer satisfactorily. In other words, the nature of the future relationship between legal intervention and the regulatory autonomy of collective-bargaining actors (*Tarifautonomie*) would have to be made explicit. One of the issues such an interaction would have to address is the right to call for industrial action at shop-floor level. At present, this right is reserved exclusively to, and sanctioned by, the industrial-relations actors above plant level. In a bargaining context where framework agreements diminish in importance, and employers exercise their option to leave their federation, negotiations and compromise have to be sought at the level of the individual firm; in the absence of the framework agreement, new modes of conflict-expression and -resolution will have to be devised, and then approved by law. Any comparative perspective across the Rhein quickly yields the sombre conclusion that where collective-bargaining actors are weak, the resulting void will be filled by state intervention in the French tradition of dirigisme (Bastian 1994, p. 115).

This leads naturally to the second area: the identification of new modes of, and arenas for, wage bargaining. The current buzzwords are decentralization of bargaining, and pluralisation of agreements. To hint at the possible curtailment, or even abolition, of framework agreements implies reconsideration of the role, resources, and authority of the bargaining actors at plant level. From a trade union perspective, such a reassessment addresses the competencies of the works councils, whose members are not always unionized or, at the opposite extreme, belong to more than one union.[20] More importantly, by delegating responsibilities and conflicts to the plant level via legal opening clauses (*Öffnungsklauseln*), a major element of competitive transparency is diminished for employers. By setting certain standards of industrial governance in framework agreements, employers within any given sector share the same point of departure on issues such as remuneration, vocational training, and pension schemes. That common ground would become increasingly narrow if and when framework agreements are transformed out of all recognition. In consequence, the levels and modes of competition between firms would be extended to such a degree that the prevailing atmosphere could become one of 'free for all'.

SUMMARY AND CONCLUSIONS

The employment initiative launched by the chairman of the IG Metall, Klaus Zwickel, in November 1995 was presented as a tripartite enterprise to halve record unemployment in Germany. The dominant trade union in the engineering sector, it sought a trade-off between job creation and wage restraint, thereby acknowledging a direct relationship between jobs on the one hand and the competitive pressures faced by the industry on the other. Subsequent union propositions detailed a Bündnis für Arbeit Ost which comprised drastic working-time reduction with partial wage compensation, and a target number for job creation. This approach slanted the focus of bargaining away from income and towards job security and job creation.

The specific details of the job-creation package proved the major bone of contention. Non-binding 'declarations of goodwill', rather than specific numbers, were the dominant responses both from private employers and from the government in its capacity of employer in the public sector. In terms of negotiating profile, the collective-bargaining organizations are not in a position to impose legal sanctions which would bind plant-level actors to precise employment targets. In other words, the degree to which bargaining representatives of the employers in the various sectors can filter employment commitments down to the local level remains a core dilemma right at the implementation stage of any redistributive labour-market policy. Equally, the institutional and legal preconditions necessary to overcome such implementation deficits can be seen as far too labour-intensive and time-consuming, so that a shelving of the proposals becomes the least risk-prone option for all of the actors concerned. Nor can one exclude the possibility that such innovative (and highly sensitive) initiatives will be taken advantage of by employers and union representatives who have very different scenarios for the essence and rationale of industrial relations in Germany.

In conclusion, it is not the intention of this analysis to paint worst-case scenarios. What it does seek to do is to ask those who advocate radical change whether they are fully aware of the implications of what it is they are proposing – the possible risks as well as the expected benefits – and to inquire as to the nature of such alternatives as they may hold in reserve. The line of argument advanced here strongly supports the need for structural reform and tangible results, but is concerned also to emphasize that this process, already in train, must be underwritten by certain fundamental prerequisites and no small degree of institutional imagination. One crucial parameter – it is by no means the only one – concerns the notion that negotiations in German industrial relations rest on co-operative problem-solving. At a time when policy-makers are highlighting the threefold challenge of globalisation, mass unemployment, and the costs of unification, such a parameter may nevertheless serve as a useful guiding light in redefining the scope and content of the social dimensions of the German social-market economy.

Notes

1. A previous version of this paper has been published as *So viel Bündnis war noch nie: The institutional architecture of an alliance for jobs in Germany*. Discussion Papers in German Studies No. IGS97/2, The University of Birmingham.
2. In February 1996, Chancellor Helmut Kohl rejected radical policies such as those implemented in Britain in the 1980s by the (then) Prime Minister, Margaret Thatcher. Kohl was quoted as saying: 'I never thought Mrs Thatcher's example was a desirable one for Germany where we have a completely different concept of social obligations' (*Financial Times*, 9 February 1996, p. 2).
3. In June 1996, the Länder government of Bavaria, represented by its head of government (Edmund Stoiber), the trade union confederation DGB, and economic-interest organizations signed an 'employment pact'. The pact stipulated a regional version of a federal 'Alliance for Jobs', and emphasized the importance of 'social consensus' in situations of economic difficulty. In terms of job creation, the pact envisaged a significant increase in part-time employment. Regarding the contentious issue of financing those commitments, the Bavarian government promised that something in excess of DM1.2bn, drawn from its privatization receipts, would be committed to the goals of the employment pact.
4. Companies which could not increase training places were to make compensatory payments into a common vocational fund.
5. This catalogue of demands makes clear that there is no valid comparison between the Bündnis initiative and the so-called 'Konzertierte Aktion' in the late 1960s and early 1970s, which was a top-down initiative, warmly welcomed by the federal government under economic conditions of low unemployment, and as a reaction to the wild-cat strikes of 1969.
6. In 1995, only a quarter of eastern companies in private ownership were members of an employers' association (*The Economist*, 1996, 10). According to a survey carried out by the *Vereinigung Mittelständischer Unternehmer* (Association of Small and Medium-sized Entrepreneurs), only 30.5 per cent of the firms surveyed followed collective-bargaining agreements strictly, while 40 per cent actually undermined the conditions set by them (*Frankfurter Rundschau*, 10 January 1996).
7. The Green Party, at its convention in March 1996, added further colour to alliance parlance in Germany by calling for a *Bündnis für Arbeit und Umwelt* (Alliance for Jobs and Environment).
8. Several local branches of the socialist-led FGTB refused to sign the accord. The opposition within the union rank-and-file came mainly from its Walloon delegates.
9. Translated as: 'never before has there been so much alliance'.
10. In July 1996, Germany had a combined total of 8.2 million people who were unemployed and recipients of social welfare.
11. More specifically, the savings package includes cuts of DM25bn by state and municipal authorities, reductions in pensions for German immigrants (mainly those from eastern Europe), and the raising of the female retirement age from 60 to 63 years. The plan to raise the pensionable age is one way of ensuring

that the pension system can survive the twin pressures of an ageing population and a shrinking labour force. Furthermore, the welfare cutbacks propose restricting the German luxury of long, government-subsidized visits to spas.

12. Surprisingly, at the Christian Democratic Union (CDU) party congress in October 1996, Kohl backtracked in his unemployment pledge, arguing that his promise would have been fulfilled if the coalition government were to achieve a one-third reduction of the jobless.
13. Revenue transfers from West to East climbed to the equivalent of \$135bn in 1995, from \$117bn in 1994, and \$97bn in 1991. The Institute for Economic Research in Halle concluded in 1995 that eastern Germany would not achieve self-sustaining growth until sometimes in the next century. In other words, nobody is saying anymore that it will be achieved 'soon'.
14. Employers' initial reaction to Zwickel's proposition reflected their interest in adjusting the 1995 two-year wage-settlement in the manufacturing industry. The compromise, which included wage increases of 3.6 per cent for 1996 and a one-hour reduction in working-time, was strongly criticized by small and medium-sized firms at the time of signing. Many of them subsequently vetoed the agreement by leaving the Gesamtmetall federation.
15. Such a reduction in labour costs was to be achieved by a 10 per cent decrease of the wage bill by means of the introduction and extension of flexible work-patterns (for example, by operating machines for longer hours without having to pay overtime rates). This element in the overall reduction was to be achieved by the works councils at plant level. A further 5 per cent was to come from the government via legislation which would slash social-security contributions. Finally, the third party to the agreement, the collective-bargaining representatives at industry level, were to agree to a 5 per cent reduction in paid 'non-work' – for example, by abolishing two days of paid holidays when a worker became a parent. Hence, all sides at the different levels of Germany's industrial relations system were to make a feasible contribution, with the thrust of the 'burden sharing' achievement coming from the local level.
16. Grass roots support for overtime reduction is not easily implemented by an engineering union that has seen more than 600 000 members leave the organization since its post-unification membership peaked at 3.7 million in 1990. In 1995 alone, the IG Metall lost 4.2 per cent of its total membership. Looking only at the eastern part, it lost 8.4 per cent of its members in 1995 (*Frankfurter Rundschau*, 12 January 1996).
17. According to economic data furnished by the federal Economics Ministry, the international role of the new Länder is growing. In 1995, they attracted DM496m in foreign investment, and themselves invested DM326m abroad – a surplus of DM 160m. The figures are comparatively small, but nevertheless show a considerable rise in both directions (*Economic Report*, 1996).
18. Consequently, the reform of collective-bargaining patterns in Germany must also take into consideration the organizational structures in which the actors play out their roles – the 17 employers' federations which are represented in the German metal and electrical industry, for example, currently negotiate and sign agreements for 21 participating regions. Streamlining these numbers in terms of mergers and organizational density is as much the order of the day as calls for increased margins of flexibility in labour markets.

19. The centralized system sets pay and working conditions for entire branches of industry. It is predicated on the capacity of unions and employers' federations to conclude pilot agreements which are subsequently incorporated into the pay-and-conditions architecture of other regions.
20. The German airline Lufthansa is a good case study on this point. In October 1996, the company signed an agreement on wages, employment guarantees, and 100 per cent sick-pay compensation with the public-sector union ÖTV. The DAG, a white-collar union whose membership consists primarily of cockpit personnel, and which had been negotiating separately from the ÖTV, refused to sign the compromise despite the fact of a co-operation agreement between the two unions. While the DAG is holding out because it represents a higher status of personnel at Lufthansa, the enterprise directors refuse to continue separate negotiations, and have argued that they will honour the new contract, irrespective of union membership cards.

Bibliography

ALBERT, M. *Capitalisme Contre Capitalisme*. Paris, Edition du Seuil, 1991.

BASTIAN, J. *A Matter of Time. From Work Sharing to Temporal Flexibility in Belgium, France and Britain*. Aldershot, Avebury, 1994.

BASTIAN, J. 'The process of social unification: more by default than by design?' *German Politics*, 1996 Vol. 5(2) (August), pp. 297–303.

BOLAFFI, A. *Die schrecklichen Deutschen. Eine merkwürdige Liebeserklärung*. Berlin, Siedler Verlag, 1995.

(The) Economist 'Divided still: a survey of Germany'. 9 November 1996.

ETUI (European Trade Union Institute) *Social Pacts in Europe*. Documentation based on an ETUI Workshop, 14–15 May 1996. Brussels: ETUI, 1996.

Financial Times, 9 February 1996, p. 2.

Focus, Marathon Ost, No. 48, (1996), pp. 20–4.

Frankfurter Rundschau, 10 January 1996, p. 11.

Frankfurter Rundschau, 12 January 1996, p. 11.

GERMAN EMBASSY *Economic Report* (3 June 1996). London, German Embassy, 1996.

GUTMANN, G. (ed.) *Die Wettbewerbsfähigkeit der ostdeutschen Wirtschaft. Ausgangslage, Handlungserfordernisse*. Berlin, Duncker & Humblot, 1995.

HOFFMANN, R. (ed.) *Social Pacts. Alliance for Employment*. Discussion and Working Paper 96.01.1 (E). Brussels, ETUI, 1996.

LEMAITRE, P. 'Bruxelles a réuni une table ronde pour mobiliser les partenaires sociaux sur un "pacte européen pour l'emploi"'. *Le Monde*, 30 April 1996.

RIDINGER, R. *Transformation im Wandel. Die Wirtschaftsstrukturen in den neuen Bundesländern*. Bonn, Bouvier, 1995.

SEGUIN, P. *En Attendant l'Emploi*. Paris, Editions du Seuil, 1996.

STREECK, W. *Social Institutions and Economic Performance: Studies of Industrial Relations in Advanced Capitalist Economies*. London, Sage, 1992.

WEGNER, M. *Bankrott und Aufbau. Ostdeutsche Erfahrungen*. Baden-Baden, Nomos Verlagsgesellschaft, 1995.

ZOHLNHÖFER, W. (ed.) *Die Tarifautonomie auf dem Prüfstand*. Schriften des Vereins für Socialpolitik 244 (Neue Folge). Berlin, Dunker & Humblot, 1996.

9 Catching Up with the West: The Achievements and Limitations of Creative Destruction

Thomas Lange and Geoff Pugh

INTRODUCTION

Unification left eastern Germany with an acute imbalance between physical and human capital. A well-educated and trained workforce is a necessary condition for physical investment to generate sustained productivity growth. This is grounded in theory as well as the experience of South Korea and Taiwan where, since the 1960s, high investment promoted by public subsidy has powered growth and convergence with the developed market economies (Rodrik 1995, pp. 53, 96, 100). Accordingly, in eastern Germany a fundamental feature of transition strategy has been government support for investment – both directly in infrastructure and indirectly through financial incentives for the private sector.

Contrary to historical precedent, however, and unique among the transitional economies, is a second feature of the transition strategy in eastern Germany, namely, initial support from government, unions and even business for high wages. While investment subsidies increased the quantity of investment, high wages were supported for their influence on the quality of investment. High wages were to ensure that the only profitable investment would be 'high-tech', thereby precluding 'low-tech' investment intended to profit from cheap labour.[1]

STRATEGIES FOR THE UPSWING

Sinn and Sinn distinguish three possible 'strategies for the upswing' (Sinn and Sinn 1992, p. 143). The first strategy is the 'maintenance strategy', in which wages would have been kept low enough to maintain eastern employment as it was at the time of GEMSU. This is the strategy that the other ex-Soviet bloc countries have had to adopt. In eastern Germany, however, it was not politically feasible. Moreover, it was not a credible strategy. It would have led to excessive migration and would also have minimised structural change and, hence, slowed growth and delayed 'catch-up'.

Second is the high-wage, high-tech strategy which was broadly supported by government, unions and business (Sinn and Sinn 1992, pp. 153, 164–8). In its effect, this was to be a process of creative destruction. This strategy allowed rapid wage convergence with western Germany by imposing wage increases far in excess of productivity increase. The rationale is that production units unable to survive higher wages 'are weeded out immediately and that reorganisation investments not worth making at these wage rates are not allowed to take place. Only the most modern factories meeting the highest Western standards are allowed' (Sinn and Sinn 1992, p. 152). This strategy presupposed both the presence of subsidies to stimulate the investment necessary to raise productivity so as to support wage growth, and also social transfer payments to subsidise jobs or compensate workers made unemployed as wages grew in advance of productivity.

Between these extremes, Sinn and Sinn argued for a third strategy, a compromise that 'could well be optimal from an efficiency point of view' (Sinn and Sinn 1992, p. 145). Their strategy of 'organic system transformation' 'is a gradual change in the price structure that keeps pace with the gradual change in the pattern of production' (Sinn and Sinn 1992, p. 145). Although wages would be higher than in the maintenance strategy, at least during its initial stages Sinn and Sinn's restricted-wage strategy would have dictated lower wages than the prevailing high-wage, high-tech strategy. It is in this sense that we use the term 'low-wage' strategy.

The essential feature of Sinn and Sinn's strategy is that wage rates must rise in accord with market forces – hence, as a consequence of capital accumulation and productivity growth rather than, as in the high-wage, high-tech strategy, in advance of capital accumulation and productivity growth. The principle of Sinn and Sinn's strategy is to maximise the role of the price mechanism in the transition process. We argue that a high-wage strategy in at least the initial stage of transformation was more favourable to rapid convergence. The principle of our counter-critique is that private decisions taken in response to current information provided by the price mechanism (for example, low wages) may lead to an outcome which is efficient in the short run but which is inconsistent with dynamic efficiency – innovation and productivity growth – in the long run.

Our approach does not neglect adjustment through the price mechanism. Instead, we adopt an eclectic approach by considering not only the cost of a high-wage, high-tech strategy but also the benefits. Analysis of convergence strategy based only on relative prices is static: as wages rise relative to productivity, output and employment are lost. These effects lead to no further changes. Our intention is to broaden the analysis to take account of benefits arising from dynamic processes, in particular the possibility that wages rising relative to productivity may, when combined with investment subsidy, contribute to cumulative causation effects that perpetuate growth. By definition, these are realised over time. Accordingly, at any one time, dynamic benefits are realised only in part: because cumulative causation perpetuates benefits, the other part exists as the present value of future benefits yet to be realised.

We argue first that there are conditions under which dynamic benefits may be promoted by a high-wage, high-tech policy but are blocked by a low-wage, low-tech strategy. Secondly, static costs and dynamic benefits coexist and the balance between them can change. This changing balance is associated with two phases in the convergence process.

In the first phase, rising wages preclude development on a low-wage, low-tech basis and, when coupled with subsidised investment, promote a high-tech growth path. In this phase, the output and employment costs of high wages are offset by dynamic benefits, which include both actual benefits currently realised and potential future benefits from ongoing cumulative processes. This phase requires wages to rise sufficiently to function as an instrument of 'creative destruction' in relation to existing low-tech, low-wage production, especially in the traded-goods sector. This phase is necessary but not sufficient to secure self-sustaining economic development on a high-wage, high-tech basis.

If wages continue to rise beyond the level required to inaugurate this first phase, 'destruction' continues unabated but with diminishing 'creative' effects. First, the more wages continue to rise above average productivity, the more output and employment are choked off in low-tech sectors in the non-traded sector. Secondly, once a high-wage, high-tech convergence path has been established, continuing wage increases are unlikely to generate further dynamic benefits. Moreover, even in the high-tech sector wage increases curtail profit growth, thereby reducing both the incentive and the means to invest which, in turn, reduce potential output and employment. Consequently, there is a point at which wage rises cease to be associated with actual and potential dynamic benefits in excess of static costs. Beyond this point, rising wages impose additional static costs that are increasingly greater than additional dynamic benefits. This defines a second phase in which wage moderation is necessary not only to secure a more favourable environment for low-tech firms in the non-traded-goods sector, but also to maximise dynamic benefits from high-tech sectors producing traded goods.

This two-phase model structures our approach to convergence strategy for eastern Germany. In the first few years of unification, rising wages together with investment subsidy precluded a low-wage, low-tech strategy while creating actual and potential dynamic benefits. These, we argue, offset static losses. However, by the mid-1990s, the costs of continued wage increase increasingly overwhelmed the dynamic benefits of the high-wage, high-tech strategy. We conclude that wage moderation is needed to realise fully the potential of a high-wage, high-tech strategy.

To analyse the first phase, we develop two models which, together, constitute a dynamic complement to the argument of Sinn and Sinn. They give first a demand-side and then a supply-side rationale for a convergence strategy in which high wages drove out of business the least efficient producers while investment subsidy secured the investment necessary to restructure the eastern economy towards high-wage, high-tech production for high-growth markets.

DEMAND – SIDE RATIONALE FOR A HIGH-WAGE, HIGH-TECH STRATEGY

An Application of Thirlwall's Growth Rule

A simple theory of growth can be derived from the principle of external balance: namely that imports (M) into a country or region in excess of exports (X) must be paid for by borrowing or inward financial transfers (i.e., by some form of capital inflow, F). We can write this as

$$M = X + F \qquad (1)$$

In which case,

$$m = \lambda x + (1 - \lambda) f \qquad (2)$$

where m, x, and f approximate the percentage rates of growth of, respectively, imports, exports, and capital inflow, and λ is the share of export revenues in total foreign exchange receipts; $(1-\lambda)$, accordingly, is the share of capital inflow in total foreign exchange receipts.[2] Equivalently, λ and $(1 - \lambda)$ are, respectively, the proportions of the import bill covered by export receipts and capital inflow.

Equation (2) can be transformed by dividing through by m and multiplying both sides by the percentage growth of GDP (y):

$$y = [\lambda x + (1 - \lambda) f]\frac{y}{m} \tag{3}$$

We can give economic interpretation to the final term on the right-hand side (y/m). The income elasticity of imports (π) measures the responsiveness of imports to a change in national income. It is calculated as the percentage change in imports divided by the percentage change in income (which causes the change in imports). Accordingly, y/m is the inverse of the income elasticity of demand: i.e., $1/\pi$. And equation (3) may be written

$$y = \frac{1}{\pi}[\lambda x + (1 - \lambda) f] \tag{4}$$

Equation (4) suggests that the growth rate of national (or regional) income is positively related to the rate of growth of exports (x) and/or the rate of growth of capital inflow (f), and inversely related to the income elasticity of demand for imports (π).

For eastern Germany, the overriding policy objective is self-sustaining growth: that is, a rate of growth of national output (y) that enables convergence at a politically acceptable rate while restricting the growth of capital inflow and ultimately reducing the major element accounted for by fiscal transfers. Indeed, within two or three years of GEMSU annual fiscal transfers of about DM 200 billion reached a politically acceptable ceiling. Moreover, current levels of private-sector investment are already so large – up to 50 per cent or more of eastern GDP – that a substantial rate of growth of capital inflow is unlikely. The corollary of no significant growth in capital inflow ($f = 0$) is that equation (4) reduces to

$$y = \frac{\lambda \chi}{\pi} \tag{5}$$

Equation (5) reproduces ThirLwall's 'growth rule' (McCombie and Thirlwall 1994). This suggests that growth and, hence, convergence in eastern Germany depends positively on the rate of growth of exports (weighted by the share of export revenues in total foreign exchange receipts), and inversely on the income elasticity of demand for imports.

Income elasticity of demand for imports tends to increase with income (increasing income generates increasing demand for product diversity and, hence, increasing demand for imports) (McCombie and Thirlwall 1994, pp. 372, 416). Consequently, it is difficult to enhance growth by influencing consumer preferences against imports and thereby reducing income elasticity of demand for imports. Instead, the engine of growth has to be exports.

With respect to both analysis and policy prescription, there is little distinction to be made between minimising income elasticity of demand for imports and maximising the rate of growth of exports. In any particular market, the rate of growth of East German exports can be reduced to the growth of income multiplied by the income elasticity of demand for East German exports in that market. Maximising export growth, therefore, also depends on the relevant income elasticity. In turn, income elasticities depend on product quality: that is, on all those product characteristics apart from price that influence consumer preferences such as reliability, durability, technical sophistication, design, after-sales service, and so on. As incomes rise, consumers substitute away from lower- towards higher-quality goods and services. In turn, the highest quality mass-produced products tend to be the product of investment in new product and process technologies. Hence, the high-tech, high-wage strategy exploits a causal link between high-tech investment, product quality, high income elasticity of demand, and high growth. Correspondingly, a low-wage, low-tech strategy would tend to lock East German industry into producing low-quality goods with a low income elasticity of demand. This is one reason why such a strategy would restrict the rate of growth and delay convergence.

Evidence on the link between technological level and growth

Empirical support for the positive link between technological level and growth rate is provided by Maurer (1994, pp. 310–11). He classifies OECD industries in the manufacturing sector according to their technological and growth characteristics. Following the standard OECD classification, industries are allocated to 'high', 'medium' and 'low-technology' sectors according to research and development 'intensities' – that is, OECD average shares of research and development expenditure in sales revenue – of, respectively, more than 10 per cent, between 0.9 and 10 per cent, and less than 0.9 per cent. The growth dynamic of each industry is proxied by a weighted average of annual export growth for 12 OECD countries over the period 1970–90 and sectors are characterised as 'high growth' (more than 5.8 per cent), 'medium growth' (3.5 to 5.8 per cent), and 'low growth' (less than 3.5 per cent).

Table 9.1 shows a positive correlation between the technological intensity and growth of industries. A corollary is that the more an economy specialises in high- or medium-tech output the more it produces for high- or medium-growth markets (Maurer 1994, p. 313).

Table 9.1 Technological level and growth in the OECD (by industry)

	High growth	*Medium growth*	*Low growth*
'High-tech'	• Computers and office machinery • Aerospace • Consumer electronics	• Pharmaceuticals	
'Medium-tech'	• Electro-mechanical* • Automobile	• Chemicals • Plastics • Oil refining • Precision engineering and optical* • Quarrying and stone working (ceramics, glass and mineral products) • Other processing industries	• Machine construction • Non-ferrous metal production • Shipbuilding • Other transport
'Low-tech'		• Food processing • Metal working • Paper and printing • Wood working and wood processing	• Iron and steel • Textiles

* See note 3 at end of chapter.
Source: Maurer 1994, p. 312.

Table 9.2 East German manufacturing output and contribution to GDP (percentages)

	Growth of real manufacturing output over the previous year	*Share of East German GDP*
1991	–	16.8
1992	5.2	16.4
1993	11.7	16.9
1994	15.5	17.9
1995	6.7	18.1
*1996**	5.25	18.6

* Estimate
Source: Deutscher Bundestag 1996, p. 72.

The data in Table 9.2 shows that since 1991 in eastern Germany the growth of manufacturing has continuously increased potentially exportable output. Moreover, Table 9.2 shows that this growth has been sufficient to increase steadily the share of manufacturing in eastern GDP. Comparison with Table 9.4 shows that while the contribution of manufacturing to GDP in East Germany is smaller than in West Germany, it is in line with the three other major economies of the European Union.

Table 9.3 shows that within manufacturing, restructuring has enabled high- and medium-tech industries with high or medium growth not only to increase output (Column 2) but also between 1991 and the first half of 1995 to increase their share in total output by about a fifth (Columns 3 and 4).[3] In comparison, machine construction – a medium-tech but low-growth industry – has undergone both reduced output and a greatly reduced share in total manufacturing output.

Since the early collapse of eastern manufacturing, restructuring to create competitive, high-wage firms has increased not only the share of

Table 9.3 Contribution of high- and medium-tech sectors to total East German manufacturing output

	Output Growth (1991 = 100)	*Share of East German Manufacturing Output (percent)* 1991	*1995 (1st half)*	*Type (according to Table 9.1)*
Computers and office machinery Electro-mechanical Precision engineering and optical	147.9	11.2	11.8	Medium-High Tech; Medium-High Growth
Automobile	172.4	10.7	13.2	Medium-Tech; High Growth
Chemicals (including pharmaceuticals)	106.9	8.5	6.5	Medium-Tech; Medium Growth
Plastics	355.7	1.3	3.4	Medium-Tech; Medium Growth
Quarrying and stone working (Ceramics, glass and mineral products)	282.9	5.1	10.2	Medium-Tech; Medium Growth
Coking plants and oil refining	117.4	3.0	2.5	Medium-Tech; Medium Growth
Sub-total		39.8	47.6	
Machine construction	72.7	18.1	9.3	Medium-Tech; Low Growth
Total		57.9	56.9	

Source: Calculated from Deutscher Bundestag 1995, p. 81.

manufacturing in total output but also the share of manufacturing accounted for by high- and medium-tech sectors with high or medium growth. Table 9.4 – also using the OECD classifications – shows that the total share of high- and medium-tech sectors in manufacturing output (56.9 per cent; from Table 9.3) is in line with West Germany and the other major industrialised economies. For reference, we list the shares of national output accounted for by manufacturing in each country. Here we have some evidence of success for the high-wage, high-tech strategy in restructuring East German industry towards knowledge-based manufacturing sectors with medium- to high-growth prospects.

SUPPLY-SIDE RATIONALE FOR A HIGH-WAGE, HIGH-TECH STRATEGY: THE ACCUMULATION OF CAPITAL AND 'LEARNING-BY-DOING'

This section explains why convergence depends on renewing the eastern capital stock at the highest technical level. Such investment increases the capital:labour ratio and embodies new technology. In addition, high-tech investment raises productivity by maximising opportunities for learning-by-doing.

Increasing productivity and growth of output are generated by process innovation and product innovation. Innovation, or technical progress in

Table 9.4 Share of medium- and high-tech sectors in manufacturing in selected industrialised countries (1990) (percentages)

	West Germany	*USA*	*Japan*	*France*	*Italy*	*UK*
High-tech	21	24	22	19	14	22
Medium-tech	34	27	33	28	26	22
Total	55	51	55	47	40	44
	Share of national output – GDP – accounted for by manufacturing (current prices) (1992)					
	26.5*	18.3†	27.9	20.5	20.5‡	19.3

* Estimate for 1996 (Deutscher Bundestag 1996, p. 72);
† 1991 data;
‡ Includes mining and quarrying.
Sources: Economic Bulletin, Vol. 32, No. 9 (September 1995), p. 13; United Nations, 1995, pp. 179–87.

the broad sense, may be seen as a series of problem-solving activities, that is, a learning-by-doing process (Ricoy 1991, p. 732). Learning-by-doing is the hypothesis that management and workers learn through experience and that experience is obtained during production. Accordingly, learning-by-doing generates dynamic economies of scale and increased productivity of labour.[4] Moreover, learning-by-doing benefits are not necessarily confined to the individual firms that expand output over time. Labour turnover is one way in which knowledge obtained within one firm can be communicated to other firms. In this case, learning-by-doing within firms entails a positive externality – that is, learning spillovers – by increasing the stock of knowledge available to all firms within the economy. Accordingly, economic growth is a learning process that enhances productivity: learning and productivity increase are endogenous to growth.

Learning-by-doing effects are not just a once-and-for-all source of growth but are a potential link in a process of unbounded growth. This process of cumulative causation sustains a virtuous circle – a self-expanding process – in which increased output induces productivity increase and thus further output increase (in principle, forever).

Learning-by-doing and cumulative causation support the dominant strategy for eastern Germany in two ways: by amplifying the productivity effect of investment; and, because these amplification effects are maximised by investment at the highest technical level. The rest of this section develops these arguments.

Promotion of Investment on the Largest Possible Scale: The Case for Investment Subsidy

In this section we explain how investment drives growth of output and employment.[5] We start with three supply-side effects whereby investment – particularly in machinery and equipment – raises productivity.

Firstly, net investment – investment in excess of depreciation – increases the capital stock per worker. Increasing the quantity of equipment at the disposal of each worker enables output per worker to rise. However, raising productivity by investing in more of the same is limited by diminishing returns to capital. Initially, this constitutes an incentive for investment in eastern Germany. With diminishing returns, the East's relatively low capital:labour ratio means that the potential return from capital investment is relatively high. Hence, precisely because eastern Germany is relatively poorly endowed with capital, it has the potential to grow at a faster rate and converge with western Germany.

Ultimately, diminishing returns dictate that productivity growth from accumulation of capital at the existing level of technology is limited. However, productivity growth generated by the accumulation of knowledge and its application to production is potentially unlimited. Positive interactions between investment and technological advance – for example, the possibility of inward investment embodying the highest prevailing levels of technology as well as learning-by-doing effects – give further and more important reasons why eastern Germany has the potential to grow at a faster rate and converge with western Germany.

Secondly, investment is the vehicle of technical progress. In two ways, investment is the means whereby knowledge is introduced into production.

Technical progress is not exogenous but is embodied in new equipment. Accordingly, investment usually improves the quality of the capital stock through the installation not just of more equipment but of better, more efficient equipment. In addition, 'the introduction of new capital may lead to better organisation, management, and the like. This may be true even if no new technology is incorporated in the capital equipment' (Wolff 1991, p. 566).

Accordingly, in eastern Germany the potential return from capital investment is relatively high, not only because of its relatively low capital:labour ratio but also because investment offers the opportunity to modernise equipment and bring production towards the technological and managerial frontiers.

Thirdly, new processes and products bring uncertainties which are resolved through experience as well as further research and development (Ricoy 1991, p. 732). Consequently, investment not only introduces knowledge into production but also requires the generation of new productive knowledge. Learning-by-doing means that 'technological advance should be correlated with the accumulation of capital stock' (Wolff 1991, p. 566). Subsidising and accelerating investment has the initial effect of raising the capital:labour ratio and so increasing productivity and output. This initial increase, however, has the potential to be amplified and perpetuated by learning-by-doing effects.

In addition, there is the 'Verdoorn or Kaldor effect, whereby investment growth may lead to a growth in demand and thereby to the maintenance of a generally favourable economic climate for investment' (Wolff 1991, p. 566). Accordingly, inward investment may be seen as powering a process in which further increases in investment and productivity growth are endogenous (that is, part of a self-generating cumulative process).

Demand-side theory reinforces the three supply-side causal links between the rate of capital:labour growth and productivity growth.[6] Together, they suggest that high-tech investment is the key to eastern catch-up. Moreover, these investment effects are to a large extent 'external' to individual firms. General learning effects and experiences with the handling of new technology (as opposed to specialised training programmes) benefit not only the firm in which they occur but also – via labour turnover – producers as a whole. Likewise, the firm increasing output benefits not only itself – say, through static scale economies – but also raises demand for other firms. In this case, investment subsidies for eastern Germany fulfil the public policy role of making good the inability of markets to stimulate private investment to a level reflecting its social return.

Promotion of Investment at the Highest Technical Level: The Case for a High-Wage Strategy

In eastern Germany, rather than maintain the existing productive apparatus through low wages, a strategy of thoroughgoing reconstruction in the presence of a high level of human capital should constitute the most favourable environment for the process of learning. In other words, the alleged need for publicly financed training as a way out of industrial decline fails to materialise. Investment in high-tech real (rather than human) capital provides a platform for skills, knowledge and experience to develop without an explicit intervention in the eastern German labour market. The more rapid is structural change, technological renewal and, consequently, growth, the speedier the corresponding learning process. In turn, this generates higher productivity growth, higher output growth and, thereby, eases the process of structural transformation.

From the point of view of firms, shock therapy, amplified by high wages but supported by investment subsidy, enforces increased efficiency of production but also enhances the learning process. From this perspective, there are three problems with a strategy based on relatively low wages and, hence, relatively low-quality output.

The first, as explained above, is that such output will be subject to relatively slow demand growth and, hence, minimal learning-by-doing effects. Secondly, if we assume that learning-by-doing on the basis of essentially unchanged technology is subject to diminishing returns then, even if demand for the products of existing and slowly changing East German technology could be increased, the benefits of learning-by-doing would still be minimal. Thirdly, and most importantly, a low-wage strategy would perpetuate existing eastern technologies so that learning-by-doing might tend to reinforce adherence to obsolete technology, thereby retarding radical restructuring and the renewal of learning-by-doing at a higher level and rate. At best, learning-by-doing in the context of an obsolete and, hence, well understood technology yields minimal benefits. At worst, it reinforces adherence to existing technology and retards change.

Learning-by-doing with obsolete technology: the best case

A large part of learning-by-doing arises from the operation of existing plant and equipment. Even that part which arises from investment decisions can be a response to shortcomings in the operation of existing technology, giving rise to learning that is concerned with incremental supplement or modification of existing processes and products. The downside of such a learning process is the possibility that the value of such learning is constrained by obsolete technology. In this case, firms – or, as in the case of eastern Germany, whole industries – can devote themselves to gaining experience, knowledge and technological mastery of processes and products that are increasingly incapable of yielding competitive advantage. In the best case, therefore, the benefits of learning-by-doing with an obsolete technology are minimal. This conclusion is reinforced if we allow for diminishing returns as the existing technology becomes more familiar and the returns from learning effects diminish over time.

Learning-by-doing with obsolete technology: the worst case

Obsolete technology not only devalues the learning process but may also be an obstacle to fundamental restructuring. Because the trajectory of change and learning is defined by existing technology, producers operating with obsolete technology can become trapped into dedicating their resources – above all, their time and energy – to the incremental improvement of relatively high-cost and low-quality output. The alternative for the producer with lagging technology is to undertake fundamental restructuring to reduce costs and enhance product quality. However, while the possibility remains of further improvement of the old technology, there is a ready case for continuing the old ways as well as a powerful argument against undertaking the cost of radical change: attempts as late as 1990 in eastern Germany to modernise hopelessly obsolete products – the Trabant amongst them – provide ample anecdotal evidence for this. Even when the arguments are compelling, it is enormously difficult to engineer radical change in place of adherence to existing technology. According to Michael Porter, corporate change is difficult and complacency more natural: consequently, 'pressure to change is more often environmental than internal' and 'outsiders … are often the innovators' (Porter 1990, pp. 51–2). In this worst-case scenario, Sinn and Sinn's 'organic' strategy, in which eastern firms survived because of low wages, would have reduced pressure for radical restructuring and encouraged micro-level inertia and resistance to change. Moreover, at the macro level, a low-wage strategy would have slowed the process of structural change, tending to restrict the eastern economy to low-wage, low-tech production and thus delaying convergence indefinitely. Conversely, allowing wage pressure as the 'environmental' agent of change and subsidising investment by western 'outsiders' entailed lost output but accelerated the pace of transformation.

Producing on the basis of low wages and obsolete technology would have risked this 'worst case' in which learning-by-doing reinforces adherence to existing technology and counteracts the incentives to change. Instead, productivity growth has been secured by allowing high wages to force producers in eastern Germany to 'forget' existing technology and to adopt state-of-the-art western technology: new and high-tech investment was necessary not only for a once-and-for-all raising of productivity to prevailing western levels but also to ensure the benefits of learning-by-doing in relation to current rather than obsolete technology.[7]

CUMULATIVE CAUSATION: VICIOUS AND VIRTUOUS CIRCLES OF GROWTH

Figure 9.1 sets out in schematic form how learning-by-doing effects compound the demand-side argument, set out earlier in this chapter, in a process of cumulative causation. Both models display mechanisms whereby investment and growth are mutually endogenous (hence, self-perpetuating). Together, they show how a low-wage, low-tech strategy generates a vicious circle of (relatively) low quality, minimal learning effects, low productivity growth and low output growth, while a high-wage, high-tech strategy generates a virtuous circle of high quality, maximal learning effects, high productivity growth and high output growth.

Figure 9.1 links investment, export performance, and economic growth into a single self-perpetuating process. The next section presents some

Figure 9.1 Vicious and virtuous circles of growth

'Low-wage, low-tech' strategy		**'High-wage, high-tech' strategy**	
Investment ⇒ Increased capital/labour ratio ⇒ Increased labour productivity ⇒ Increased output		Investment ⇒ Increased capital/labour ratio ⇒ Increased labour productivity ⇒ Increased output	
But process technology still obsolete and output of relatively low quality		*Increasing proportion of technology at or approaching world's-best standard*	
Best Case			
Channel 1	**Channel 2**	**Channel 1**	**Channel 2**
⇒ Obsolete, hence familiar technology	⇒ Relatively low quality ⇒ Relatively low export growth & high income elasticity of demand for imports	⇒ Learning-by-doing at a higher technical level	⇒ Relatively high quality ⇒ Relatively high export growth & low income elasticity of demand for imports
⇒ Relatively little learning possible	⇒ Relatively low growth of demand and output	⇒ Learning by-doing effects maximised	⇒ Relatively high growth of demand and output
⇒ Relatively low productivity effect from 'learning-by-doing'		⇒ Relatively high productivity effect from 'learning-by-doing'	
⇒ Relatively low output growth		⇒ Relatively high output growth	
⇒ Relatively slow growth of (induced) investment		⇒ Relatively high growth of (induced) investment	
Worst Case *'Learning-by-doing' reinforces adherence to obsolete technology* ⇒ Restructuring delayed ⇒ Growth slowed still further ⇒ (Induced) investment reduced still further			

informal evidence that in eastern Germany a joint process is underway of investment in medium- and high-tech manufacturing, improving export performance and high levels of growth.

Empirical evidence on investment, export performance, and growth

Table 9.5 shows the sectoral composition of investment in eastern Germany for each year 1991–4. Although, in this period, manufacturing investment declined steadily from 30 per cent of total investment in the enterprise sector (excluding housing) to 24 per cent, in each year it was considerably in excess of the share of manufacturing output in GDP (see Table 9.2). Over time, this should increase manufacturing output and develop eastern Germany's export base.

Table 9.6 shows that in 1994 nearly two-thirds of investment in manufacturing was in high- and medium-tech industries, whereas from 1991 to 1993 the proportion was consistently over 60 per cent. Hence, given the correlation between the extent to which industries are information-based and their growth (see Table 9.1), western investment is developing an export base mainly in high- and medium-growth industries.

Table 9.7 shows that by Spring 1996, East German enterprises depended for somewhat more than half of their turnover on East German customers, about one quarter on West Germany and one sixth on true exports.[8] In a number of respects, the export data is encouraging.

Table 9.5 Investment by sector, 1991–1994 (DM Million)

	1991	*1992*	*1993*	*1994*	*Percentage increase (1991–1994)*
Agriculture, forestry and fishing	950	1 090	1 300	1 500	58
Utilities	8 940	12 690	15 500	17 500	96
Mining	1 420	1 440	1 500	1 600	13
Manufacturing	18 510	22 500	23 700	24 600	33
Construction	3 610	4 440	4 500	5 500	53
Trade	4 360	5 330	5 700	6 000	38
Transport and communications	16 140	22 512	24 900	26 700	65
Banking and insurance	1 380	2 110	2 100	1 600	16
Housing	15 900	23 910	31 400	44 900	182
Other services	6 430	8 630	13 400	16 900	163
Total Enterprise Sector	77 640	104 652	124 000	146 800	89
Other (state and private non-profit sector)	14 920	23 250	26 500	32 200	116
Total Enterprise sector	92 560	127 902	150 500	179 000	93
(excluding housing)	61 740	80 742	92 600	101 900	65

Source: Statistisches Bundesamt *Das Gesamtergebnis* (1995), (Table 28).

Table 9.6 Manufacturing investment by technological category, 1994 (DM Million)

	*High-tech**	*Medium-tech*	*Low-tech*
Total investment	2340	13 530	8730
Share of manufacturing investment	10%	55%	35%

* Includes electro-mechanical and precision engineering; see footnote 3 at end of chapter.
Source: Calculated from Statistisches Bundesamt *Das Gesamtergebnis* (1995), (Table 28).

Table 9.7 Commodity composition of East German exports

	Spring 1996: percentage of business turnover arising from sales in east Germany, west Germany, and other countries		
	East Germany	*West Germany*	*Other countries*
Construction	92	8	0
Raw materials and semi-manufactures (Produktionsgüter)	73	16	11
Services	65	27	8
Consumer goods	37	42	21
Investment goods	32	39	30
Total	56	27	17

Source: Survey of 498 East German enterprises conducted in Spring 1996 by the Institut der deutschen Wirtschaft, Köln.

While at the end of 1995 the volume index for export orders was still only at a little more than 80 per cent of the 1991 level, this comparison hides the reorientation of East German exports from undemanding Comecon markets to fiercely competitive markets in industrialised western countries.

The importance of western medium- and high-tech investment in rebuilding East Germany's export capacity is revealed by the commodity structure of the turnover of eastern enterprises. Table 9.7 shows that the more technologically intensive goods (especially investment goods) are showing signs of export capability distinct from lower-tech sectors dependent on regional markets.

Table 9.8 Export and growth performance

	Spring 1996: Percentage of business turnover arising from sales in east Germany, west Germany, and other countries[1]				*Growth record (Percentage change)*[2]		*Population (million) (1990)*[3]
	(I) East Germany	*(II) West Germany*	*(III) Other countries*	*(IV) 'Exports' (II + III)*	*(V) Growth of real GDP (1991–1995)*	*(VI) Growth of real GDP (1994/1995)*	*(VII)*
Thuringia	32	43	25	68	+ 40	+ 4.6	2.5
Saxony	42	33	26	59	+ 35	+ 7.4	4.9
Brandenburg	60	25	16	41	+ 31	+ 4.9	2.7
Saxony-Anhalt	61	23	16	39	+ 30	+ 4.3	3.0
Mecklenburg-West Pomerania	64	25	12	37	+ 24	+ 5.9	2.3
Berlin (East)	77	15	7	22	+ 32	+ 5.0	3.2 (Berlin)
East Germany	42	33	26	59			
Hessen					+ 8.0	+ 2.3	5.5
Schleswig-Holstein					+ 7.0	+ 2.2	2.6
Hamburg					+ 7.0	+ 2.1	1.6
Lower Saxony					+ 6.0	+ 2.1	7.2
Bavaria					+ 6.0	+ 1.6	10.9
Germany					+ 6.0		
North Rhine-Westphalia					+ 3.0	+ 1.6	16.7
Rhineland-Palatinate					+ 2.0	+ 1.1	3.6
Bremen					+ 2.0	+ 1.8	0.7
Baden-Würtemberg					+ 1.0	+ 1.3	9.3
Saarland					+ 1.0	+ 2.0	1.1
Berlin (West)					–4.0	–1.5	3.2 (Berlin)

Sources:

[1] Survey of 498 East German enterprises conducted Spring 1996 by the Institut der deutschen Wirtschaft Köln

[2] Volkswirtschaftliche Gesamtrechnung der Länder (compiled by the Institut der deutschen Wirtschaft Köln)

[3] Owen-Smith 1994, p. 40.

Table 9.8 shows a strong positive correlation between growth and export performance. In the five years 1991–5, Thuringia and Saxony had the highest growth of the five new Länder and by the beginning of 1996 sales on the West German market or exports accounted for more than half of enterprise turnover. In turn, this is related to the relatively high proportion of investment-goods producers in these states. Moreover, with the exception of Berlin (East) – with an industrial structure in this period dominated by services and construction – there is a perfect rank correlation between 'export' performance (Column IV) and real GDP growth (Column V). The robustness of this developing export capability is indicated by a survey of business confidence published in May 1996 by the Institut der deutschen Wirtschaft, Köln. The survey of 498 eastern enterprises confirmed the downturn in eastern Germany. Striking, however, is the continued optimism with respect to exports to industrialised western countries (that is, excluding exports to former-Comecon countries). Figure 9.2 summarises the main results of this survey. It shows the balance of optimistic and pessimistic expectations with respect to the main indicators of

Figure 9.2 Survey of business confidence, May 1996 (balance of optimistic and pessimistic expectations)

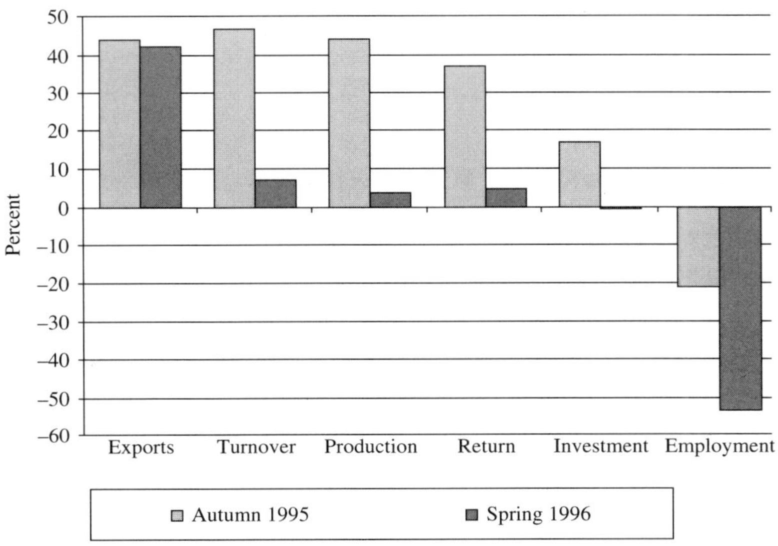

Source: IWD, 16 May 1996, p. 8.

economic health (a negative balance on, say, investment, means that more firms intend to reduce than to increase investment).

Amidst this general anticipation of worsening business conditions, eastern enterprises expect to be able to maintain the dynamic of export growth to industrialised western countries established during the years 1993–5 (in 1995 increasing by 15 per cent compared to West Germany's 6 per cent). This is a more sanguine view than that of the German Institute for Economic Research (DIW), which is supported by data indicating that eastern firms account for only 2 per cent of German exports and little more than 1 per cent to industrialised western countries.

However, widely cited data of the kind reported in Table 9.9 gives a too-pessimistic impression. The decline in eastern exports as a share of total German exports is explained by continued growth of West German exports to former Comecon members at the same time as exports from East German suppliers shrank. Meanwhile, the increased share of eastern firms in total German exports to western industrial markets as reported in Table 9.9 is possibly a serious underestimate. As the DIW report notes, intra-firm deliveries are not taken account of in this data. Consequently, because a large part of the East German economy is made of branch plants of West German firms, an unquantifiable but certainly large part of eastern output is delivered to western parent firms. These deliveries from East to West can subsequently be exported directly – after minimal further value added (for example, packaging) – or indirectly – having entered as intermediate goods into products finally exported – but are not counted as eastern exports.

THE LIMITS OF A HIGH-WAGE STRATEGY

Barry and Bradley's comments on the strategic choices facing the EU's Southern periphery are relevant to eastern Germany:

Table 9.9 East German exports as a share of German exports

Share of East German firms	*1991*	*1992*	*1993*	*1994*	*1995*
• in total German exports	2.6	2.1	1.9	1.8	1.9
• in exports to western industrial countries	0.8	0.8	0.8	1.0	1.2

Source: DIW 1996, p. 55 (Table 23).

> Do they permit the fairly rapid destruction of their indigenous, inefficient, labour-intensive, low-wage sector and facilitate its replacement by an efficient capital (or R&D) intensive, high-wage sector? As in the Irish and Spanish cases, this route appears likely to entail substantial structural unemployment and an associated high tax burden if social welfare systems are put in place.
>
> (Barry and Bradley 1994, p. 23)

In comparison with Greece and Portugal, eastern Germany is privileged with respect to the existing level and rate of accumulation of physical infrastructure and human capital and, above all, inward investment. This has enabled eastern Germany to avoid condemning a large part of its population to the status of working poor occupying 'low-skill, low-productivity, low-pay', 'bad' jobs. The downside is a high long-term unemployment rate supported by the German system of social insurance.

In the first five years of unification, the prevailing high-wage, high-tech strategy supported by publicly subsidised inward investment and fiscal transfers has enabled dramatic restructuring and productivity growth. However, as productivity rises, increasingly the problem in eastern Germany is not the average productivity level but the proportion of the population employed at this level. Again, comments of Barry and Bradley are relevant:

> Average productivity levels in Spain and Ireland are now not far behind the EU average, but there is still some leeway to make up. However, the greater part of the shortfall in average living standards in these countries is due to the fact that in both an exceptionally low proportion of the population is employed at these productivity levels.
>
> (Barry and Bradley 1994, p. 22)

Table 9.8 shows that in the five years 1991–5 growth in the five new Länder was both higher and more even (ranging from 24 to 40 per cent) than in the western Länder (ranging from 1 to 8 per cent after excluding West Berlin). However, during 1995 the pace of eastern Germany's catch-up slowed significantly. Construction output was stagnant, while manufacturing in general and investment goods in particular underwent declining growth rates. The pessimistic results of the Spring 1996 business survey evidence reported in Figure 9.2 indicated a downturn persisting into 1996. This has been confirmed by a sharp decline of annual GDP growth. In the convergence process, we can distinguish the period 1992–4 in which the annual rate of real GDP growth in East Germany was on average 8.2 per cent higher than in West Germany. From 1995 to 1997 the difference has shrunk to 1.3 per cent (Deutscher Bundestag, 1996, p. 22). Indeed, the estimated difference for 1996 of 0.5 per cent and a forecast for 1997 of –0.25 per cent suggests that convergence has stalled.

The main proximate causes of stalled convergence were firstly slower growth in western Germany, and secondly the stabilisation of inward fiscal transfers at around DM 200 billion per annum. This is probably the extreme upper limit of what is politically feasible:

> Yet the most that a constant volume of government support can do is to help maintain the level of output achieved in the wake of the impulses originally induced. No additional expansionary effects are being generated by this support.
>
> (*Economic Bulletin*, January 1996, p. 11).

The underlying cause is that convergence is still not a self-sustaining process. Given that a declining proportion of inward fiscal transfers is devoted to investment, to increase or even maintain the level of investment requires investment-led growth independent of government incentives. This dynamic is precluded, however, by lack of profitability. Corporate investment in Germany is particularly sensitive to profitability as both incentive and means, because most investment is financed from retained earnings (Pugh 1997, pp. 89–92). In eastern Germany, the astounding fact is that 'firms as a whole are not realising any profits per working hour at all. There can consequently be no investment dynamic in the absence of government incentives' (Economic Bulletin, January 1996, p. 11). The Spring 1996 business survey demonstrates a sharp decline in the balance of firms with positive rather than negative expectations about profitability (returns) 'to which corresponds the clear decline in enterprise investment plans' – indeed, comment the editors of the Report, 'for the first time since the survey began the balance of enterprises intend to reduce their investment' (iwd, 16 May 1996, p. 8).

Productivity has risen rapidly. In particular, between the beginning of 1991 and the end of 1994, manufacturing productivity (net output per working hour) more than tripled. Yet both at the level of the eastern economy as a whole and at the sectoral level of manufacturing labour costs have risen at least as fast (Economic Bulletin, September 1995, p. 7; January 1996, p. 13; and November 1996, p. 24). Consequently, there is no gap between productivity and hourly labour costs to generate profit and, hence, investment financed out of retained earnings.

Many of the benefits of high wages in combination with subsidised investment depend on unmeasured – and possibly unmeasurable – externalities and, hence, are difficult to compare with the costs of this strategy. However, it is likely that by the mid-1990s the benefits of further wage increases are exceeded by the costs. In the early years of unification, wage increases could be justified as an instrument of 'creative destruction' that precluded eastern Germany from becoming trapped in a vicious circle of low wages, low skills, low productivity, and low growth. After five years these benefits have been secured: wages, skills, productivity, and growth are all relatively high. Consequently, it is likely that the potential for further benefit from wage increase has been exhausted. Conversely, the costs of this strategy continue: unit labour costs remain at such a high level that eastern firms, especially new small- and medium-size firms, cannot earn sufficient profit to finance the investment necessary for self-sustaining recovery. Indeed, given that the growth of fiscal transfers and externally-financed inward investment have reached their limits, the costs of continued wage increase tend to intensify in terms of curtailed growth and prolonged convergence. Additional wage increase, therefore, is likely to generate increasingly more cost than benefit. This suggests a strategic reorientation towards wage restraint. The initial high-wage strategy must give way to something like Sinn and Sinn's 'organic' or restricted wage growth strategy.

Notes

1. 'Low- medium- and high-tech' refer both to the extent to which particular industries – especially in manufacturing – are knowledge based (that is, R&D intensive) and to the extent to which investment within any industry is in leading-edge technologies (that is, those embodying the latest technical and managerial 'know-how'). These concepts are clarified further on in the chapter.
2. Equation (2) applies the rule that the growth of a sum is the weighted average of the rates of growth of the components.
3. Table 9.3 does not account accurately for the separate shares of medium- and high- technology output in East German manufacturing. First, because definitional discrepancies prevent a complete and exact maping of industrial sectors from the German data (e.g., coking plants and oil refining) on to the indicative categories of Table 9.1 (e.g., oil refining). Secondly, the technology-intensity categories group activities that can be very different: within, say, a generally medium-tech sector (e.g., chemicals), there might be high-tech sub-sectors (e.g., pharmaceuticals), which are over- or under-represented in a particular location. And, thirdly, classification systems differ: for example, electro-mechanical and precision engineering are

sometimes listed as high-tech (e.g., *Economic Bulletin*, Sept. 1995, p. 9) and sometimes as medium-tech (e.g., Maurer, 1994, p. 312).

4. See Vassilakis 1991, p. 151: 'Empirical studies of the production process in various industries have demonstrated a positive association between current labour productivity and measures of past activity like past cumulative output or investment.' On the economic logic of this empirical relationship, see Ricoy 1991, p. 732.
5. This section focuses on the causal link between investment and productivity growth which, necessarily, generates output growth. Empirical evidence for a causal link between investment and employment growth is furnished by Dinenis and Funke who, in a study of UK and West German manufacturing, discover that the investment rate 'has a positive impact upon manufacturing employment in both countries' (1994, p. 418).
6. For empirical support for this link, see Wolff 1991.
7. Balasubramanyam et al. (1994 and 1996) provide econometric evidence on the contribution to growth of learning-by-doing effects.
8. Collection of data on intra-German trade was suspended at the end of 1994. Consequently, only business survey evidence is available on eastern 'exports' to western Germany.

Bibliography

BALASUBRAMANYAM, V. N., SALISU, M and SAPSFORD, D. *Foreign direct investment and growth in EP and IS countries*. Lancaster University Department of Economics Working Paper, EC18/94, 1994.

BALASUBRAMANYAM, V. N., SALISU, M. and SAPSFORD, D. *Foreign direct investment and growth: new hypotheses and evidence*. Lancaster University Department of Economics Working Paper, EC7/96, 1996.

BARRY, F. and BRADLEY, J. *Labour Market Performance in the EU Periphery*. Centre for Economic Research Working Paper, WP 94/3, March 1994.

DEUTSCHER BUNDESTAG. *Jahresgutachten 1994/1995 des Sachverständigenrates zur Begutachtung der gesamtwirtschaftlichen Entwicklung*. Unterrichtung durch die Bundesregierung. Bonn, 1995.

DEUTSCHER BUNDESTAG. *Jahresgutachten 1995/1996 des Sachverständigenrates zur Begutachtung der gesamtwirtschaftlichen Entwicklung*. Unterrichtung durch die Bundesregierung. Bonn, 1996.

DINENIS, E. and FUNKE, M. *Factor Prices, Employment and Investment in UK and West German Manufacturing*. The Manchester School, vol. LXII, no. 4, Dec. 1994 pp. 412–24.

DIW, 'Gesamtwirtschaftliche und unternehmerische Anpassungs fortschritte in Ostdeutschland: Vierzehnter Bericht' *Wochenbericht* (WB), vol. 63, no. 27, 1996.

ECONOMIC BULLETIN. DIW (The German Institute for Economic Research). Gower Press, monthly, various issues.

IWD (Institut der deutschen Wirtschaft) *Informationsdienst*. Köln; various issues.

MAURER, R. 'Die Exportstärke der deutschen Industrie – Weltmarktspitze trotz technologischen Rückstands?', *Die Weltwirtschaft*, no. 3 (September) 1994 pp. 308–19.

McCOMBIE, J. and THIRLWALL, A. *Economic Growth and the Balance of Payments Constraint*. Macmillan, London, 1994.

OWEN-SMITH, E. *The German Economy*. Routledge, London, 1994.

PORTER, M. *The Competitive Advantage of Nations*. Macmillan, London, 1990.

PUGH, G. *The Investment Diversion Effects of German Unification*. In Hölscher, J. and Frowen, S. (eds) *The German Currency Union of 1990*. Macmillan, London, 1997.

RICOY, C. J. *Cumulative Causation*. In Eatwell, J., Milgate M. and Newman, P. (eds) *The New Palgrave Dictionary of Economics*. Vol. 1. Macmillan, London, 1991. pp. 730–5.

RODRIK, D. 'Getting interventions right: how South Korea and Taiwan grew rich', *Economic Policy*, no. 20, April 1995 pp. 55–107.

SINN, G. and SINN, H-W. *Jumpstart: The Economic Unification of Germany*. MIT Press, Cambridge, Mass., 1992.

STATISTISCHES BUNDESAMT *Volkswirtschaftliche Gesamtrechnung*. 1995.

UNITED NATIONS *Statistical Yearbook*. UN, New York, 1995.

VASSILAKIS, S. *Learning-by-doing*. In Eatwell, J., Milgate M. and Newman, P. (eds) *The New Palgrave Dictionary of Economics*. Vol. 3. Macmillan, London, 1991, pp. 151–2.

WOLFF, E. 'Capital Formation and Productivity Convergence Over the Long Term', *American Economic Review*, vol. 81, no. 3, 1991, pp. 565–79.

10 Economic Aspects of German Unification: Lessons for European Integration

Eric Owen Smith

INTRODUCTION

The speed of political events which preceded German unification precluded rational economic judgements about the nature of German Economic, Monetary and Social Union (GEMSU). In any case, economists were divided about whether the inevitable shock which would accompany GEMSU should be cushioned or introduced at one fell swoop (Owen Smith 1997). At the other end of the spectrum, the tortuous and protracted process of European economic integration has exposed conflicting national interests and differing economic paradigms. It is inevitable that these two very different processes would produce comparisons (Kloten 1995). In the first section, therefore, the principal differences between GEMSU and European integration are reviewed. This is followed in the second section by a critical appraisal of GEMSU. The main monetary, fiscal and social-policy implications are then analysed in a third section. It will be demonstrated, by summarising arguments made more extensively by this writer elsewhere (Owen Smith 1998a), that a number of features of the German economy have already been adopted, or would lend themselves to adoption, at the European Union (EU) level. The final section of this chapter is largely confined to a review of the economic aspects of GEMSU and European integration. It boils down to a contrasting picture of homogeneity and heterogeneity.

PRINCIPAL DIFFERENCES

The basic forms of economic integration are a free trade area, a customs union, a common market and/or a monetary union. Three different forms of monetary union can be distinguished. First, the exchange rates of participating currencies are fixed and this initial parity is maintained in perpetuity (Lythe 1995, p. 152). This most likely involves financing facilities to ease monetary and trade adjustments. It certainly requires the pooling of reserves and operating a common external exchange rate policy (ibid.). In the literature this form has been a called *currency union*. The second form of monetary integration involves the freedom of capital movements and the unification of financial institutions and markets to foster that freedom. In policy discussions this form of monetary integration was called *financial integration*: it is what the European Council had in mind when it enacted the Single European Act, or EC 1993. This second form of integration does not require the first form of integration. In fact the two can be considered as independent policy choices. Their separate nature can be adduced from the turbulence in the Exchange Rate Mechanism (ERM) and concurrent tribulations in the German financial sector during the preparations for EC 1993. The third form of monetary integration involves unification at the policy level and may or may not go beyond monetary policy. It is this form of integration which has been called *monetary union*. In recent policy discussions this term has meant the co-existence of a currency union and the complete integration of financial markets. A currency union would be an essential prelude to the introduction of a common currency. Prior to the exchange-rate turbulence which dramatically commenced in September 1992, only the drachma remained outside the ERM: significantly Greece still had a relatively high rate of inflation. But the state of the ERM in 1992–3 made the agonising over European Economic and Monetary Union (EMU) something of a charade. Nonetheless, EC 1993 had sought to revive the goal of EMU by writing into the EEC Treaty a binding commitment on the part of the Member States to work progressively to bring it about.

By virtue of the 'big bang' approach the aims of GEMSU were unambiguously spelt out, whereas EC 1993 may have been the ultimate goal of some EC members. Following Molle (1990, pp. 12–13), the cumulative sequence of:

- a free-trade area (all internal tariff barriers removed),
- a customs union (common external tariffs), and
- a common market (labour and capital mobility)

had been largely achieved by the time EC 1993 was finally implemented. However, economic and monetary union (vesting economic and monetary policy decision-making powers in supra-national authorities) was unacceptable to many policy-makers in the member states. Tichy (1993, pp. 167–8) defines the forms of integration reviewed above in rather more detailed terms. However, he emphasises that ultimately the critical test is the extent to which trade is created rather than diverted.

GEMSU, then, was a wide-ranging treaty which encapsulated the monetary, economic and social features necessary for the introduction of West Germany's Social Market Economy (SME) into East Germany. EC 1993 and EMU, on the other hand, are based on a phased process of European economic and monetary union. A social dimension to the process of European integration was added by the 'Social Charter', which was later embodied as a 'Chapter' in the Maastricht Treaty. Hence, at the time of GEMSU all three parts of the European process of integration were at various stages of implementation and negotiation. The degrees of enthusiasm among members ranged from a desire for rapid integration on all fronts to a cautious and even sceptical approach. For example, a convergence of economic policies and indicators was viewed, not least by the Bundesbank (BBk), as being an essential prior condition – and proposals were drawn up by the central bankers of the then EC for a European central bank which had much in common with the ethos of the BBk. The convergence of monetary policy applied particularly to low rates of price inflation and low levels of public debt. Since GEMSU seriously undermined the Bundesbank's stabilisation policies in this sense, it became even more sceptical about EMU.

The Maastricht Treaty contained extremely rigorous conditions on economic and *monetary* integration. These conditions were convergence in inflation, exchange and long-term interest rates at levels achieved by the EU's best performers, along with budget deficits no greater than 3 per cent of GDP and debt/GDP ratios not exceeding 60 per cent. Not only did GEMSU threaten the likelihood of Germany's achieving these targets, but it effectively meant that, given free capital and labour mobility, only those economies with fairly equal living standards could realistically aspire to economic and monetary integration in the 1990s. Ireland, Spain, Portugal and Greece, with annual per capita incomes below DM 20 000 in 1991, would find that labour and, possibly, capital investment would tend to flow to more affluent economies. Britain was on the borderline (DM 26 660) while West Germany's DM 31 990 was deflated to DM 27 510 when the East was included (*Die Welt* 23 November 1992). In fact, *Die Welt* (ibid.) graphically summed up this effect on the West German economy as 'relegation to the second division'. (The headline was also used – even more implausibly – in 1993 to illustrate the prospect of the French Franc succeeding the DM as the anchor currency of the ERM – ibid., 17 June.)

Before and even after GEMSU, therefore, it was at the very least conjectured that economic and monetary union between countries or regions with differing levels of development, economic structure and degrees of stability should be tackled in stages. In essence, this was the approach recommended in the Delors' report. If, however, the monetary union is implemented as a 'big bang' at the start of the unification process, it will be very difficult to make rapid corrections and counter adverse trends as they develop. In particular, it is no longer possible to use exchange rates to facilitate the process of adjustment, and there is by definition only *one* authority in monetary policy. For East Germany this meant there was no question of the exchange rate gradually adjusting – instead, East Germany moved without any transitional period from a non-convertible currency to a strong currency with international convertibility. Given the political imperatives of unification, and also given the problems in East Germany, there was no time for an alternative course. East German confidence had to be strengthened quickly to counter westward-flowing emigrants. Exchange rate risks for potential investors had to be rapidly reduced to get the necessary capital flowing into East Germany. It must also be borne in mind that even prior to GEMSU there had been an accelerating decline in East German industrial production.

There was thus no policy option in terms of choosing the adjustment process. Predictably, higher living standards caused an exodus of labour from East to West, thus contributing to the decline in East German industrial production prior to GEMSU. In the four months from October 1989 to January 1990 alone, more than 300 000 emigrated from East to West Germany, whereas in the first six months of 1990 this flow amounted to 200 000. The outflow fell back sharply following free elections and GEMSU. But this meant that the process of adjustment would fall on prices and employment. If migration had continued on the scale just indicated, however, the political, social and economic implications for both parts of Germany would have been incalculable. On the price front, commentators envisaged a rapid adjustment process in the East, with the West avoiding unacceptable inflationary pressure by re-routing traded goods which would otherwise have been exported.

The rapid adjustment hypothesis is particularly interesting. A substantial proportion of profits from industry and other sources in the East had been earmarked under central planning for the purpose of subsidising rents, food, fares, culture, a huge housing programme and social services. Some of these non-traded goods were heavily subsidised. Hence, as these subsidies were removed the prices of these goods would rise. On the other hand, these price rises would be more than offset as the prices of many traded goods fell because western products became available, thereby removing extreme shortages. Hence both the price level and structure generally adjusted quite rapidly – perhaps too rapidly for the East Germans (Lythe 1995, p. 157). Far from having an inflationary impact in its year of implementation, GEMSU as such probably had a disinflationary bias (MRDB 8/91: table VIII[10]). But what other lessons can be learned from this ambitious case of integration?

A CRITICAL APPRAISAL OF GEMSU

When East Germany was incorporated into West Germany in 1990, the West German economy occupied a dominant position within the EU and in the wider global economy. East Germany constituted only 30 per cent of the new DM area; its share of total population was only 21 per cent; by 1993 its GDP was only 9 per cent of the united German GDP, while its share of industrial production had shrunk to 5 per cent of the German total. By 1996, only 18 per cent of the labour force was located in the East but 28 per cent of national unemployment.

Exchange rate determination is arguably the most important lesson from this leap into full union. Put at its simplest, the GDR had in effect employed long-run average shadow export pricing of GDR Mark 3.73: DM 1 (Akerlof et al. 1991, pp. 17–18). Even short-run average cost pricing meant, in DM terms, an average loss of 84 per cent on each item exported to non-Communist economies (ibid.). The politics of GEMSU meant flows were converted at GDR Mark 1: DM 1, and stocks generally at GDR Mark 2: DM 1. This clearly resulted in most eastern German products being price uncompetitive, especially given that they were now officially priced in the world's hardest currency and the former GDR's export markets were in the reserve-impoverished Comecon. The compromise rates thus created problems for producers and, for that matter, both gains and losses for consumers and savers (Lythe 1995, pp. 160–2). (Because savings were so much higher in the East, the compromise exchange rates reduced the wealth of eastern households by about a third – ibid., p. 164.)

In addition, eastern German products were also uncompetitive on qualitative grounds – a characteristic that reflected the technological backwardness of the industrial base. This was in complete contrast to the viable industrial base which existed when the SME emerged in West Germany. Apparently this lack of knowledge about eastern competitiveness, along with an underestimation of industrial profitability, were based on the absence of reliable western intelligence of the situation in the East

(Prützel-Thomas 1995, pp. 120–5). Yet had it been possible to retain two segmented labour markets at the time of GEMSU, the average lower productivity level in eastern Germany would have been reflected by lower money wage rates converted at 1:1. But segmentation was by definition ruled out. Either there would be a high degree of migration and commuting to higher-paid jobs in western Germany, or money wage rate equalisation, initially through subsidisation, would have to occur (Owen Smith 1994, p. 317). After all, the rational interests of western German employees lay in preventing low-wage competition.

Eastern German industrial production consequently plummeted to a third of its former level within a year of GEMSU, a fall even more catastrophic than the five-year Great Depression of 1928–33 (Sinn and Sinn 1992, pp. 29–30). Commuting and migration to western Germany, job creation and training schemes, early retirement and short-time working did not prevent a headline unemployment rate of 17 per cent (ibid,; Owen Smith 1994, p. 259). When such state-supported schemes are included, the proportion rose to 28 per cent in 1994 (Houpt 1995, p. 255) Actual unemployment probably peaked at three times the official figure (Steinherr 1994, p. 27). Total exports fell by 60 per cent during 1989–91, and three-quarters of this decrease was due to the decline in Comecon trade (ibid.). One-third of the fall in industrial production was due to the decline in exports, and the other two-thirds by the shift within eastern Germany to foreign products (ibid.). Such a series of repercussions begs the following central question. Could a more rapid and thorough recovery be anticipated in eastern Germany than in the relatively more gradualist Poland, Hungary and the then Czechoslovakia – three aspirant members of the EU?

Major blunders were also made in the fields of monetary and fiscal policies, both of which have implications for the German model. Within the paradigm of this model the monetary policy reactions were predictable, whereas the fiscal policy mistakes were avoidable. The latter errors emanated from the Paretian promise made by members of the Federal coalition parties prior to the first all-German elections. It was contended that GEMSU would make no one in western Germany worse off, but everyone in the eastern part of the newly united economy better off. The mounting debt required to finance transfers to eastern Germany, which was in turn initially financed by borrowing, ultimately led to rising short-term interest rates and taxation. Two income tax surcharges of 7.5 per cent, a one percentage point increase in the top rate of VAT to 15 per cent, and increases in the excise duty on hydro-carbon oils were necessary. Raising taxes to reduce the public deficit was justifiable – if arguably suboptimal – under the circumstances. Even so, the overall tax rate, at about 45 per cent, was not seriously out of line with the average for 13 OECD countries (although the USA, Japan and the UK were significantly below the average of 43.1 per cent in 1993 – OECD 1994, p. 96). On the grounds of inflation, however, the hike in short-term term interest rates by the BBk is more difficult to justify. Analogies may be drawn with the first two crude-oil-price shocks (Owen Smith 1994, pp. 158–60). At their peak, current real short-term rates in 1974, 1981 and 1992 were respectively –0.9, 0.2 and 3.2 per cent (Owen Smith 1997). There could surely not have been such a vast difference in the implied expected rates of inflation.

Analysis of the wider exchange-rate implications of the BBk's interest-rate policies is rendered more difficult by the apparent stubborn refusal of other ERM members to agree to a realignment. In discussing Steinherr, de Cecco compares the manner in which GEMSU was implemented with the decision in the USA rapidly to increase public expenditure in the 1960s, without a commensurate increase in taxation (de Cecco in Steinherr 1994). He traces the destruction of the Bretton Woods international monetary regime to this policy scenario. Because the necessarily huge rise in public expenditure which accompanied GEMSU could not be monetised through a compliant central bank, the rise in interest rates induced a large inflow of capital. Since international investors were guaranteed instruments denominated in a high interest, low-inflation and revaluing currency, they were enticed to invest in Germany. De Cecco (ibid.) plausibly sees the ERM as being the 'first international victim' of this policy. Domestically, the boom in western Germany ended and unemployment rose. Significantly, capital controls had been an important element in the success of the European Monetary System (EMS) during the 1980s (Higgins 1993, p. 33). It follows that there are clear policy implications for the system's reform (ibid., p. 37). The three options are: (1) reduce capital mobility; (2) accept a single monetary policy; (3) allow exchange rates to adjust freely. In other words, GEMSU and unsound macro-economic policies undoubtedly contributed to strains within the ERM, but fundamental reform may be required as a precursor to EMU.

There were further differences between the emergence of the SME and GEMSU (Owen Smith 1993 and 1997). Briefly put, they can be summarised as follows. Markets still functioned, albeit imperfectly, after the Second World War. Federal subsidies and tax relief induced investment during the 1950s. Following GEMSU, the German government procrastinated over the property-rights question and also failed to offer significant subsidies for investment in real capital (Thornton, in Steinherr 1994, p. 6). Hölscher (1994) usefully postulates three stylised facts for the development of the SME. They are the 1948 Currency Reform, the 1950

EPU credits and the 1953 London Treaty. Notice how West Germany gained extremely beneficial relief from internal and external debts, along with invaluable balance-of-payments assistance. Yet one of the most impressive accomplishments during the GEMSU process was western German thoroughness in drawing up various accounts setting out the degree of eastern German indebtedness. This was a major contributory factor to their becoming collectively known as 'Besserwessie' in eastern Germany – a corruption of the German term for 'know-all' (*Besserwisser*). Moreover, some western German commentators insisted on market principles for eastern Germany that had been ignored in western Germany for decades (Owen Smith 1997; Smyser 1993, p. 167). A good half of the savers' conversion loss was probably siphoned off by the BBk, the privatisation process transferred whole enterprises – probably 90 per cent of eastern productive assets – to western German ownership without according an opportunity for share ownership to easterners, and the restitution process transferred a large part of housing wealth to western Germany – and not without an element of farce: there were more claims than pieces of property (Hall and Ludwig 1995, pp. 500–2; Kurz 1993, p. 135; Sinn and Sinn 1992, pp. 74, 117; Smyser 1993, p. 178). The Deutsche Bank accepted DM 12 billion in eastern deposits, but made loans of only DM 6.8 billion (Smyser 1993, p. 157). By the end of 1993, only DM 14.2 billion had been invested in enterprises privatised by the Treuhand – compared to investment promises of over DM 200 billion in that institution's books (Prützel-Thomas 1995, p. 123). At the very heart of this catalogue of East/West flows lies the issue of physical property rights; but was the very process of unification made possible only by the 'bankruptcy' of the former GDR (ibid., p. 125)? Hence, if the eastern Germans believed that the adoption of the DM would make them wealthier in the short term, they were cruelly disabused (Flockton 1992, p. 60). GEMSU was implemented in a manner which inevitably made eastern Germans 'victims' (de Cecco in Steinherr 1994, p. 2).

IMPLICATIONS FOR EUROPEAN MONETARY, FISCAL AND SOCIAL POLICIES

The European Monetary Institute, the forerunner of the European Central Bank (ECB), is situated in Frankfurt am Main – a city which is also the seat of the Deutsche Bundesbank. It is not surprising that this is the only major European institution to be located in Germany. The ECB will certainly be a clone of the BBk. Above all, it will enjoy an identical degree of independence from political influence. Moreover, the BBk is more centralised than its predecessor (Bank deutscher Länder). It is owned by the Federal government. Its eight-strong directorate – notwithstanding their subsequent independence – are Federal appointees. Länder representation on its governing Council was reduced to nine as a result of GEMSU and its attendant threat of an unwieldy Council. Together with the directorate, therefore, the policy-making Council now consists of 17 members. In order to achieve its sole goal of price stability, it uses its contemporaneous interest-rate instruments and currently targets the monetary aggregate M3 (Owen Smith 1994, pp. 143–78). To gain the BBk's support, the Euro would have to be a 'strong' currency. Yet the strength of the DM contributed to the record post-war unemployment in western Germany in 1996. Hence, because the DM is a major trading, investment and reserve currency, the fortnightly deliberations of its Council are an internationally important event. Domestically, the BBk 'punishes' the wage bargainers and government if they are perceived to be endangering price stability (Carlin and Soskice 1997, p. 70). In short, the fundamental macroeconomic policy dynamic in Germany is monetary policy.

A number of issues would have to be resolved before the ECB could be modelled on the BBk. First, if all 15 EU members were in a position to move simultaneously to the third and final stage of EMU, all 15 central-bank presidents or governors would be accorded a Council seat. Yet, BBk experience with GEMSU indicates that very few additional places would be available for other representatives. Secondly, what type of securities would be acceptable collaterals for discounting by the ECB? Because of its restrictive approach to dealing in public-sector debt, the BBk has evolved its own 'flexible' securities for this purpose (Owen Smith 1994, pp. 150–1). Thirdly, would politicians retain the right to negotiate exchange-rate treaties? If so, central bankers would be perturbed by the possibilities of imported inflation.

Next consider fiscal policy. Because GEMSU incorporated East Germany into an existing economic, monetary and social union, tax rates were already established – albeit that some transitional arrangements were made. Such a degree of tax harmonisation was not, of course, made possible by EC 1993. VAT rates still differ widely within the EU, as do excise duties. Citizens of member states living near Luxembourg, for example, make considerable savings by purchasing motor-vehicle fuel and tobacco products in the Grand Duchy – in some cases merely by crossing a road or bridge!

There is an even greater problem. The establishment of a centralised ECB is at an advanced stage of preparation. By way of complete contrast, the EU's fiscal powers are relatively negligible. In 1992 its budget totalled ECU 61.1 billion – about the same size as the combined general-government and the Treuhand privatisation agency's budgetary deficits in Germany, and not a great deal larger than the solidarity-surcharge enhanced Federal unshared tax yield in that year (Owen-Smith 1994, pp. 110–11; MRDB 1/94, p. 75* and 4/95, p. 55*; OECD 1994, p. 153). Even more significantly, it was trivial compared to the magnitude of flows from western to eastern Germany (Ifo 1994, p. 5). By 1997 (in real terms) the EU's budget will total ECU 74.5 billion, 28.4 per cent (gross) of which will be contributed by Germany (von Laun 1994, p. 55). This 22 per cent budgetary expansion is, however, dwarfed by the costs of GEMSU – an exercise analogous to including Sweden and Greece (to say nothing of the central European aspirant members) in EMU. In short, it is the degree of dissimilarity in economies which determines the degree of fiscal transfers required and thus the costs of transformation. That said, private and public investment flows to the five new Länder, though large, are not disproportionate relative to both population and other regions in unified Germany (Hall and Ludwig 1995, pp. 497–8). There is still chronic under-investment and a lack of marketing techniques in eastern Germany (Houpt 1995, pp. 255, 259). A policy prescription advanced is that the East should show more flair by investing in the service sector – an area where Germany as a whole is weak (ibid., p. 262).

On the expenditure side, CAP still accounts for a half of the total EU budget, with Germany faring better than the UK. At an early stage in the emergence of the SME, German farming interests were soon able to evade market forces, and accommodating the French farmers as European integration progressed meant that agriculture would remain protected and subsidised (Nicholls 1994, p. 345). It is astonishing that only German agriculture achieves what other economic sectors can only dream about: potential losses which would occur as a result of the revaluation of the DM are in effect written off by the CAP (FAZ 18 May 1995). In fact, despite her comparative disadvantage, Germany became a major food exporter (Flockton 1992, p. 58). Reform of such a fiscal arrangement is supposedly to be undertaken by 1999, although in the spring of 1995 Bavarian farmers demonstrated against the loss of southern EU markets as a result of the revaluation of the DM no longer being unaccompanied by the CAP's Monetary Compensatory Amounts. Indeed, food prices throughout the EU were set at German levels, by far the highest in Europe. Pegging farm prices to the DM, which was introduced on German insistence in 1984, was brought to an end only after it had cost EU taxpayers ECU 35 billion. *The Economist* (8 July 1995) predicted that food stocks in the EU will rise again unless prices are further reduced. Given the electoral and lobbying power of German farmers that seems unlikely. The two policy options for European integration therefore appear to be either delaying any further EU enlargement, or not permitting new members into the CAP until after a long transitional period. This latter option effectively means according virtual associate membership to successful applicants from central Europe.

Within the EU the quantitative and qualitative magnitudes of both revenue raising and expenditure are thus respectively too insignificant or misdirected to provide any countervailing power to the envisaged degree of centralisation in monetary policy. Price stability will therefore be the only policy goal, even if employment creation by public-sector spending is considered a viable alternative policy scenario. Any clone of the BBk will normally view public-sector expenditure as suboptimal.

On the other hand, the German model has a potentially useful device for fiscal equalisation – although the donor Länder within the Federal Republic were critical of the system even before GEMSU. This model demonstrates the fairly obvious proposition that each level of government must be allocated a revenue flow which corresponds to its implicit expenditure commitments (vertical equalisation). It also indicates the need for fiscal transfers from more affluent to less affluent areas, especially in the event of an economic, monetary and social union (horizontal equalisation). There are several points worthy of note. Above all, the Federal share of VAT has fallen over the years, not least as a result of 'compensating' the western Länder for the full inclusion of the new Länder in the system as from 1 January 1995. (Between 1990 and 1994 these obligations were met out of the German Unity Fund, to which the Federal government was by far the largest contributor.) The shortfall was in turn partially met by increasing the independently levied Federal duty on hydro-carbon oils, the revenue from which almost doubled between 1989 and 1994 (MRDB 4/95, p. 55*). An income-tax solidarity surcharge was re-introduced as from 1 January 1995, again amounting to 7.5 per cent.

It should also be noted that the tax revenue of local authorities is insufficient to cover expenditure needs. They admittedly retain 86 per cent of their trade-tax yield whose fundamental reform is under active consideration (Owen Smith 1994, pp. 100–1, 107–8; FAZ 29 April 1995). Interestingly enough, the larger local authorities are pressing for a constitutionally guaranteed share of VAT revenue in return for the complete abolition of the trade tax. When the payroll element of this tax was abolished in 1979, the local authorities received an additional percentage point share in the income-tax yield. But the trade tax not only undermines industrial competitiveness. The virtual cap on further increases means that alternative sources of revenue have to be found. Above all, fee income from services such as sewage disposal totalled DM 34 billion in 1994, having grown by almost 50 per cent in the period 1989–93 (*Die Zeit* 15/94).

Articles 106(3) and 107(2) of the basic law respectively require the Federal and Länder governments to promote uniform living standards throughout the Republic, achieving this by means of fiscal equalisation between financially strong and financially weak Länder. There are three fundamental lessons. First, GEMSU was also a costly exercise in this respect. Secondly, Bremen and Saarland – the two weakest Länder in western Germany – remained eligible for additional assistance between 1995 and 1998. Thirdly, both the Federal and the richer Länder governments were significant contributors. Basically, the 'fiscal power' of any Land is its tax revenue-raising powers. If this indicator exceeds the Land's 'equalisation indicator', the Land becomes a net contributor and vice-versa. The first round of equalisation process then results in each Land being brought up to a minimum share of 95 per cent of the average tax revenue raised by the Länder. Next, the second round of Federal grants-in-aid would normally bring every Land up to a minimum revenue level of 100 per cent of average revenue. The Federal cost of this exercise alone was DM 25.327 billion. This statistic consists of the second round Federal grants, plus a number of special grants designed to reduce the administrative and financial burdens of transition between 1995 and 2004 (BMF 1993, p. 42). In addition, the new Länder will receive infrastructure-renewal grants, also for the period 1995–2004. This all results in a rough equalisation of the old Länder relativities (Bremen and Saarland receive supplementary assistance).

Integrating the new Länder into the fiscal equalisation system will cost the Federal government DM 41.9 billion annually during the decade 1995–2004. This consists of DM 16.6 billion in forgone VAT revenue, plus DM 18.7 billion in grants-in-aid and DM 6.6 billion infra-structure assistance. Grants-in-aid to the old Länder will cost the Federal government an additional DM 6.9 billion, although these will decline after 1998. The old Länder will in addition contribute a gross DM 15.7 billion to the costs of integration: DM 2.9 billion in forgone VAT revenue, plus horizontal equalisation payments of DM 12.8 billion. Hence, over the next few years the total equalisation flow to eastern Germany from the Federal and old Länder governments amounts to DM 57.6 annually (Ifo 1994, p. 5). The German Unity annuities increase this sum to DM 67.2 billion (ibid.). Total transfers are even higher. In net terms – that is, eliminating double counting by deducting the Federal government's tax yield in eastern Germany and deducting privatisation revenue from the losses of the privatisation agency – transfers between 1991 and 1994 totalled DM 626 billion (Deutsche Bank Research 1994, p. 21). As well as the continuing costs of the now-defunct privatisation agency, there is a social-insurance transfer which in 1993, for example, cost DM 42 billion (Ifo 1994). This latter cost, given the advanced social policy embodied in the SME, was inevitably high. Summarising, a net annual transfer of DM 130 billion was expected in 1996 (BTS 3 May 1996).

The introduction of the single market in 1993 was seen by the EC as generating the need for the protection of fundamental social rights because of the threat of cross-border mergers and the attendant process of concentration (Owen Smith 1994, p. 310). Although this was the genesis of the Social Charter, it is necessary to recall that such developments date from the Treaty of Rome itself. This notion of countervailing power is also a built-in feature of the SME. In any case, the firm is not the black box assumed in neo-classical economic theory; social efficiency is as important as economic efficiency (FitzRoy and Kraft 1987, p. 496; and 1993, pp. 366; 374–5; Owen Smith 1997). Contrary to the predictions of property-rights theory, employee participation in managerial decision-making may improve efficiency (Gurdon and Rai 1990).

Article 118 of the Treaty of Rome requires the EC to promote co-operation between member states 'in the social field'. In the present context it is instructive to note that social security, the right of association and collective bargaining between employers and employees are all among the several policy-areas specified. Similarly, Annex 1 to the Maastricht Treaty requires the Community (Article 2[1]) to support and complement the activities of member states in, for example, informing and consulting employees. Article 2(3) mentions such items as 'the social protection of employees', 'co-determination' and, in effect, the need to determine common conditions of employment within the EU. Annex 1 is more popularly known as the 'Social Chapter' – from which the then UK government 'opted out'. During the 1980s, however, the European Court of Justice (ECJ) forced this government to introduce amendments to its Equal Pay and Sex Discrimination legislation. Moreover, in 1994 the House of Lords ruled that, by EU standards, the UK's virtual exclusion of part-time employees from employment protection legislation was illegal.

On the other hand, it can be quite easily shown that the German model scores highly on all of these social-policy features. But it is not meant to imply that the various social-policy features of this model are the subject of perfect economic and social consensus. There are several outstanding examples of conflict in what has nevertheless been a remarkably consensual society in the post-war period. First, some of the economy's largest employers and their associations resorted to litgation over the property-rights implications of the 1976 Codetermination Act. Significantly, the case was heard by the Federal Constitutional Court, and its verdict went against the employers (Berghahn and Karsten 1987, pp. 124–6). Second, in 1984, during the lengthy strike in support of the 35-hour week, the employers and the Federal Labour Office took legal action in order to prevent employees indirectly affected by strike action in another district from drawing short-time benefits (ibid., pp. 98–9; Owen Smith et al 1989, pp. 205–6). The issue here was whether the neutrality of the Office during an industrial dispute was impaired. It duly reached the Constitutional Court in 1995. Whereas the Court thought the contested provisions acceptable at that juncture, it also envisaged their statutory revision at some future date (SZ 5 July 1995). Third, in 1993 the largest employers' association (*Gesamtmetall*) repudiated the agreement to bring about a step-by-step equalisation of money wage rates between eastern and western Germany, followed by its unprecedented announcement that the wage agreement in western Germany was to be terminated (Bastian 1995; Sadowski *et al.* 1994, p. 533). These events confirmed the view that trade unions were on the defensive (Silvia and Markovits 1995a and 1995b). Over the last two decades, the costs of social insurance, assistance and welfare have also become critical policy issues (Owen Smith 1998b). Since social-insurance costs are principally met by equal contributions from employers and employees, unemployment among the indigenous labour force – particularly in construction – has increased as a result of their counterparts from member states with less-developed systems not having to meet these high non-wage costs when in Germany. This problem of social dumping is exacerbated by the lower wages paid to EU citizens working in Germany. This latter reason lies behind the German government's desire to see a single market for labour whereby local rates of pay would have to be paid by all employers. The EC supports this initiative (*TU Information Bulletin* 1/95).

CONCLUSION: HOMOGENEITY VERSUS HETEROGENEITY

The SME can be defined in general terms. Freedom, efficiency and equity all receive equal weight (Wiseman 1989). The SME was the product of opposition to both fascist and communist economic systems, as well as to the *laissez-faire* school epitomised by von Hayek (Nicholls 1994, pp. 102–3, 146; Owen Smith 1994, pp. 16–20). To Anglo-American economists the Germans do all the wrong things: they protect their companies from hostile take-overs; they cosset their employees with generous social-security provisions; they allowed employees to have a say in business long before the social chapter was enacted in the Maastricht Treaty; they face heavy taxation; monopolies dominate important sectors of the economy; and the role of local and national government is extensive. An independent central bank is also a product of German history, that is to say, two humiliating inflations. International financial markets hold this bank – the Bundesbank – in such high esteem that the exchange rate Deutsche Mark has been continually revalued. The highly regulated dual system of vocational training is jointly provided by the state and employers. In short, by Reagan–Thatcher standards, the German economy should be a major disaster area. Yet the industrial wasteland of East Germany has been incorporated into the Federal Republic as a result of German Economic, Monetary and Social Union (GEMSU). After some needless prevarication, during which theoretical Anglo-Saxon neoclassical competitive models were considered for the former East Germany, fiscal transfers from western to eastern Germany have financed fundamental infrastructure reforms (Owen Smith 1997). But European integration represents a far greater degree of heterogeneity than that exemplified by GEMSU.

Indeed, it is the degree of heterogeneity which bedevils European integration. Dyker (1992, p. 1) gives an excellent perspective of European problems in this respect. Europe is unique among the high-income regions of the world. It is extraordinarily heterogeneous, boasting some 50 major nationalities (not all enjoying separate statehood), and nearly as many languages. Economic development has therefore proceeded in the face of a whole range of cultural and linguistic barriers. Yet in spite of the comparative poverty of Europe in raw materials, her economies typically trade a relatively high proportion of their GNP.

There are further differences. If the Brandenburgers had agreed to amalgamate with the Berliners, united Germany would have been a federation of 15 states – precisely the same number as the current membership of the EU. Quite apart from the strong political motivation underlying GEMSU, however, there were obvious historical, cultural and geographical features which favoured integration. Historically, Article 116 of the West German constitution even accorded German nationality to all those living within the area of the former Third Reich. In many respects, these factors bind Germany as much to central and eastern Europe as to the western part of the continent. Such unifying factors are almost completely absent within the EU. Indeed, the point made at the outset about heterogeneity can be usefully supplemented at this juncture.

Of greater significance in terms of the Maastricht Treaty is the even more pronounced degree of heterogeneity as far as the criteria for 'optimal' currency unions are concerned. Perhaps above all else, the formidable strengths of the BBk and the DM are *the* features of the German model which will most affect EMU. The titles of contributions to the policy debate in this area are as evocative as those which address the German financial system (Goos 1994; Hafer and Kutan 1994; Smeets 1990). The fact that these strengths had their origins in a draconian Allied currency reform and an undervalued international exchange rate are nearly always overlooked. The contrast with GEMSU could not be greater. Nonetheless, the emergent strong economic and political position of the DM implies that any optimal currency union with which Germany is associated would have to be based on strict price stability.

Tichy (1993, p. 172) estimates that this union could be comprised of Germany herself, along with the Netherlands, Austria, probably Belgium, and Switzerland. Presumably the exclusion of Luxembourg is an oversight. But the inclusion of Switzerland is at once incongruous and unrealistic: her international 'neutrality' and cumbersome political decision-making process, as well as the costless benefits endowed by being an outsider with access to EU markets, all indicate that she will retain her present position. In addition, she has important holdings within the EU.

France, on the other hand, has incurred high opportunity costs, not least in terms of unemployment, in maintaining a 'fort franc' stance. Short of dramatic policy changes, she may qualify for this currency union. Meanwhile, in spite of a great deal of trepidation within Germany, the Maastricht criteria were virtually met in 1994 (BBk Report 1994, p. 105). This is unless one assumes that the annual 3 per cent inflation rate in western Germany, compared to an EMU threshold value of 2.6 per cent, was sufficient to deny her membership. Moderate wage claims, increased productivity and under-utilised production capacity all contributed to 'the fight against inflation' (ibid., p. 103). Since this is central bankers' code for falling real wages accompanied by rising unemployment, it brings the implications of the present plans for EMU into sharp relief. Ultimately, corporatism and consensus is preferable to the consequences of competition and external flexibility in the labour Market. The bottom line is that without the addition of the German model's fiscal and social policies, politically stable and viable progress toward European integration will not be feasible.

Bibliography

AKERLOF, G. A., ROSE, A. K., YELLEN, J. L. and HESSENIUS, H. 'East Germany in from the Cold: The Economic Aftermath of Currency Union', *Brookings Papers on Economic Activity*, vol. 1, 1991. pp. 1–105.

BASTIAN, J. 'Brothers in Arms or at Arms? IG Metall in 1994: Confronting Recession and Unification', *German Politics*, vol. 4, 1995. pp. 87–100.

BERGHAHN, V. R. and KARSTEN, D. *Industrial Relations in West Germany*. Berg. Oxford, New York, Hamburg, 1987.

BMF, *Finanzbericht 1995*, Das Bundesministerum, Bonn, 1994. BTS – *Berliner Tagesspiegel* (various), Berlin.

CARLIN, W. and SOSKICE, D. 'Shocks to the System: the German Political Economy Under Stress', *National Institute Economic Review*, vol. 1, 1997. pp. 57–76.

Deutsche Bank Research 'East Germany: Progress and Problems', *Bulletin*, 17 October 1994, pp. 19–25

DIE ZEIT (various), Hamburg.

DYKER, D. A. *The National Economies of Europe*. Longman. London, New York, 1992.

FAZ – *Frankfurter Allgemeine Zeitung* (various), Frankfurt a.M.

FITZROY, F. and KRAFT, K. 'Efficiency and Internal Organization: Works Councils in West German Firms', *Economica*, vol. 54, 1987. pp. 493–504.

FITZROY, F. and KRAFT, K. 'Economic Effects of Codetermination', *Scandinavian Journal of Economics*, vol. 95, 1993. pp. 365–75.

FLOCKTON, C. 'The Federal Republic of Germany'. In Dyker, D. A. (ed.) *The National Economies of Europe*. Longman. London, New York, 1992. pp. 32–68.

GOOS, B. 'German Monetary Policy and the Role of the Bundesbank in the ERM', *Economic and Financial Review*, vol. 1, 1994. pp. 3–12.

GURDON, M. A. and RAI, A. 'Codetermination and Enterprise Performance: Empirical Evidence from West Germany', *Journal of Economics and Business*, vol. 42, 1990. pp. 289–302.

HAFER, R. W. and KUTAN, A. M. 'A Long-Run View of German Dominance and the Degree of Policy Convergence in the EMS', *Economic Inquiry*, vol. XXXII, 1994. pp. 684–95.

HALL, J. and LUDWIG, U. 'German unification and the "market adoption" hypothesis', *Cambridge Journal of Economics*, vol. 19, 1995. pp. 491–508.

HIGGINS, B. 'Was the ERM Crisis Inevitable?', *Economic Review (Federal Reserve Bank of Kansas City)*, vol. 78, 1993. pp. 27–40.

HÖLSCHER, J. *Entwicklungsmodell Westdeutschland: Aspekte der Akkumulation in der Geldwirtschaft*. Duncker & Humblot Berlin, 1994.

HOUPT, A. E. 'The Transformation of the Eastern German Economy', *Intereconomics*, vol. 30, 1995. pp. 253–62.

Institut für Wirtschaftsforschung 'Die Neuordnung des bundesstaatlichen Finanz ausgleichs im Spannungsfeld zwischen Wachstums- und Verteilungszielen', *Ifo-Schnelldienst*, 3/94, pp. 3–11.

KLOTEN, N. *Deutsche und Europäische Währungsunion. Ein Vergleich*. In Heckel, M. (ed.) *Die innere Einheit Deutschlands inmitten der europäischen Einigung*. J. C. B. Mohr (Paul Siebeck), Tübingen, 1995.

KURZ, H. D. (ed.) *United Germany and the New Europe*. Edward Elgar. Aldershot, 1993.

LAUN, K. VON 'Europäische Union: Die Finanzlast für die Bundesrepublik', *Orientierungen zur Wirtschafts- und Gesellschaftspolitik*, vol. 59, 1994. pp. 55–61.

LYTHE, C. 'What does the experience of German monetary union tell us about the theory of monetary union?', *International Review of Applied Economics*, vol. 9, 1995. pp. 150–68.

MOLLE, W. *The Economics of European Integration*. Dartmouth Publishing. Aldershot, 1990.

MRDB: Deutsche Bundesbank *Monthly Report* (various).

NICHOLLS, A. J. *Freedom with Responsibility: The Social Market Economy in Germany 1918–1963*. University Press Oxford, 1994.

OECD, *Economic Surveys* (Germany). Paris (various).

OWEN SMITH, E. *'The German Economy' in Western Europe*. 2nd ed. Europa Publications. London, 1993.

OWEN SMITH, E. *The German Economy*. Routledge. London, 1994.

OWEN SMITH, E. 'Incentives for Growth and Development'. In Frowen, S. F. and Hölscher, J. (eds) *The German Currency Union of 1990 – A Critical Assessment*. Macmillan, 1997.

OWEN SMITH, E. 'The German Model and European Integration'. In Larres, K. (ed.) *Germany since Unification: Domestic and External Consequences*. Macmillan, 1998a.

OWEN SMITH, E. 'The Demographic Timebomb, the Welfare State and United Germany' In: Shackleton, J. R. and Lange, T. (eds), *The Political Economy of German Unification*. Berghahn Books. New York, 1998b.

OWEN SMITH, E., FRICK, B. and GRIFFITHS, T. *Third Party Involvement in Industrial Disputes: A Comparative Study of West Germany ad Britain*. Avebury Press. Aldershot, 1989.

PRÜTZEL-THOMAS, M. 'The Property Question Revisited: The Restitution Myth', *German Politics*, vol. 4, 1995. pp. 112–27.

SADOWSKI, D., SCHNEIDER, M. and WAGNER, K. 'The Impact of European Integration and German Unification on Industrial Relations in Germany', *British Journal of Industrial Relations*, vol. 32, 1994. pp. 523–37.

SILVIA, S. J. and MARKOVITS, A. S. 'The New World of German Trade Unions: Still Essential Pillars of "Modell Deutschland"?', *Business and the Contemporary World*, vol. VIII, 1995a. pp. 52–66.

SILVIA, S. J. and MARKOVITS, A. S. 'The Reform of the German Trade Union Federation', *German Politics*, vol. 4, 1995b. pp. 64–85.

SINN, G. and SINN, H.-W. *Jumpstart: the Economic Unification of Germany*. MIT Press. Boston, Massachusetts, 1992.

SMEETS, H.-D. 'Does Germany Dominate the EMS?', *Journal of Common Market Studies*, vol. XXIX, 1990. pp. 37–52.

SMYSER, W. R. *The German Economy: Colossus at the Crossroads*. 2nd ed. Longman. Harlow, 1993.

STEINHERR, A. 'Lessons from German Unification', *CIDEI Working Paper*, no. 33, December 1994.

SZ – *Süddeutsche Zeitung*, München (varcons).

TICHY, G. 'European Integration and the Heterogeneity of Europe'. In Kurz, H. D. (ed.) *United Germany and the New Europe*. Edward Elgar. Aldershot, 1993. pp. 163–80.

WISEMAN, J. 'Social Policy and the Social Market'. In Peacock, A. and Willgerodt, H. (eds) *German Neo-Liberals and the Social Market Economy: Origins and Evolution*. Macmillan. London, 1989. pp. 160–78.

11 Lessons from German Unification for European Integration? A Conceptual Approach

Anja Hochberg

AN INTRODUCTORY OVERVIEW

German unification and European integration represent two separate though related unification processes with some remarkably comparable features, but also with some distinctively different characteristics. German and European integration differ in the speed and extent of transformation engendered: in just a few years, it is expected that the economic system of the former GDR will have been transformed into the so-called 'social market economy'. European integration, while its completion is likely to take longer, also reaches for a new qualitative dimension, but, quite different from East Germany's transformation, Europe's essential underlying economic principles of operation will remain almost entirely in place.

The following analysis is based on certain similarities between these two unification processes, such as the need for determination of a development path, and the question whether and within which limits an optimum currency area can be defined. Thereafter, we shall look at both historical events as examples of crisis likely to spur new developments. From this starting point, we shall venture to look at key lessons from German unification for a more successful European integration.

SOME FUNDAMENTAL, BUT NOT REALLY SURPRISING LESSONS

First and foremost, socio-economic integration cannot be decreed by political pressure. This simple primary lesson, general as it may sound, should not be underestimated. Having observed the unfortunate effects of a poorly prepared, politically motivated rush towards German unity, reasoned caution is of crucial importance for the development of workable solutions for European integration. Its central issues are easily identifiable: the economic mechanism, its political structure, and the speed of movement towards EMU (Tichy 1993). But an early recognition that, at the end of the day, only economic elements will remain as legitimate forces driving integration should not mislead us into some sort of economic determinism. Far more useful is a comprehensive view such as the one proposed by Reinike (1992).[1] The necessity of a 'holistic' approach is reinforced by the character of EMU, because it represents a profound systemic transformation due to the radical changes about to occur in the economic and political structures of a Europe with a single currency. Or, as Stares (1992, pp. 4) sums it up:

> integration cannot be rushed or carried out haphazardly, or the effort will almost certainly be fruitless, if not counterproductive. Rather, integration must proceed from a basic appreciation of the multifaceted nature of a functioning market economy at both the micro and the macro level of human interaction, including the legal and administrative, economic, and social and psychological dimension.

The Enduring Debate between Monetarists and Economists

The trivial lesson that integration is highly interdependent also begs application to the eerily familiar debate between monetarists and economists which has been raging on for decades. Economists demand convergence of economic fundamentals and co-ordination of economic policy as a necessary precondition of EMU. Therefore, economists view monetary union as the culmination of an all-encompassing convergence process. Quite in opposition to this economists' approach, monetarists say that it is the institutional framework that is first and foremost required in order to promote economic harmonisation. Therefore, they see monetary integration as a necessary starting point, not as a result (Thomasberger 1993, p. 161). In reality, European monetary relations and their institutional and legal arrangements have always reflected some form of compromise between competing monetarist and economist approaches (Christophersen 1994), a fact that became most obvious in the Werner Report as well as in the Delors Report.

In light of the overwhelming evidence rendered by empirical forces driving economic reasoning and logic, we see no choice but to side squarely with the economist perspective. Ironically enough, the German Bundesbank, when discussing EMU, has always taken this approach

(Hankel 1991). There was but one single exception to this strategy: the political decision to start German Economic Monetary and Social Union with monetary unification (Apolte and Cassel and Cichy 1994, p. 111).[2] However, the Bundesbank recognised this almost immediately as a disastrous mistake.

> Pöhl recently warned the Commission of the European Communities as well as the other central bankers and ministers at the intergovernmental conference, to learn from the past, especially from the mistakes with GEMSU [German Economic, Monetary and Social Union].
>
> (Kaufmann 1993, p. 214)

After this historical experience, one almost automatically has to reject the recent proposal of de Grauwe (1996) which called for a strengthening only of the EU's monetary institutions.

Historical evidence suggests a critical reflection on the proper approach to EMU. The establishment of common institutions like the European Central Bank and a common currency can not and will not, without the presence of indispensable economic convergence, result in anything realistically resembling a successful union.

The Applicability of Optimum Currency Area Theories

Integration processes can be assessed by clear economic criteria. In this respect, the Optimum Currency Area literature is quite helpful in defining determinants that qualify a country as a good or wanting candidate for monetary union. The basic idea is to identify any factors that could be a viable substitute for the loss of exchange rates as instruments of adjustment. Despite the obvious partial weakness of this theory, which does not really deal with deeper implications of the unification shock itself and with the role of trading partners (Lythe 1995), it offers a reasonable starting point for assessing feasibility of EMU. Broadly speaking, five central criteria are recognised as paramount (Thomasberger 1993, p. 161): factor mobility, openness of the economy, probability of similar and symmetric shocks, diversification of production and the mechanism of fiscal equalisation.

After extensive studies of the realities of German Economic, Monetary and Social Union (GEMSU), Lythe (1995) found, that – by standards of theoretical forecasting – East and West Germany would both have been considered good candidates for a currency union.

> Labour was very mobile, and Eastern German consumers were swift to move into the same product markets as their Western German counterparts. The two Germanys both had a production structure that was diverse and they were at least broadly similar. Both pre-union economies were quite open, and Eastern Germany in particular had a lot to gain from reduced transaction costs. The only problem appeared to be those of differences in growth rate of output and export, and these should have had the effect of curbing the rate of growth in Western Germany.
>
> (Lythe 1995, p. 165)

But these initially clearly favourable economic preconditions were in reality soon countervailed by the detrimental consequences of the politically determined fixing of an 'agreed' exchange rate – we shall look at this issue shortly.

Although, at least in the view prevailing throughout the Optimum Currency Area literature, both Germanies were almost universally recognised as reasonable candidates for unification, they experienced unexpectedly high adjustment costs. What, then, would be the likely prospects for EMU as it is scheduled to proceed to date? As Altmann (1994, p. 315) summarily concludes, the EU as a whole surely cannot hope to qualify as an optimum currency area. In his analysis, only very few countries (Belgium, Luxembourg, the Netherlands and Germany) meet 'substantially', but not entirely, the bulk of recognised requirements for an optimum currency area, whereas the rest of member states does not. Being well aware of the fact that both integration processes have, in part, divergent features, Tsoukalis (1993, p. 212) concluded that

> economic integration inside the EC has not yet reached the level where capital and especially labour mobility could act as near substitutes for changes in the exchange rate; or that wage or price movements in different countries correspond to changes in productivity rates so as to make exchange rate realignments redundant; or even that the EC economy is sufficiently homogeneous so that different countries and regions are not frequently subject to asymmetric external shocks.

Of course, this will hardly lead anyone to suggest abandoning the project of EMU. However, it does lend heavy support to the view that it might be wiser to establish Economic and Monetary Union only between those candidates who already positively satisfy at least the key criteria of basic economic convergence (Herr and Westphal 1991, pp. 75; Altmann 1994, p. 315).

UNIFICATION PROCESSES AS CRISES

Another quite important conclusion can be drawn from the observation that every unification process takes on the character of a crisis. From an evolutionist economist's perspective, crisis does not deserve, as it so commonly is, to be labelled as a bogeyman. It creates fluid conditions conducive for change as the economy, and sometimes society at large, undergoes something akin to zero base budgeting of many hitherto established preferences and values. Sure, German unification amounted to a serious shock that strongly influenced every area and dimension of society. Nevertheless, it did not cause the emergence of new, unprecedented problems. Rather, it swept problems into the limelight that had long been inherent in the organisational structures of German society.

Economic Challenges of German Unification

The German economy has faced problems mainly in the area of market organisation. Its status quo was challenged in the extreme by the demanding task of transforming the entire East German economy. Some criticism raised the spectre of missed opportunities to reform the system of market organisation in West Germany at the same time while implementing a new organisational framework for the East German economy. (Apolte, Cassel and Cichy 1994, p. 107)[3] In that respect, the process of European integration had better be understood as a historic opportunity to eliminate deficiencies that have been lingering in existence for a long time.

Prospects of European Integration

Likewise, already existing and recognised problems at the European level are invariably likely to become intensified over the course of EMU's establishment, particularly the inconsistencies and inefficiencies of the distribution aspects of some important EU policies, such as the EU's much maligned agricultural, social and regional policy.

Consider first the Common Agricultural Policy (CAP). The overall strategic problems of the CAP, mainly characterised by a struggle for shares of funds, are concentrated in the following areas: first and foremost, the policy is far too expensive as two-thirds of the current Community budget is spent on CAP; second, it contains openly discriminatory measures against non-members who are important trading partners; third, it provokes unequal distribution effects because of its regressive income policy; and fourth, it must in all fairness be judged a rather inefficient way of subsidising, given the remarkably unsatisfactory transfer ratios (Tsoukalis, 1993).

On the largely undisputed assumption that a centralised monetary policy will become necessary within EMU, redistribution policies have to balance the expectedly uneven distribution of unification gains. If this is so, then CAP requires fundamental reform in order to be able to fulfil its task under the changed conditions of EMU.

Unfortunately, much the same is to be said about regional policy. EU regional policy has resulted in only limited impact reducing divergence (Armstrong and Vickerman, 1995). It is generally suspected that EMU may actually even exacerbate the problem of interregional disparities.[4] There are, of course, some positive effects associated with Economic and Monetary Union: lower costs of borrowing, elimination of currency related international transaction costs, reduced uncertainty about exchange rates and inflation, hence increased investment, innovation and growth.

There are, however, also some quite severe disadvantages to be weighed. Let us first consider the loss of use of exchange rates as a proven mechanism for adjustment to internal and external shocks: once EMU is established, adjustment will have to occur via real variables, such as the level of wages and unemployment, or through migration. Given the rigid structure of labour markets throughout Europe, it is highly unlikely indeed that real wages could adjust as flexibly as would be required. The second problem would be the probable convergence of inflation, internal and external balance and public debt. This will involve a generally deflationary bias on the part of the regions that could slow down the economic development in many of them. Obviously, the effect of EMU on the regions is closely related to the question of whether or not Europe as a whole is an optimum currency area. It is safe to draw at least one conclusion already: EU regional policy will have to be substantially intensified, and it will have to be much more clearly focused on the problems that are likely to emerge in EMU's wake. In its working paper *The Social Consequences of Economic and Monetary Union*, the European Parliament (1994, pp. xii) openly acknowledged that the extent of regional transfers undertaken pursuant to the resource flow principle is a matter of political choice which should depend on an assessment of the distribution of overall costs and benefits of integration; the scale and the effects of migration; and the degree of homogeneity in terms of citizenship, culture and language; and the economic efficiency of transfers. In any event, a special Community effort may become necessary as the costs of EMU during transition will be high and are expected to burden the weaker members to a disproportionally greater extent.

Inevitably, the increased importance of fiscal policy has to be closely co-ordinated with monetary policy in order to avoid dangerous implications for credibility and performance in the area of inflation control. The Bundesbank's approach as outlined by König and Willeke (1995) seems to provide a functionally appropriate framework.[5]

But even for the purposes of formulating fiscal policy, the experiences of GEMSU can serve as a useful illustration. Gargantuan transfer payments and remarkable regional policy efforts have been necessary to contain the most socially harmful and divisive impacts of unification. Ironically enough, German unification lead to some increased convergence in the rest of Europe, but not in a way conventional wisdom would have expected: due to changes in the balance of trade and the currency evaluation, Germany 'improved' convergence conditions, if only by moving itself closer toward the weaker countries.[6]

Another problematic area where pre-existing problems could be substantially worsened following EMU is social policy. The overall objective of social policy could be defined as achieving an increase in competitiveness under the assumption of equal importance of economic and social efficiency (Owen Smith 1994, p. 17). Considering the diversified aspects of social policy such as minimum wages, worker's participation and the harmonisation of national rules and regulations, there are some strategic deficiencies that have to be solved in a manner compatible with integration. Once again Tsoukalis (1993, p. 175):

> Large differences in productivity levels and economic conditions more generally continue to compensate in most cases for the large disparities in wages and working conditions. If harmonisation and the establishment of minimum standards were to proceed irrespective of economic realities, the cost for the less developed countries and regions could be very high. Social regulation cannot be determined in complete defiance of the market.

In so identifying the main problem areas for European integration, we may confidently describe it as a crisis bearing the seed of opportunity. After all, the success or failure of EMU will depend heavily on how, and how quickly, current problems of European integration can be resolved. EMU, by and of itself, does indeed represent a new quality of European integration. However, the actual fundamentals in economic convergence, monetary arrangements and innovative institutional problem solving capacities need to be put in place – and the time for it is now.

POLICY IMPLICATIONS FOR EUROPEAN INTEGRATION

Mindful of all the arguments brought forth above, it would seem that only a staggered approach towards Economic and Monetary Union promises to be feasible. Schwarz (1995) juxtaposes two proposals: 'Core-Europe' versus 'Variable Geometry'. In order to avoid further alienation of those member states that will not be able to join the EMU 'Club' in the first instance, the principle of variable geometry would need to be applied. It might turn out to be the only way to guarantee that economic and political integration between all Member States will continue to proceed and that, sooner or later, all of them will be able to enjoy the benefits of a single currency.

Venturing even further from here, we need to look at some practical implications. The first important point is the political necessity to create equal opportunity at the outset of EMU. This mainly concerns the problem of fixing the final exchange rate when merging national currencies into the Euro. The fatal consequences of a wrong decision in this regard have become painfully visible in the experiences of the new Länder (Sinn and Sinn 1992, p. 34).[7]

In that respect, it seems useful to compare the experiences with German currency reform of 1948 and GEMSU.[8] The 1948 currency was undertaken at the end of a cathartic restructuring period and under conditions of a substantially *undervalued* post-war currency. Quite contrary to that, the German–German currency union 1990 represented the starting point of a vast industrial restructuring in East Germany. This restructuring task was at that time made even more difficult because the DM was comparatively quite substantially *overvalued* in terms of West German–East German relative prices.[9]

Therefore, the answer to the question as to at what exchange rate countries should enter European currency union will prove to be of overriding importance for the success of the entire EMU venture: the final exchange rate will have to balance different national levels of productivity and nominal wages subtly but appropriately in order to contribute to the elimination of significant differences in unit costs. By doing so, improvements in competitiveness are likely to depend primarily on continued increases in productivity (Herr and Westphal 1991, p. 101).[10]

The final exchange rate will also have to be geared toward minimising inflationary potential caused by the conversion event itself. And it will have to ensure that the new currency is accepted by the people (König and Willeke 1995, p. 29). With respect to ensuring such acceptance, there is a growing consensus about a visible and rather urgent need to improve tangibly the efficiency and, more specifically, the political marketing skills of EU institutions in charge.

The assessment of the role of trade relations under the Optimum Currency Area theory should be of considerable value for predicting possible impacts of EMU. Differences in the structure of external economic relations will affect the likelihood of asymmetric shocks within the Union as was demonstrated by Lythe (1995, p. 165).[11] If we further consider the structurally important fact that the ratio of intra-community trade varies within a range roughly between 50 per cent (UK and Germany) and 72 per cent (Belgium, Luxembourg and Ireland), it is safe to expect some serious tensions to surface rather quickly and sharply.

That leads us directly to issues of fiscal federalism. Fiscal federalism is of indisputably outmost importance to economic unification and involves, at the same time, the development of concomitant political structures. As already shown in the context of our analysis of redistribution mechanisms, the development of EU institutions must not be allowed to lag behind economic development. Otherwise, Economic and Monetary Union could easily be abused as a fake substitute for full institutional and structural convergence.[12]

Looking at fiscal federalism, Stehn (1993, pp. 33) points to several necessary corrections and additions to the Maastricht Treaty. If the treaty is to fulfil its equalising task and, at the same time, if it is to be economically efficient, public perception will have to distinguish separate areas and aspects of decentralisation and centralisation: therefore, increased fiscal federalism does not automatically imply a reinforced position for the Brussels bureaucracy, resulting in inevitable welfare losses.

The future design of the European Central Bank also still calls for a clear solution. In this respect, it is worth while to be critical of the broad range of issues of security and external exchange rate policy as yet unresolved, whereby the matter of the external exchange rate policy seems to carry the most ominous consequences. If the European Commission had responsibility for determining the external exchange rate, then internal monetary policy (and, to some undeniable extent, fiscal policy as well) could easily be counteracted. But if that were to happen, the European

Central Bank would lose some of its reputation and credibility, which would likely result in higher interest rates and an increase in unemployment. Yet another issue to be pondered is the regrettable failure to prohibit the use of indices in the Statute of the European Central Bank which could in time jeopardise price stability. Such a prohibition of indices could, on one hand, enable a decoupling of potential inflationary cycles, and it could, on the other hand, also force monetary authorities to counteract widening differences in inflation (Schlesinger 1993, p. 5).

So far, our focus has been on the internal dimension of EMU. But if we wish to see a more complex picture of the lessons of GEMSU for EMU, we cannot neglect to take also the external dimension into account. Assuming a 'core Europe' of member states establishing EMU among each other, how will likely increased import demand and, simultaneously, raising interest rates affect the other EU countries which have by then not been able to meet EMU criteria yet? Both effects could readily be studied in the case of GEMSU (Sinn and Sinn 1992; European Commission 1990; Hasse, 1993). The actual final impact of both effects will depend (a) on the future nominal exchange rate as discussed by Schäfer (1993, p. 217) and (b) on the shaping of redistribution policies as already mentioned earlier above.

Another crucial decision will be necessary as to how EMU shall be financed. If it is to be done by borrowing, then we may safely expect interest rates to rise, which would predictably put some revaluation pressures on the Euro. The economic effects for core-and non-core countries will in this case depend on their monetary relations with the core, especially on the exchange rate system then in place. If the link between non-core currencies and the Euro will be loose (as free floating exchange rates will be highly improbable considering trade relations), then it is rather likely that exports of non EMU-Members would have to increase due to the following devaluation of non-core currencies. Conversely, if non-members were to peg their currencies more or less rigidly to the Euro, then a recession resulting from a rise in non-core currencies' interest rates with the aim to maintain or regain parity is another likely possibility. In light of these disconcerting prospects, it might be wise to abide by some of history's lessons when dealing with plans for the EU's further enlargement in the relatively near term.

To sum up: integration and unification should be considered catalysts that tend to merely reinforce problems already previously in existence. Partial failures of the market mechanism are becoming more and more obvious in times of crises, such as those brought on by major structural and societal change. Due to a necessary paradigm shift from a supply-side concept toward a preference for increasingly keynesian intervention, the Commission will very likely find itself motivated to act (Pilz and Ortwein 1992; Krelle 1992).[13] Till now, the Commission's policy was mostly based on supply-side economics – a fact easily supported by taking a look at the Internal Market programme. This fundamental question about the basic economic policy theory promptly results in the familiar and highly controversial wage debate: do high wages hinder economic development? At this point, we come full circle: what lessons does German unification with its decidedly mixed practical experiences in that area hold for formulating consistent and effective policies (Löbbe 1993; Betz and Hausknecht 1991; Kalmbach 1993; Schmidt and Sander 1993)?

Notes

1. This holistic approach can be summarised as follows:

   > a modern market economy is the principal form of social organization governing advanced industrial democracies. It is a complex organisation based not only on the interaction of individual economic preferences, but on social relationship and patterns of behavior, legal norms and mechanisms, and political forces and institutions, all of which interact in a structured manner to produce the relatively consistent behaviour characteristic of any large institution. Moreover, any change in the economic circumstances under which individuals interact will also have a major impact on the political, legal, and social structures in which economic activities are embedded. In other words, change in one area cannot be seperated from change in the others; on the contrary, it may often be the cause. (Reinicke, W. H. [1992], p. 178)

2. From the point of view of the New Political Economy, this decision of the Bundesbank is seen as fully rational. For the argument, see Gawel and Thöne 1996.
3. 'Als verpaßte ordnungspolitischen Chancen wird einerseits der Verzicht darauf verstanden, die Gunst der Stunde der Vereinigung zu nutzen und eine Reihe von ordnungspolitischen Altlasten der Bundesrepublik zu beseitigen; andererseits fällt darunter aber auch die Unterlassung einer hinreichenden ordnungspolitischen Flankierung des Transformationsprozesses in den neuen Bundesländern, nachdem die bedingungslose Übertragung der in den alten Bundesländern gewachsenen Sozialen Marktwirtschaft politisch entschieden war.' (Apolte, Cassel and Cichy 1994, p. 107)
4. Even if some recent publications (De Nardis and Goglio and Malgarini 1996) predict an increasing stability for the regions due to diversified regional specialisation. However, this cannot be held for many regions which are lagging behind and are characterised by mono-structures.
5. Krichel, Levine and Pearlman (1996, pp. 28–54) developed a model showing that in the case of a monetary union, the best scenario consists of

an independent central bank which 'removes the incentives for the governments to engineer surprise inflation by credible inflation targeting'.

6. The traditional meaning of convergence is rather the rapprochement of the economies which are lagging behind.
7. For a discussion of the currency conversion controversy in great detail, see Sell (1995), who also denied the character of both Germany as an optimum currency area.
8. For a comprehensive presentation of the different German currency reforms, see Schlesinger 1993, pp. 3–6.
9. Interesting insights into the process of determination of the final exchange rate for the former GDR are provided by Kloten 1995, pp. 53–58.
10. 'Der Umstellungssatz jeder EWS-Währung müßte so gewählt werden, daß die Unterschiede zwischen den nationalen Produktivitätsniveaus und Nominallohnniveaus ausgeglichen werden. Indem somit das Problem der Unterschiede in den Lohnstückkostenniveaus eliminiert werden würde, würde die Entwicklung der Wettbewerbsfähigkeit der einzelnen Regionen in einer Whrungsunion nur noch von den Produktivitätssteigerungsraten abhängen. (Herr and Westphal 1991, p. 101)
11. Where ... the partners in a monetary union are both open but trade with different economies, there may be tensions in the monetary union from shocks affecting one member's trading partners more than others. (Lythe 1995, p. 165)
12. For more detail see Klatt 1993; Appleton, 1992.
13. For the political conception and strategy see Pilz and Ortwein (1992), p. 50. For the necessity to increase the role of the state, see Krelle (1992), p. 55.

Bibliography

ALTMANN, J. 'Ist die Europäische Union ein optimaler Währungsraum', *Wirtschaftsdienst*, 6/94, HWWA-Institut für Wirtschaftsforschung, Hamburg.

APOLTE, T. and CASSEL, D. and CICHY, E. U., *Die Vereinigung: Verpaßte ordnungs politische Chancen*. In Gutmann, G. and Wagner, U. (eds) *Ökonomische Erfolge und Mißerfolge der deutschen Vereinigung – Eine Zwischenbilanz*. Stuttgart, 1994. pp. 105–30.

APPLETON, J. M. 'European integration and the German Länder: Lost competence or found opportunity.' In Mattox, G. A. and Shingleton, A. B. (eds) *Germany at the Crossroads. Foreign and Domestic Policy Issues*. Oxford, 1992, pp. 51–66.

ARMSTRONG, H. W. and VICKERMAN, R. W. (eds) *Convergence and Divergence Among European Regions*. European Research in Regional Science 5, London, 1995.

BETZ, K. and HAUSKNECHT, A. Die wirtschaftlichen Folgen des Helmut Kohl. In Westphal, A., Herr, H., Heine, M. and Busch, U. (eds) *Wirtschaftspolitische Probleme der deutschen Vereinigung*. Frankfurt a.M. and New York, 1991.

CHRISTOPHERSON, H. 'The transition to Economic and Monetary Union', *Europe Documents,* 20 April 1994, no. 1880, pp. 1–4.

DE GRAUWE, P. 'The Economics of Convergence: Towards Monetary Union in Europe', *Weltwirtschaftliches Archiv,* 1996, vol. 132(1) pp. 1–27.

DE NARDIS, S. and GOGLIO, A. and MALGARINI, M. 'Regional Specialisation and Shocks in Europe: Some Evidence from Regional Data', *Weltwirtschaftliches Archiv*, 1996, vol. 132(2), pp. 197–214.

EUROPEAN COMMISSION. *The Community and German Unification.* COM (90) 400 final. Brussels, Luxembourg, 1990.

EUROPEAN PARLIAMENT, DIRECTORATE GENERAL FOR RESEARCH. *Working Paper: The Social Consequences of Economic and Monetary Union.* Final Report. Social Affairs Series, E-1, Luxembourg, 10/1994.

GAWEL, E. and THÖNE, W. 'Zur Neuen Politischen Ökonomie der deutsch–deutschen Währungsunion', *Kredit und Kapital,* vol. 29, 1996, no. 1, pp. 1–31.

HANKEL, W. 'Eine Mark und ein Markt für Deutschland: Ordnungspolitische Aspekte der deutschen Währungsunion.' In Westphal, A., Herr, H., Heine, M. and Busch, U. (eds) *Wirtschaftspolitische Probleme der deutschen Vereinigung.* Frankfurt a.M. and New York, 1991. pp. 28–45.

HASSE, R. 'German–German monetary union: main options, costs and repercussions.' In Ghanie Chaussy, A. and Schäfer, W. (eds) *The Economics of German Unification.* London and New York, 1993. pp. 26–59.

HERR, H. and WESTPHAL, A. 'Probleme der monetären Integration Europas. Die Europäische Währungsunion und die deutsche Vereinigung.' In Westphal, A. and Herr, H. and Heine, M. and Busch, U. (eds) *Wirtschaftpolitische Probleme der deutschen Vereinigung.* Frankfurt a.M. and New York, 1991. pp. 75–114.

KALMBACH, P. 'On alternative strategies of wage policy in Eastern Germany.' In Kurz, H. D. (ed.), *United Germany and the New Europe.* Aldershot, 1993. pp. 119–133.

KAUFMANN, H. M. 'From EMS to European Economic and Monetary Union with German Economic and Monetary Union as a major sideshow.' In Kurz, H. D. (ed.), *United Germany and the New Europe.* Aldershot, 1993. pp. 200–16.

KLATT, H. *German Unification and the Federal System.* In Jeffery, C. and Sturm, R. (eds), *Federalism, Unification and European Integration* London, 1993. pp. 1–21.

KLOTEN N. 'German Unification: A Personal View', *Central Banking*, Autumn 1995, vol. 6, no. 2, pp. 53–8.

KÖNIG, R. and WILLEKE, C. 'German monetary unification', *Central Banking*, Summer 1995, vol. 6, no. 1, pp. 29–39.

KRELLE, M. 'The political economy of the new Germany.' In Stares, P. B. (ed.), *The new Germany and the new Europe*. Washington, 1992. pp. 55–92.

KRICHEL, T. and LEVINE, P. and PEARLMAN, J. 'Fiscal and Monetary Policy in a Monetary Union: Credible Inflation Targets or Monetized Debt?', *Weltwirtschaftliches Archiv,* 1996, vol. 132(1), pp. 28–54.

LÖBBE, K. 'Tarifpolitik im vereinigten Deutschland: Gratwanderung zwischen Einkommens- und Beschäftigungsziel.' In Siebert, H. (ed.), *Die zweifache*

Integration: Deutschland und Europa. Workshop zur Strukturberichterstattung. Institut für Weltwirtschaft an der Universität Kiel, Tübingen,1993. pp. 135–61.

LYTHE, C. 'What does the experience of German monetary union tell us about the theory of monetary union', *International Review of Applied Economics,* 1995, vol. 9, no. 2, pp. 150–68.

OWEN SMITH, E. *The German Economy*. London, 1994, p. 17.

PILZ, F. and ORTWEIN, H. *Das vereinte Deutschland. Wirtschaftliche, soziale und finanzielle Folgeprobleme und die Konsequenzen für die Politik*. Stuttgart, 1992.

REINIKE, W. H. 'Towards a new European political economy.' In Stares, P. B. (ed.), *The new Germany and the new Europe*. Washington, 1992. pp. 177–217.

SCHÄFER, W. 'The Unification of Germany, the Deutschmark, and European Monetary Union.' In KURZ, H. D. (ed.), *United Germany and the New Europe*. Aldershot, 1993. pp. 217–30.

SCHLESINGER, H. 'Währungsreformen und Währungsunionen – sind sie Lehrbeispiele für eine Europäische Währung?', *Auszüge aus Presseartikeln*, Deutsche Bundesbank, Frankfurt a.M. November 1993, no. 79, pp. 3–6.

SCHMIDT, K.-D. and SANDER, B. 'Wages, productivity and employment in eastern Germany.' In Ghanie Ghaussy, A. and Schäfer, W. (eds) *The Economics of German Unification*. London, 1993. pp. 60–72.

SCHWARZ, H.-P. 'United Germany and European Integration', *SAIS Review,* Fall 1995, vol. XV, pp. 83–101.

SELL, F. L. 'The Currency Conversion Controversy', *MOST,* 1995, vol. 5, no. 4, pp. 27–53.

SINN, G. and SINN, H. W. *Kaltsstart. Volkswirtschaftliche Aspekte der deutschen Vereinigung*. Tübingen, 1992.

STARES, P. B. (ed.) *The New Germany and the New Europe*. Washington, 1992.

STEHN, J. 'Theorie des fiskalischen Förderalismus: Ein Referenzmaßstab zur Beurteilung der Beschlüsse von Maastricht.' In Siebert, H. (ed.), *Die zweifache Integration: Deutschland und Europa*. Workshop zur Strukturberichterstattung. Institut für Weltwirtschaft an der Universität Kiel, Tübingen, 1993. pp. 33–48.

THOMASBERGER, C. *Europäische Währungsintegration und globale Währungskonkurrenz*. Tübingen, 1993.

TICHY, G. 'European Integration and the Heterogeneity of Europe.' In Kurz, H. D. (ed.), *United Germany and the New Europe*. Aldershot, 1993. pp. 163–80.

TSOUKALIS, L. *The new European Economy. The Politics and Economics of Integration*. Oxford, 1993.

Name Index

Notes: 1. Entries include authors' names where they appear in the main text or in notes, but not where they appear in bibliographies.
2. Page numbers in **bold** type refer to illustrative figures or tables and to authors of papers in this book.

Subject Index

Notes: 1. Page numbers in **bold** type refer to illustrative figures or tables.
2. Entries in **bold** type refer to chapter or section headings
3. Entries refer to authors' notes as well as to the main text.
4. Entries refer to post-1990 united Germany unless otherwise indicated.